ILLUSTRATIONS OF THE HISTORY AND PRACTICES OF THE THUGS

ILLUSTRATIONS OF THE HISTORY AND PRACTICES OF THE THUGS

AND NOTICES OF SOME OF THE PROCEEDINGS OF THE GOVERNMENT OF INDIA, FOR THE SUPPRESSION OF THE CRIME OF THUGGEE

THORNTON

GYAN

Published by

Gyan Publishing House
5, Ansari Road
Daryaganj, New Delhi-110002
Phone: 011-47034999, 9811692060
E-mail: books@gyanbooks.com

Distribution Network
gyanbooks.com
India, USA, Canada, UK, Australia, France

ISBN : 978-81-212-3569-3 (PB)
First Published, London, 1851

2nd Impression 2020

Printed at: Gyan Press, Delhi.

Illustrations of the History and Practices of the thugs
Author: Thornton

ILLUSTRATIONS

OF THE

HISTORY AND PRACTICES

OF THE

THUGS.

AND NOTICES OF SOME OF THE PROCEEDINGS OF THE GOVERNMENT OF INDIA, FOR THE SUPPRESSION OF THE CRIME OF THUGGEE.

LONDON:
NATTALI AND BOND,
23, BEDFORD STREET, COVENT GARDEN.
1851.

INTRODUCTION.

THE limited portion of information recently obtained in this country as to the existence and practices of the classes of Assassins known by the name of Thugs, has had the effect of directing public curiosity to the subject; and the following pages have been compiled with a view to the gratification of that feeling. The best authorities have been consulted; and the general views which are presented to the reader may claim at least the praise of accuracy.

As the object of the writer was to convey information, and to afford as just, and, at the same time, as vivid a picture as possible of the strange state of society which it was his duty to exhibit, he has in many instances given the confessions or depositions of members of the Thug fraternity in their own language, in preference to rendering them into his own. This plan, it was, conceived, would afford to the reader a degree of insight into the characters and feelings of these murderers, superior to that which could be derived from the perusal of a mere narrative.

The authorities for the facts related are, in many instances, referred to: but it would be unjust to close these remarks without a general acknowledgment of the services rendered by Captain Sleeman to the cause of justice and good government, as well in the collection and diffusion of information respecting the Thugs, as in more active labours for their suppression. To the researches of that Gentleman, all writers on the subject, in common with the author of this volume, must be deeply indebted.

ILLUSTRATIONS

OF THE

HISTORY AND PRACTICES

OF THE

THUGS.

CHAP. I.

THE existence of large bodies of men having no other means of subsistence than those afforded by plunder, is, in all countries, too common to excite surprise; and, unhappily, organized bands of assassins are not peculiar to India! The associations of murderers known by the name of Thugs present, however, so many remarkable points of character and manners, that curiosity may reasonably be excited to inquire into the history, and ascertain the feelings, opinions, and motives of persons differing, in many respects, so widely even from all other followers of their own horrible occupation.

In different parts of India, these ruffians assume, and have been designated by, various names, derived either from the mode by which they dispatch their victims—from the purpose for which they destroy life,

life, or from the arts by which they inveigle their prey to destruction. In the more northern parts of India, these murderers are called Thugs, the name by which they are most generally known among Europeans. This term signifies "deceiver." In some provinces to the southward, according to Dr. Sherwood, they have obtained the name of Phansigars, or "stranglers," from the Hindostanee word *phansi*, a "noose." By the same authority it is stated, that in the Tamul language they are called Ari Tulucar, or Mussulman "noosers"; in Canarese, Tanti Calleru, implying "thieves who use a wire or cat-gut noose"; and in Telagu, Warlu Wahndlu, or Warlu Vayshay Wahndloo, meaning "people who use the noose."

It is remarkable, that, after an intercourse with India of nearly two centuries, and the exercise of sovereignty over a large part of the country for no inconsiderable period, the English should have been ignorant of the existence and habits of a body so dangerous to the public peace. This, however, seems to have been the case: and it may be regarded as affording a strong proof, how little progress was made by the Europeans, during a long series of years, in knowledge of the people among whom they resided, and over whom they exercised the functions of rulers.

There is reason to conclude, that the British Government knew nothing of the Thugs until shortly after

after the conquest of Seringapatam, in 1799, when about a hundred were apprehended in the vicinity of Bangalore. They did not engage general attention; nor would it appear that they were suspected to belong to a distinct class of hereditary murderers and plunderers, settled in various parts of India, and alike remarkable for the singularity of their practice and the extent of their depredations. In the year 1807, between Chittoor and Arcot, several Thugs were apprehended, belonging to a gang which had just returned laden with booty from an expedition to Travancore; and information was then obtained, which ultimately led to the developement of the habits, artifices, and combinations of these atrocious delinquents.

The Thugs that invested the south of India some years ago were settled in Mysore, on the borders of that province and the Carnatic, in the Balaghat districts ceded to the Company by the Nizam in 1800; and they were particularly numerous in the Poliums of Chittoor. The sequestered part of the country which comprehended these Poliums maintained little intercourse with the neighbouring districts, abounding in hills and fastnesses; and, being immediately subject to several Polygars, afforded the Thugs a convenient and sure retreat. The protection of the Polygars was extended to them, in common with other classes of robbers, in consideration of a settled

 contribu-

contribution, or, which was more frequent, of sharing in the fruits of their rapacity.

It is impossible that such criminals as the Thugs, living by systematic plans of depredation, could long remain in the same place in safety, unless their practices were encouraged or connived at by persons in authority. Hence, after the establishment of the Company's Government over the Carnatic and the districts ceded by the Nizam, and the consequent extinction of the power and influence of the Polygars, some of whom had succeeded in rendering themselves virtually independent of the former government, many of these murderers changed their abodes, and assumed other names: others, who remained, endeavoured to shelter themselves by subterfuge and dissimulation.

While they lived under the protection of Polygars and other petty local authorities, and among people whose habits were in some respects analogous to their own, it was unnecessary to conceal that they subsisted by depredation. They and their families lived peaceably with their neighbours, whom they never attempted to molest. Between them there subsisted a reciprocation of interest, in the purchase and disposal of the plunder which the Thugs brought with them, on returning from their expeditions. Conscience in the East is neither very delicate nor very enlightened; and if any scruples arose, the countervailing profit would more

more than balance them. The Thugs at all times engaged in the tillage of land, even under the native chiefs, when they had settled habitations. They either sowed the lands, or prepared them for seed, during the season that they remained at home; and left the care of them to their women and children, in their absence. This peaceful pursuit afforded them a screen, on the extension of the English Government, and, while pursuing their criminal practices, enabled them to appear dependent on honest and laudable industry.

According to Dr. Sherwood, who wrote in 1816, and whose acquaintance with Thuggee appears to have been founded principally upon observations made in the territories subject to the Presidency of Fort St. George, a gang consisted of from ten to fifty, or sometimes a greater number. Captain Sleeman states, that the gangs have often contained two or three hundred; but, in such instances, they commonly follow each other in small parties of ten or twenty, upon roads parallel to each other, being prepared to concentrate, on any point, when necessary. Different parties frequently act in concert, apprising one another of the approach of travellers whose destruction promises a valuable booty. They assume the appearance of ordinary inoffensive travellers: sometimes they pretend to be traders; and, if enriched by former spoliations, travel on horseback, with tents, and pass for wealthy merchants,

merchants, or other persons of consequence. Sometimes they commence their route in more humble characters; but acquiring, in their rapacious progress, horses and bullocks, these at once furnish them with the means of transporting the remainder of their plunder, and of making pretensions to higher degrees of wealth and station.

Thugs are accustomed to wait at choultries, on the high roads, or near towns where travellers rest. They arrive at such places, and enter towns and villages, in straggling parties of three or four persons, appearing to meet by accident, and to have no previous acquaintance. On such occasions, some of the gang are employed as emissaries, to collect information, and especially to learn if any persons with property in their possession are about to undertake a journey. They are often accompanied by children of ten years of age and upwards; who, while they perform menial offices, are gradually initiated into the horrid practices of Thuggee, and contribute to prevent suspicion of their real character. Skilled in the arts of deception, they enter into conversation, and insinuate themselves by obsequious attentions into the confidence of travellers of all descriptions, to learn from them whence they came, whither and for what purpose they are journeying, and of what property they are possessed. When, after obtaining such information as they deem requisite,

site, the Thugs determine to attack a traveller, they usually propose to him, under the specious plea of mutual safety, or for the sake of society, to travel together; or else they follow him at a little distance, and, when a fit opportunity appears for effecting their purpose, one of the gang suddenly throws a rope or sash round the neck of the unfortunate victim, while the rest contribute, in various ways, to aid the murderous work.

Intrepidity does not appear to be a characteristic of the Thugs; and, in truth, it is a quality not to be looked for in assassins by profession. A superiority in physical force is generally regarded as an indispensable preliminary to success. Two Thugs, at the least, are thought necessary for the murder of one man; and more commonly three are engaged. Some Thugs pride themselves upon being able to strangle a man single handed; and this is esteemed a most honourable distinction. To ascribe to a Thug this power, is the highest compliment that can be paid him. A single Thug who had succeeded in pulling a man from his horse, and strangling him, conferred a distinction upon his family which ennobled it in the eyes of their fellows for many generations. Such a man was Buckshee, and a few others; but the majority of the Thugs are, and ever have been, firm adherents of the maxim, that "discretion is the better part of valour."

Some

Some variations have existed in the manner of perpetrating the murders; but the following seems to be the most general. While travelling along, one of the gang suddenly throws the rope or cloth round the neck of the devoted individual, and retains hold of one end; the other end being seized by an accomplice. The instrument of death, crossed behind the neck, is then drawn very tight, the two Thugs who hold it pressing the head of the victim forwards: a third villain, who is in readiness behind the traveller, seizes him by the legs, and he is thus thrown on the ground. In this situation there is little opportunity of resistance. The operation of the noose is aided by kicks inflicted in the manner most likely to produce vital injury, and the sufferer is thus quickly dispatched.

The best precautions are taken to guard against discovery or surprise. Before the perpetration of the murder, some of the gang are sent in advance, and some left in rear of the place, to keep watch, to prevent intrusion, and to give warning, if occasion requires, to those engaged in the act. Should any persons unexpectedly appear on the ground before the murdered body is buried, some artifice is practised to prevent discovery; such as, covering the body with a cloth, while loud lamentations are made, professedly on account of the sickness or death of one of their comrades; or one of the watchers will fall down, apparently writhing with

with pain, in order to excite the pity of the intruding travellers, and to detain them from the scene of murder.

Such are the perseverance and caution of the Thugs, that, in the absence of a convenient opportunity, they have been known to travel in company with persons whom they have devoted to destruction, for several days before they executed their intention. If circumstances favour them, they generally commit the murder in a jungle, or in an unfrequented part of the country, and near a sandy place or dry water-course. Particular tracts are chosen, in every part of India, where they may exercise their horrid profession with the greatest convenience and security. Much-frequented roads, passing through extensive jungles, where the ground is soft for the grave, or the jungle thick to cover them, and where the local authorities took no notice of the bodies, were favourite spots. The Thugs speak of such places with the same affection and enthusiasm as other men would of the most delightful scenes of their early life.

In these chosen spots, a hole, three or four feet in depth, usually forms the grave of the unhappy traveller, who is placed in it with his face downwards. The barbarous character of the Thugs is displayed in their treatment of the wretched remains of the murdered persons. Though death brings a termination of suffering, it does not put an end

to

to the outrages of the murderers. Long and deep gashes are made in various parts of the bodies: sometimes the limbs are disjointed, and the figure distorted into unusual positions. These outrages arise from various motives. Their intention generally is, to expedite the decomposition of the body, and to prevent its inflation, which, by causing fissures in the superincumbent sand, might attract jackals, and thus lead to the discovery of the corpse. Sometimes, however, these deeds have been the result of disappointment, and the emanations of a petty and unmanly revenge. When the amount of plunder is less than had been expected, the villains have frequently vented their displeasure in wanton indignities on the unconscious remains of the dead.

If, when a murder is perpetrated, a convenient place for interring the body be not near, or if the Thugs be apprehensive of discovery, it is either tied in a sack, and carried to some spot where it is not likely to be found, or is put into a well. In Oude, where the fields are almost all irrigated from wells, the bodies were generally thrown into them; and when the cultivators discovered these relics of crime, they hardly ever thought it worth while to ask how they came there, so accustomed were they to find them. In Bengal and Behar, where the most frequented roads pass along or frequently across rivers, the bodies are cast into those rivers.

If

If none of these expedients be advisable, a shallow hole is dug, in which the corpse is buried, till a fit place for interring it can be discovered; when it is removed, and cut in the manner already mentioned. If compelled to perform the interment under circumstances which subject them to the risk of observation, the Thugs put up a screen on the wall for a tent, and bury the body within the enclosure; pretending, if inquiries are made, that their women are within the screen. If the traveller had a dog, it is killed, lest the affection of the animal should cause the discovery of the body of his murdered master. The office of mangling the dead body is usually assigned to a particular person of the gang. The Thugs are always provided with knives and pickaxes, which they conceal from observation.

It will thus be seen, that the system of the Thugs is well devised to secure that concealment so necessary to the continued success of their horrid practices. The mode of destroying their victims, and of disposing of their remains, almost preclude the possibility of rescue or escape, of witnesses to the deed, of noise or cries for help, of effusion of blood, and, indeed, of any trace of the crime. An impenetrable veil of darkness is thrown over their atrocities.

It has been supposed, that formerly a long string with a running noose was used by the Thugs for seizing

seizing travellers, and that they robbed on horseback. These practices do not at present, however, appear to be common. They sometimes use a short rope, with a loop at one end: but a turban, or sash, are more usually employed, as these answer the atrocious purpose in view as well as a regularly-prepared noose, and have the additional recommendation of exciting no suspicion. When a waist-cloth or sash is used, it is previously doubled to the length of two feet, or two feet and a half: a knot is formed at the double extremity, and a slip-knot tied about eighteen inches from it. In regulating the distance of the two knots, so that the intervening space, when tightly twisted, may be adapted to embrace the neck, the Thug who prepares the instrument ties it upon his own knee. The two knots give a firm hold of the cloth, and prevent its slipping through the hands in the act of applying it. After the person attacked has been brought to the ground, the slip-knot is loosed by the Thug who has hold of that part of the cloth: and he makes another fold of it round the neck; upon which placing his foot, he draws the cloth tight, in a manner similar to that—to use the expression of a Thug informer—"of packing a bundle of straw."

If, which scarcely ever happens, a traveller escape from the persons attempting to strangle him, he incurs the hazard of being dispatched by one of the parties on watch. These men have swords,

swords, and will endeavour to cut down any man who escapes from the stranglers. Should he finally escape, or should any other circumstance occur to excite alarm or apprehensions of being seized, the gang immediately disperses, having previously agreed to re-assemble, at an appointed time, at some distant place.

Travellers resting in the same choultry with Thugs are sometimes destroyed in the night. On these occasions, a person is not always murdered when asleep; as, while he is in a recumbent posture, the stranglers find a difficulty in applying the cloth. The usual practice is, first, to awaken him suddenly, with an alarm of a snake or a scorpion, and then to strangle him.

In attacking a traveller on horseback, the Thugs range themselves in the following manner: one of the gang goes in front of the horse, and another has his station in the rear; a third, walking by the side of the traveller, keeps him engaged in conversation, till, finding that he is off his guard, he suddenly seizes the victim by the arm, and drags him to the ground, the horse at the same time being seized by the foremost villain: the miserable sufferer is then strangled in the usual manner.

Against Thugs, it must be obvious, that arms, and the ordinary precautions taken against robbers, are unavailing. When a person is armed with a dagger, it is usual for one of the villains to secure his

his hands. It sometimes happens, that entire parties of travellers, consisting of several persons possessed of valuable effects, are, while journeying in imaginary security, suddenly cut off; and the lifeless and despoiled bodies being removed and interred, not a vestige of them appears. Instances have occurred, of twelve and fourteen persons being simultaneously destroyed; but such occurrences must be rare.

Occasionally, the booty obtained is considerable. Near Sadras, about eleven years ago, three *golah* peons were killed, having on them money, in different coins, to the amount of 16,000 rupees. In 1805, five persons were killed in Coimbatoor, and cash to the amount of 2500 pagodas, the property of the Collector of the district, was taken. In the same year, two respectable natives proceeding on horseback from Madras to the Malabar coast, with five attendants, were all killed. In 1807, five persons, besides two others who had joined them on the road, were killed near Bangalore, and robbed of property to the amount of 1000 pagodas, belonging to an officer of Engineers. And in 1815, three persons were killed in the district of Masulipatam, and 2500 rupees taken. Very frequently, however, the property taken is but small; and such are the cruelty and cupidity of these wretches, that, on the presumption of every traveller possessing concealed treasure, or some property, however trifling,

trifling, the greatest apparent indigence does not always afford security.

The plunder was sometimes carried home; sometimes disposed of on the road. If the murdered person resided near the place of his assassination, the property was carried to a distance: if, as was more commonly the case, he was a stranger, the ruffians did not scruple to offer the fruits of their rapine in the immediate vicinity of their crime: the only precaution taken was, that the place of sale should be in advance of that where the murder was committed, and not a village where the traveller had previously been seen.

The mode of dividing the plunder is probably various. Dr. Sherwood says, that formerly, if good horses, shawls, or other valuable articles, were among the booty, they were commonly reserved for the Polygar, in payment of protection. A portion of the plunder was usually appropriated to defraying the expenses of religious ceremonies; and, sometimes, a part was also allotted for the benefit of widows and families of deceased members of the gang. The residue of the booty, being divided into several parts, was generally shared as follows;—to the leader, two shares; to the men actually concerned in perpetrating the murder, and to the person who cut the dead body, each one share and a half; and to the remainder of the gang, each one share.

According to Captain Sleeman, when there are ten

or more articles of the same kind, the tenth is assigned to the leader, before the general division takes place: if the nature of the property does not admit of decimation, one anna in the rupee is assessed upon its value, for the benefit of the leader. After this deduction, and the payment of a small extra allowance to the stranglers, grave-choosers, diggers, and other officers, the remainder is divided by lot, called, in the Thug dialect, *Kouree, Phenkua, Marna*, or *Dalna*. It is usual to make three allotments of the spoil, and to divide the gang into three equal parties. A cowry is then given to each party, by whom it is marked. The cowries are then placed in the hands of a man who is kept ignorant of the parties to whom they respectively belong; and the final decision is made by his placing one of the cowries upon each parcel of the plunder. The parties then take possession of the shares thus consigned to them, and divide the produce among the individuals.

The operations of the Thugs are facilitated, and their designs cloked, by a peculiar dialect: they have recourse, also, to a variety of signs, both for concealment, and for the purpose of communicating with comrades beyond the influence of speech. Drawing the back of the hand along the chin, from the throat outwards, implies that caution is requisite—that some stranger is approaching. Putting the open hand over the mouth, and drawing it gently

gently down, implies that there is no longer cause for alarm. If an advanced party of Thugs overtake any traveller whom they design to destroy, but have need of more assistance, they make certain marks on the roads, by which those of the gang who follow understand that they are required to hasten forwards. A party in advance also leaves certain marks, where a road branches off, as intimations to those who are behind. They draw their feet along the dust, in the direction they have taken; and if their friends are to follow quickly, they leave the dust piled up at the end of the line where the foot drops, or make a hole in the dust with the heel. If the road afford no dust, they leave two stones, placed one upon the other, in the line they have taken; and strew a few leaves of trees along the road. If their co-adjutors are to make haste, they make a very long line of leaves. They have many other signs, for similar purposes.

Of the number of persons who fall victims to these lawless associations, it is obvious that no estimate can be proved, deserving of the slightest confidence. The number has, without doubt, varied greatly at different periods. There is reason to believe, that from the time of the conquest of Mysore in 1799, to 1807 and 1808, the practice, in that part of India, reached its height, and that hundreds of persons were annually destroyed. In one of his reports, the Magistrate of Chittoor observes: "I believe that some of the Phansigars have been concerned in above two hundred murders: nor will this estimate appear extravagant, if it be remembered, that murder was their profession, frequently their only means of gaining a subsistence: every man of fifty years of age has probably been actively engaged during twenty-five years of his life in murder; and, on the most moderate computation, it may be reckoned that he has made one excursion a year, and met each time with ten victims."

Francis Bartolomeo says: "During a residence of thirteen or fourteen years in India, I never heard of any traveller being robbed or murdered on the highway;"—but other travellers, whose experience was less agreeable, attest that the practice of Thuggee is not of recent introduction. Thevenot, in the following passage, evidently alludes to it:— "Though the road I have been speaking of, from Delhi to Agra, be tolerable, yet hath it many inconveniences. One may meet with tigers, panthers, and lions upon it; and one had best, also, have a care of robbers, and, above all things, not to suffer any body to come near one upon the road. The cunningest robbers in the world are in that country. They use a certain slip with a running noose, which they can cast with so much sleight about a man's neck, when they are within reach of him, that they never fail, so that they strangle him in a trice. They have another cunning trick, also, to catch travellers

travellers with. They send out a handsome woman upon the road, who, with her hair dishevelled, seems to be all in tears, sighing and complaining of some misfortunes which she pretends has befallen her. Now, as she takes the same way that the traveller goes, he easily falls into conversation with her, and, finding her beautiful, offers her his assistance, which she accepts: but he hath no sooner taken her up behind him on horseback, but she throws the snare about his neck and strangles him; or at least stuns him, until the robbers, who lie hid, come running to her assistance, and complete what she hath begun. But, besides that, there are men in those quarters so skilful in casting the snare, that they succeed as well at a distance as near at hand; and if an ox, or any other beast belonging to a caravan, run away, as sometimes it happens, they fail not to catch it by the neck."

The modern Thugs have recourse to numerous artifices to entrap their victims; but there is reason to think that the allurements of female fascination are now not often resorted to. Their customs with regard to their women, however, vary much. The Thugs, who reside in fixed habitations, rarely allow their women to accompany them. The wandering bands, who seem to retain more of the usages of their ancestors, are attended and aided by their females.

To a European reader it must appear extra-

 ordinary,

ordinary, that the constant disappearance of such numbers of natives should have excited so little interest and inquiry, as not to have led to a general knowledge of these combinations of criminals. Such ignorance, perhaps, could not have prevailed in England, where it might be supposed that the absence, if unaccounted for, of even a single person, must produce suspicion, with consequent investigation and discovery. But even in England it has recently been made evident, that numbers of persons may disappear from the scene of their ordinary avocations without producing much surprise or any alarm. In India, the probability of such disappearance is far greater; and such an event, unless occurring to a person of some consequence, would scarcely be known beyond the precincts of the place of residence, or the village of the unfortunate sufferer, nor much observed there. Many that fall victims to the Thugs are the subjects of other and distant states: many have no settled abodes. It must also be remembered, that the Thugs usually refrain from murdering the inhabitants of towns and villages near which they are halting; neither are they accustomed to murder near their own habitations; circumstances which not only prevent suspicion attaching to them as the murderers, and to the local authority as protecting and sharing the booty with them, but tend to throw it upon others, who reside near the spot to which a traveller

traveller may have been traced, and where he was last seen. Besides, a person setting out on a journey is often unable to fix any period for his return; and though he should not revisit his home at the expected time, his delay will, for a while, excite little alarm in the minds of his friends. He is supposed to be unexpectedly detained—to be ill—to have met with some ordinary accident—to have deserted his family—to have died. Should suspicion arise that he has been murdered, the act is attributed to ordinary highway robbers; and it is but seldom that minute inquiries can be instituted by his bereaved relatives. But supposing that this is done, and the progress of the missing traveller traced to a particular place, and not beyond it, still suspicion would be apt to attach to any, rather than to a few apparently inoffensive travellers—journeying either for the purpose of traffic, as is imagined, or, as is often pretended, to see their relations, or to be present at some marriage; and who, if ever noticed, have perhaps been long since forgotten. If, notwithstanding all these improbabilities, suspicion should fall upon the actual perpetrators, where could they be found?

Thus with respect to Sepoys, who, having obtained leave of absence, never rejoined their corps, the conclusion generally formed has been, that they had deserted; when, in various instances, they had fallen sacrifices to the wiles of the Thugs. The

The same observation is particularly applicable to golah peons, charged with the conveyance of money and valuables; many of whom having disappeared, no doubt was entertained that they had absconded, and appropriated the property to their own use. Even the apprehension which an indistinct idea of danger tends to create in the minds of these and other travellers would render them only more liable to fall into the snare: less persuasion would be requisite to induce them to join a party of Thugs, prompted by the belief that they were thus providing, in the most effectual manner, for their own safety.

The profession of a Thug, like almost every thing in India, is hereditary—the fraternity, however, receiving occasional reinforcements from strangers: but these are admitted with great caution, and seldom after they have attained mature age. Rank is acquired by methods not dissimilar to those which procure the same advantage elsewhere. On Captain Sleeman's inquiring, of an approver, what gave a man the rank of Jemadar, the latter answered, that a man who has always at command the means of advancing a month or two's subsistence to a gang, will be called so;—a strong and resolute man, whose ancestors have been for many generations Thugs, will soon get the title;—or a very wise man, whose advice in difficult cases has weight with the gang;—or one who has influence over local authori-

ties,

ties, or the native officers of courts of justice ;—or a man of handsome appearance and high bearing, who can feign the man of rank well. By such means a man is enabled to get around him a few who will consent to give him the fees and title of Jemadar; but it requires very high and numerous qualifications to gain a man the title of Subahdar. Wealth, influence, talents, and high descent, it thus appears, have the same power among Thugs which they have elsewhere; and, in the absence of all these, impudent pretension will answer the purpose of the adventurer who has confidence enough to assume it. In this respect, at least, the polity of the Thugs presents but a counterpart of what is passing elsewhere.

In contemplating the organization of these hordes of murderers, it is difficult to conceive how they continue to subsist. It might be hoped, that when the villains who have grown grey in the practice of assassination descend with their weight of crime to the grave, some difficulty would be found in perpetuating the succession—that the profession would decay, from the reluctance of the young and uncontaminated to enter it. The initiation, however, is progressive; and the force of habit gradually overcomes the natural repugnance which, in every human breast, would at first withdraw the hand from the destruction of human life. The children of Thugs, during their more tender years, are, it appears,

appears, kept in ignorance of the occupation of their fathers. After a time, they are permitted to accompany them; but a veil is thrown over the darker scenes of the drama. To the novice, indeed, the expedition presents nothing but an aspect of pleasure. He is mounted on a pony; and being, by the laws of the Thugs, entitled to his share of the booty, he receives a portion of it, in presents suited to his years—the delight attending the acquisition being unalloyed by any consciousness of the means by which it has been obtained. The truth reveals itself by degrees. In a short time, the tyro becomes aware that his presents are the fruits of robbery. After a while, he has reason to suspect that robbery is aggravated by a fouler crime: at length, suspicion passes into certainty: and finally, the pupil is permitted to witness the exercise of the frightful handicraft which he is destined to pursue. The moral contamination is now complete; but it is long before the disciple is entrusted with the performance of the last atrocity. He passes through a long course of preparatory study; being first employed as a scout, next as a sexton, then as a holder of the limbs, before he is in any case thought worthy of being elevated to the dignity of a strangler.

A too precipitate disclosure of the frightful truth has sometimes produced fatal consequences. The following affecting story, related by a Thug who had become approver against his comrades, will illustrate

illustrate this; and there is reason to believe that the case is not altogether without parallel. It is admitted, indeed, that others have occurred resembling it in kind, though falling short of it in degree:—"About twelve years ago," said the narrator, "my cousin, Aman Subahdar, took out with us my cousin Kurhora, brother of Omrow approver, a lad of fourteen, for the first time. He was mounted upon a pretty pony; and Hursooka, an adopted son of Aman's, was appointed to take charge of the boy. We fell in with five Sieks; and when we set out before daylight in the morning, Hursooka, who had been already on three expeditions, was ordered to take the bridle, and keep the boy in the rear, out of sight and hearing. The boy became alarmed and impatient, got away from Hursooka, and galloped up at the instant the '*I hirnee*,' or signal for murder, was given. He heard the screams of the men, and saw them all strangled. He was seized with a trembling, and fell from his pony: he became immediately delirious, was dreadfully alarmed at the turbans of the murdered men, and, when any one touched or spoke to him, talked wildly about the murders, screamed as if in sleep, and trembled violently. We could not get him forward; and, after burying the bodies, Aman, myself, and a few others, sat by him while the gang went on: we were very fond of him, and tried all we could to tranquillize him, but he never recovered his

his senses, and before evening he died.—I have seen many instances of feelings greatly shocked at the sight of the first murder, but never one so strong as this. Kurhora was a very fine boy; and Hursooka took his death much to heart, and turned Byragee. He is now at some temple on the banks of the Nerbudda river."

One of the most remarkable features in this narrative is the expression of affection for the unhappy boy, by a man steeped in blood and guilt. The difficulty of supposing the better affections of the heart to subsist in conjunction with the exercise of the trade of murder led Captain Sleeman to ask the individual who related the story, if the children of Thugs continued to reverence their fathers after they became acquainted with their occupation. The answer was brief and decisive, and apparently given without any feeling that the fact averred required explanation, or was calculated to excite surprize. The party interrogated calmly replied, "The same: we love them, and they love us." Such is the inconsistency of human nature!

The indiscriminate slaughter in which these miscreants might be tempted to indulge, is in some degree restrained by superstition. It is deemed unlucky to kill certain castes and classes; and their members are therefore usually respected. The most important and extended exception to the general rule of murder is that of the female sex. Thugs, who

who have any real regard to the principles which they profess to respect, never take the lives of women. It cannot, however, be supposed that such a rule should be invariably observed by such persons as form the society of Thugs; and, in fact, it is constantly violated. "Among us," said one of the approvers interrogated by Captain Sleeman, "it is a rule never to kill a woman; but if a rich old woman is found, the gang sometimes get a man to strangle her, by giving him an extra share of the booty, and inducing him to take the responsibility upon himself. We have sometimes killed other prohibited people, particularly those of low caste, whom we ought not even to have touched."

The Thugs of Hindostan, it is said, are less scrupulous about the murder of women than those of the Deccan; and even with the former, the practice is alleged to be rather of recent origin. It has been seen, that age has had some share in determining the fate of females; and it appears, from the confessions of some of the criminals, that the possession of beauty has been allowed to operate as a protection. Feringcea, a Hindostan Thug, says: "I and my cousin Aman Sabahdar were with a gang of 150 Thugs, on an expedition through Rajpootana, about thirteen years ago, when we met a handmaid of the Peshwa Bajee Row's, on her way from Poona to Cawnpore. We intended to kill her and her followers; but we found her very beautiful;

beautiful; and after having her, and her party, three days within our grasp, and knowing that they had a lac and a half of rupees' worth of property, in jewels and other things, with them, we let her and all her party go: we had talked to her, and felt love towards her, for she was very beautiful."—Beauty, however, does not always disarm these murderers. Another beautiful female, respecting whom the same witness was questioned, was sacrificed without remorse. Feringcea endeavoured to throw the guilt of this transaction upon the Mussulmans of the gang, and to exonerate those of his own creed from participation. "We none of us," said he, "ventured near the palanquin: the Mussulmans were the only men who approached her before the murder."—The comparative forbearance of the Hindoos, in all similar transactions, is a point that was strongly urged by many of the witnesses. Being questioned as to the murder of a female named Kalee Bebee, which had excited some interest, the account given was such as to clear the Hindoo portion of the gang from the guilt of engaging in the act, and even to represent them as actively opposing it; but it does not appear that their conscientiousness extended to the length of finally declining all participation in the spoil, and a few superstitious ceremonies soon reconciled all differences. If the evidence of the approver is to be credited, disputes arose between the Mussulmans and

and the Hindoos, both before and after the murder. The Mussulmans insisted upon killing the lady, as she had four thousand rupees' worth of property with her: the Hindoos would not agree. She was killed, however, with all her followers, twelve in number: but it is added, that, in the first instance, the Hindoos refused to take any part of the booty—that the two parties even came to blows;—at last, the Hindoos gave in, and consented to share in all, but the clothes and ornaments which the women wore. This compromise between cupidity and superstition put an end to the dispute for a time; but when Pursaram Benhman, one of the Hindoo conspirators, returned home, Rae Sing, his brother, refused to eat, drink, or smoke with him, till he had purged himself from this great sin; and he, with two others, gave a feast that cost them a thousand rupees each. This feast, at which four or five thousand Brahmans were assembled, made all right.

Some associations pride themselves upon their purity in this respect. One of the Behar Thugs being asked if that body ever murdered women, answered, with much warmth, "Never! we should not murder a woman, if she had a lac of rupees upon her." A member of the Doab fraternity, who was present, immediately added, "Nor would the Doab Thugs, if she had two lacs upon her."

Among the privileged classes, are, washermen and poets, professors of dancing, blacksmiths and

carpen-

carpenters, musicians, oil-venders, and sweepers, Ganges water-carriers if they have the water actually with them, but if their pots be empty they are subject to the general law of destruction, Madaree Fakeers, and, in some districts, Sieks. The maimed and the leprous are also spared; but perhaps the origin of the latter exemption is ascribable to the fear of contamination, rather than to humanity. The sacred cow, in the eyes of all Hindoos who have any pretensions to consistency, is a protection to its possessor: art is however sometimes resorted to, for the purpose of removing this impediment to business. A party of Thugs projected the murder of fourteen persons, including several women; but the design could not be carried into effect, because the victims had a cow with them. With some difficulty, they were persuaded to sell the cow to the Thugs; who, to induce the travellers to consent to the sale, pretended that they had vowed to make an offering of a cow at Shaphore, and were much in want of one. The cow was actually presented to a Brahman at Shaphore; and the obstacle being removed, the whole of the unsuspecting travellers, including the females, were, two or three hours afterwards, strangled. Such are the fruits of the horrible creed which overspreads and darkens so large a portion of the East!

CHAP. II.

THE practice of Thuggee is not confined to adventurers upon land. The rivers of India are infested by bands of fresh-water pirates, having similar habits to those of the land Thugs, holding the same feeling, and differing only from them in a few trifling particulars. These ruffians go in considerable parties, and have generally several boats at the ghât at the same time. Their murders are always perpetrated in the day-time. Those who do the work of the boatmen are dressed like other boatmen; but those who are to take a part in the operations are dressed like travellers of great respectability; and there are no boats on the river kept so clean and inviting for travellers. When going up the river, they always pretend to be men of some consideration, going on pilgrimage to some sacred place, as Benares, Allahabad, &c. When going down, they pretend to be returning home from such places. They send out their Sothas, or inveiglers, well dressed, upon the high roads; who pretend to be going by water to the same places as the travellers they fall in with. On coming to the ghât, they see these

these nice-looking boats, with the respectably-dressed Thugs amusing themselves. They ask the Manjee (captain) of the boat to take them and the travellers on board, as he can afford to do so cheaper than others, having, apparently, his boat already engaged by others. He pretends to be pushed for room; and the Thugs pretend to be unwilling to have any more passengers on board. At last he yields to the earnest requests of the inveiglers, and the travellers are taken up. They go off into the middle of the river; those above singing and playing, and making a great noise; while the travellers are murdered inside, at the signal, given by three taps, that all is clear, and their bodies thrown into the river. The boat then goes on to some other ghât, having landed the inveiglers again upon the roads.

The peculiarities by which the river Thugs are distinguished from their fellows on shore will be best illustrated by the testimony of one of the latter class, who was consequently well qualified to observe and report on the subject. This person, who had been admitted as evidence against some votaries of Thuggee, stated, that his personal knowledge of the river Thugs was confined to a single occasion. His relation was as follows:—"About fourteen years ago, I had been on an expedition from Chupra to Moorshedabad. We were twenty-two Thugs, under Sewbuns Jemadar, who was a Rajpoot. Two of our gang, Khoda Buksh and

and Alee Yar, had often served with the river Thugs, and used to interest us by talking about their modes of proceeding. On the other side of Rajmahul we fell in with two of these Thugs. They had two bundles of clothes, and pretended to be going on a pilgrimage; and had with them five travellers, whom they had picked up on the road. Sewbuns recognised them immediately, and Alee Yar and Khoda Buksh found in them old acquaintances. They got into conversation with them; and it was agreed that Sewbuns, I, and Dhorda Kormee should go with them, and see how they did their work, while the rest of the gang went on along the bank of the river. We embarked at Rajmahul. The travellers sat on one side of the boat, and the Thugs on the other; while we were all three placed in the stern; the Thugs on our left, and the travellers on our right. Some of the Thugs, dressed as boatmen, were above deck, and others walking along the bank of the river, and pulling the boat by the goon or rope; and all, at the same time, on the look out We came up with a gentleman's pinnace and two baggage-boats, and were obliged to stop and let them go on. The travellers seemed anxious; but were quieted by being told that the men at the rope were tired and must take some refreshment. They pulled out something, and began to eat; and when the pinnace had got on a good way, they resumed their work,

and

and our boat proceeded. It was now afternoon; and when a signal was given above that all was clear, the five Thugs who sat opposite the travellers sprung in upon them, and, with the aid of others, strangled them. They put the roomal round the neck from the front, while all other Thugs put it round from behind: they thus push them back, while we push them forward. Having strangled the five men, they broke their spinal bones; and then threw them out of a hole made at the side, into the river; and kept on their course; the boat being all this time pulled along by the men on the bank."

The division of the booty seems to have been characterized by a very moderate portion of good faith. The witness continued:—"The booty amounted to about two hundred rupees. We claimed and got a share for all our party; and Sewbuns declared that we were twenty-nine, while we were really only twenty-three, and got a share for that number: he cheated them out of the share of six men. We landed that night, and rejoined our gang; and operated upon the roads leading along the river Ganges till we got to the Mormakeya ghât, where there is an invalid station, about four cose the other side of Bar. Here we fell in with the same party of *Pungoos* or river Thugs, who had three travellers with them. I did not join them this time; but Sewbuns, with two other members

members of our gang, went on board, and saw them strangled."

Another witness gave testimony nearly similar. Like the former, he had enjoyed but a single opportunity of observation. He said: "I had been on one expedition with Dilawur Khan, and one with Futteh Khan; and after these, I went with Bhowur Khan and Moradun, two Lodaha Thugs, and joined Jhoulee Khan the Fair, and Gholamun. Jhoulee Khan had a man to carry his bundle, by name Nathoo; as he was to act this season with Jypaul Kaet, a Jemadar of the Pungoos or river Thugs. He acted as their *Sotha,* or inveigler, this season. We joined Jypaul at the Mormakeya ghât, where he had two boats at the different ghâts, two and three cose from each other. Jhoulee Khan brought two *Beetoos* to the boat, which Jypaul commanded in person; and Bhowur Khan and I embarked with them. As soon as we had all got on board, Jypaul said, in Rumasee, "Let the Boras (Thugs) separate themselves from the Beetoos (those not Thugs):" and we did so, leaving the two travellers together. Four men were on the bank, pulling along the boat: one was at the helm, acting at the same time as the *Bykureea* or spy, and seven of the gang were below with us and the travellers. We had got on about a cose, when the Bykureea at the helm, seeing all clear, called out '*Bhugna ko pawn do,*' 'Give my sister's son pawn.' This was their

 mode

mode of giving the *I hirnee,* or signal; and the two Beetoos were strangled. After strangling them, they broke their spinal bones, by putting their knees upon their backs, and pulling up their heads and shoulders. After doing this, they pushed the bodies out of a kind of window in the vessel's side. Every boat has two of these windows, one on each side; and they put the bodies out of that towards the river. They break the spinal bones to prevent all chance of the people recovering and giving evidence against them. We generally stab the dead bodies through, on both sides, under the arm-pits; but they are afraid to cut or stab the body, lest there should be signs of blood upon the water, as the corpses pass other boats that are following them on the river. We got only sixteen gundas of pice, two brass lotahs, and the old clothes which the two men wore: it was hardly worth dividing. But coming on near Monghere, Jhoulee Khan, with whom we had landed and gone along the road near the river, inveigled another man, a Beetoo from Bengal, going to Guya on pilgrimage, who yielded sixteen gundas of rupees; and we six got fifteen of them among us; at least, Jhoulee Khan shared only fifteen with us. The traveller was disposed of in the same manner as the others, I believe; but I did not go on board this time. Jhoulee Khan and Bhowur Khan embarked with him, and brought back our share of the booty. After this affair I left them near Monghere,

as

as I got very little; and grew melancholy, as there were no Thugs of my own clan or district. They were all Bungoos and Loduhas."—The sentiment of this ruffian must be felt to be truly affecting!

The following report of a case of river Thuggee, drawn up by the Magistrate of Furreedpore, may be sufficient to complete the picture:—

"In July last, two men, one a Mussulman, the other a Hindoo, left Dacca together for Furreedpore, where they never arrived. Inquiries were made in both Zillahs, through the police, but without effect. It was stated that they had fifteen rupees with them, and that there were two other passengers on the same boat. In September, a man named Bholanath Chung was brought to me: he stated, that, in Magh of that year, he and several others went to Rungpore with two tobacco-merchants as passengers, strangled them with angoochas, and threw them into the river, and got forty rupees from them. His relation, Suroop Chung, he said, knew more of this, and might know something of the Dacca case. Suroop was sent for; and came and deposed that he and five others were at Dacca in a pulwar. They took two passengers on board, to bring them to Furreedpore—one a Mussulman, the other a Hindoo; took them to a Chur sand-bank about two hours' journey distance from Dacca, there strangled them with angoochas, threw the

the bodies overboard, and went back, through Dacca, to Naraigunje: got fifteen rupees, and other property, from them: two of the leaders of the gang dressed themselves up as Brahmins, and seated themselves in the boat as passengers, to inspire confidence. They afterwards added, that there were two boats, one a panchway with five men in it, besides the pulwar. These men, he afterwards reported, were in the panchway close to Furreedpore, having come for passengers at the Doorga Poojah. They were seized, four in number. At first, all told contradictory stories as to where they had been, &c.; afterwards, three confessed;—two, to having been Mullahs (sailors) of the boat on which the two missing passengers left Dacca, with other particulars; the third, to having told a false story at the request of the others. His brother was one of the party at Dacca; but being sick, had staid at home, and he had taken his place. In the boat was found a doty, recognised by the friends of the Hindoo; also a Mussulman dress and piece of cloth, recognised by the friends of the missing Mussulman; but the latter could bring no witness to swear to them. There were also found in the boat two Brahminical threads; though all the boatmen were Chandals. The Nazir and a Mohurir were sent to take up all the persons implicated in these confessions. Two others, who were taken up, confessed; and one produced from his house a lota, which

which he said had been his share of the spoil. This had before been mentioned as having been with the deceased, and was identified by three or four witnesses. The brother of one of the missing men, who had accompanied them to the boat, deposed that the panchway which was seized near Furreedpore was the same as that in which the missing men went. He also swore that he believed that two of the prisoners were two of the men he saw in the boat; the one, one of the Brahmin passengers; the other, one of the Mullahs (sailors). Suroop, who first gave information and had been promised pardon, was admitted as a witness against the others, of whom eight were made over for trial.

"In the above case, a man named Surbul Dam was named in Suroop's confession. On being taken up in the Mofussil, he denied; but when examined by me, though he denied all knowledge of the Dacca case, he confessed, that in May and June he went with a numbers of others in three boats, one a pulwar; that they first took on board, in Mymunsing (close to the borders of Furreedpore), two Tanties (weavers), on pretence of buying cloths from them; that he went on shore for a short time; and on coming back, saw the cloths, but not the Tanties. The cloths were divided among the party, and he concluded the Tanties were murdered. They went to Rungpore; and they were coming back when they fell in with a boat laden with tobacco and hemp, going

going to Seraigunje. There were five men in it. They kept with this boat for a day or two. At last, on pretence of singing *Hurry Soot*, they got the five men of the tobacco-boat to sit down with them in a circle, and then strangled them all with angoochas; one man performing the operation on each, whilst the others held their hands and feet and pressed upon their stomachs. They threw the bodies into the river; and went down the stream till evening with both boats; when they put the hemp and tobacco into their own pulwar, and sunk the boat of the men they had murdered, by breaking two holes through the bottom of it with a hatchet. They returned, and sold the tobacco and hemp at Manickgunje, in this district.—The persons implicated by this statement were all taken up: three confessed, according to the statement of Surbul Dam, but more clearly. They also said, there were only two boats, and in all ten men; which, on comparison of the statements, was evidently the true one. One of these was Bholanath, the first informer. Both he and another, Kissen Mohun, said they saw the two Tanties strangled. One other man owned having been a party to the sale of the hemp and tobacco which they brought from Rungpore: he was one of the leaders of the gang. In nearly all their houses a bundle of tobacco was found. On inquiry, the heirs of the two Tanties were discovered: they were residents in Furreed-

Furreedpore: their brothers went to a place in Mymunsing to sell some cloths, and never returned: the time of their disappearance, and places they were coming from and going to, agreed with the statements of the prisoners. They did not effect a sale of their cloths at Mymunsing, and were coming back with them. Some very fine pieces of cloth, found in the prisoners' hands, bore the same mark as that used by the deceased; but they could not be identified by oath. The heirs of the five men in the tobacco-boat were likewise found: four of them resided in Mymunsing they hired out their boat and services to a Mahajun merchant at Seraigunje; went with a cargo of salt to Rungpore, and were coming back with tobacco and hemp when they were thus murdered. The fifth person was a man sent by the Gomashta to pilot them. Intelligence had duly been given to the police at Rungpore; and the magistrate of that district reported, that a boat, answering in description to the one described by Surbul Dam, had been found, with two holes cut through the bottom. The place where it was found agreed also with Surbul Dam's statement. The boat was sent for; and also the Rungpore Gomashta, who proved the despatch of the hemp and tobacco. The sale of it at Manickgunje was proved by the merchant who effected it: four of the prisoners were identified as parties to the sale, which was regularly entered in the books. The

boat

boat was identified, both by the relations of the deceased who owned it, and by the witnesses who were admitted as King's evidence against the others. It had been repaired, but the original size of the two holes had been marked out. Two men were admitted as witnesses against the others: eight were made over for the murder of the two Tanties and the five tobacco boatmen; and one for receiving and assisting at the sale of the tobacco. In the house of one of the non-confessing prisoners, in the Dacca case, was found a brass Belu; which was recognised by a Gwala at Furreedpore, as having been with his brother when he and two others left Furreedpore for Mymunsing in January 1834: they have never since been heard of. It is regularly entered in the list of property lost, which was given in when they were declared missing. Unfortunately, no other witness to the property has yet been found."

CHAP. III.

THE dark and cheerless night of superstition, which has long clouded the moral vision of India, has given rise to institutions and practices so horrible and fantastic, that, without the most convincing evidence, their existence could not be credited by minds trained under happier circumstances than those which prevail in the East. That giant power, which has held the human race in chains wherever the pure and unadulterated doctrines of Revelation have not penetrated, has in India revelled in the wantonness of prosperity; the foundations of delusion have been laid wide and deep; the poison of a false and brutalizing creed has been insinuated into every action of daily life; the most obvious distinctions of right and wrong have been obliterated; and men have been encouraged to believe, that, while stifling the best and strongest feelings of nature, and violating the plainest rules of social duty, they were but fulfilling their destined part in the scheme of the world, and even paying homage to those invisible forms which they were bound, both by conscience and interest, to reverence.

The

The fact of the existence of the cold-blooded miscreants who in India make a trade of assassination, is sufficiently horrible : but when it is added, that their occupation is sanctified by the national religion—that the Thugs regard themselves as engaged in the especial service of one of the dark divinities of the Hindoo creed—that the instruments of murder are in their eyes holy—and that their faith in the protection of their goddess, and the perpetuity of their craft, is not to be shaken—we must be struck by the reflection, that we have opened a page in the history of man, fearful and humiliating beyond the ordinary records of iniquity.

The genius of Paganism, which has deified every vice, and thus provided a justification of the indulgence of every evil propensity, has furnished the Thugs with a patron goddess, worthy of those whom she is believed to protect. Of Kalee, the deity of destruction, they are the most devout and assiduous worshippers: in her name they practise their execrable art; and their victims are held to be immolated in her honour.

This horrible divinity they believe to have formerly co-operated more directly with her votaries the Thugs, by disposing of the bodies of those whom they destroyed. Kalee, however, chose to be secret in her operations; and the Thugs were prohibited from looking back, to see what she was about. All was well, so long as they observed

observed this rule; but the services of the goddess as a sextoness were lost through the carelessness or indiscreet curiosity of one of the association. Of the circumstances attendant on this mischance, there are different versions; and at least two are in pretty general circulation. According to one, prevalent in the Deccan, a party of Thugs, having destroyed a traveller, left the body, as usual, unburied, in perfect confidence of receiving the wonted aid from the goddess. A novice, however, unguardedly looking behind him, saw the patroness of the Thugs in the act of feasting on the corpse, one half of it hanging out of her mouth. According to another report, the person looking back was a slave; and the goddess was engaged, not in satisfying the demands of hunger, or gratifying a taste for luxury, by swallowing the murdered traveller, but in tossing the body into the air;—for what purpose does not appear. The offence to the goddess is said, also, to have been aggravated by the fact, that she was not attired with sufficient strictness to satisfy her sense of decorum. Both tales agree, in representing the goddess as highly displeased, and as visiting her displeasure upon her servants, the Thugs, by condemning them to bury their victims themselves. According to the Southern version indeed, like a wise and beneficent potentate, she tempered justice with mercy; for though she refused any longer to relieve

relieve the earth of the loathsome burdens with which her worshippers encumbered it, she was so considerate as to present her friends with one of her teeth for a pickaxe, a rib for a knife, and the hem of her lower garment for a noose. Whether or not this origin of the pickaxe be generally received, it is certain that this instrument is held by the Thugs throughout India in the highest veneration. Its fabrication is superintended with the greatest care; and it is consecrated to the holy duty to which it is destined, with many ceremonies. In the first place, a lucky day must be fixed upon: the leader of the gang then instructs a smith to make the required tool, and the process is conducted with the most profound secrecy. The door is peremptorily closed against all intrusion; the leader never quits the forge while the manufacture is going on; and the smith must engage in no other work, till his sacred task is completed. The pickaxe being made, must next be consecrated. Certain days of the week are deemed more auspicious for this purpose than the rest: Monday, Tuesday, Wednesday, and Friday, enjoy the distinction. Care is taken that the shadow of no living thing may fall on the axe, as this would contaminate the devoted implement, and frustrate all the pains that had been taken in its formation. A Doctor most deeply versed in the learning of the Thugs undertakes the solemn office of consecration.

cration. He sits down with his face to the West, and receives the pickaxe in a brass dish. The instrument which is to supply the want occasioned by the cessation of the goddess's personal labours is first washed in water, which is received into a pit dug for the purpose. The pickaxe then receives three further ablutions; the material employed in each being more expensive and valuable than that used in the first. The second washing is made with a mixture of sugar and water; the third with sour milk; and the fourth with ardent spirits. The pickaxe is then marked, from the head to the point, with seven spots. In performing this operation, the material used is neither very valuable nor very dignified, it being nothing but common red-lead. The brass dish, on which the pickaxe was handed to the officiating Thug, now comes into play again: the pickaxe is placed upon it, with a cocoa-nut, some cloves, white sandal-wood, sugar, and a few other articles. A fire is next kindled, and the fuel must consist of dried cow-dung, and the wood of the Mango or Byr tree. All the articles deposited in the brass pan are, with the exception of the cocoa-nut, thrown into the fire; and when the flame rises, the Thug priest, holding the pickaxe with both hands, passes it seven times through the fire. The cocoa-nut is now stripped of its outer coat, and placed on the ground. The comptroller of the pickaxe, holding it it by the point, then says, "Shall I strike?" The bystanders signifying their assent, he strikes the cocoa-nut with the butt end of the pickaxe, and breaks it, exclaiming, "All hail, mighty Davy (the goddess), great Mother of us all!" The surrounding spectators respond, "All hail, Davy! and prosper the Thugs!" This is a most interesting and exciting moment to the Thugs; for upon the hardness of the nut, the skill of the operator, and the accidental circumstances which may affect the force or direction of the blow, depend the realization of the hopes of the community. If the cocoa-nut be not severed at one blow, all the labour is thrown away; the goddess is understood to be unpropitious; another day must be selected for the repetition of the ceremonies, and all the trouble be incurred again. If, however, the nut is cleft at once, the proof of the approval of the goddess is indisputable. The whole of the shell, and some of the kernel of the nut, is thrown into the fire; the pickaxe is carefully tied up in a clean white cloth, and, being placed on the ground to the West, the assembled spectators, turning in that direction, prostrate themselves in adoration before "that which their own fingers have made"; that which the labour of the smith might have fashioned with equal facility into an object of reverence or of contempt; and which, while it receives divine honours, is destined to assist in a series of acts, at once horrible

by

by their guilt, and disgusting by their loathsomeness.

The ceremony of prostration concluded, all present receive a portion of the cocoa-nut: the fragments are then collected, and thrown into the pit which had been previously prepared, lest, if they remained on the ground, the sacred relics might be outraged by the defiling touch of some human foot.

These ceremonies, elaborate as they are, suffice only for a single expedition. At the commencement of every fresh series of adventures, they must be repeated.

When the sacred pickaxe is thus prepared, the next point is, to place it in safe custody: it is not every Thug who can be trusted with it. The person who bears it is selected, principally, for his shrewdness, caution, and sobriety. It is, however, only when on a journey that it is entrusted to human care at all. When in camp, it is deposited in the earth, under the especial protection of the goddess. When buried, it is always placed with the point towards the direction in which the party intend to proceed; and they have the fullest confidence, that if another course is to be preferred, the point will be found to have veered round so as to indicate the better way. Certain classes of the Thugs, when halting, throw their instrument into a well; and the received belief is, that, when wanted, it will come up of itself, if summoned in due form.

 Of

Of course, the instructed know better ; but all *profess* implicit belief in the miraculous egress of the pickaxe from the well into which it is thrown. One of the Thugs, interrogated by Captain Sleeman, said: "We have all of us seen the sacred pickaxe spring in the morning from the well into which it had been thrown overnight, and come to the hands of the man who carried it, at his call : nay, we have seen the pickaxes of different gangs all come up of themselves, from the same well, at the same time, and go to their several bearers." On being reminded of the extraordinary feats performed by jugglers, the Thug replied, with great energy : "What ! shall not a hundred generations of Thugs be able to distinguish the tricks of man from the miracles of God ? Is there not the difference of heaven and earth between them ? Is not one a mere trick ; and the other a miracle, witnessed by hundreds assembled at the same time ?" —Captain Sleeman then said to another Thug: "Sahib Khan, you are more sober than Nasir ; have you ever seen it ?" The answer was : "On one expedition only. I was obliged to fly from Telingana when Major Parker and Captain Sheriff made their inroad upon us (Gurdee), and I went and joined the Arcot gangs. During a whole expedition that I made with them, Imam Khan and his brother carried the pickaxes ; and I heard them, repeatedly, in the morning call them from the well into which they had thrown them overnight, and saw the

pickaxes

pickaxes come of themselves from the well, and fall into their aprons, which they held open *thus*"—here he exhibited the mode.

No one acquainted with the almost superhuman dexterity of Indian jugglers will feel much surprise at these feats. Their prevalence only shews the extent to which delusion may be carried, in a country where human intellect has been long prostrated by a brutalizing superstition.

When the pickaxe is buried, no foot must touch the earth which covers it; nor must it, at any time, be approached by an unclean animal, or any object which bears contamination. After each time that it has been used for the preparation of a grave, it must be submitted to the purification of the bath.

If the pickaxe fall from the hand of the man who bears it, dismay spreads through the gang. The omen is regarded as of the most fearful description: its horrors are aggravated by the uncertainty, as to the nature of the approaching evil, and even as to the party upon whom it is to descend. The omen may indicate the death of the individual who had the care of the sacred weapon, and who, through heedlessness, or misfortune, or unavoidable fatality, suffered it to drop from his embrace: or it may forebode some dreadful reverse to the fortunes of the gang. Measures are immediately taken to frustrate the evil token; and the first step is, to deprive the unhappy pickaxe-bearer of his office.

 The

The enterprise in hand, whatever it might be, is immediately abandoned; and the pickaxe must undergo a fresh consecration. Even these precautions are insufficient to restore things to their original state: the misfortune operates, upon the gang to whom it happens, as a sentence of excommunication from the society of all faithful Thugs. No other party will ever associate with one whose pickaxe has fallen, lest they should be involved in the evil which is apprehended to the "doomed ones."

The pickaxe affords the most solemn sanction of an oath among these murderers; and if any sanction can bind their consciences, it is, perhaps, the only one capable of effecting that purpose. Compared with it, neither the water of the Ganges weighs with the Hindoo, nor the Koran with the Mussulman. When the sacred pickaxe is not at hand, recourse is had to various expedients to remedy the want, and to give validity to the administration of an oath. A piece of cloth is made up into the form of the pickaxe, and duly consecrated: the person sworn then places his hand upon it, or holds it in both hands; and, after the administration of the oath, drinks water in which the representative of the revealed instrument has been washed. In other instances, he goes before the image of the goddess, with the emblem of the pickaxe in his hand, and there takes the oath. If a cloth a cloth is not conveniently to be had, even mud, moulded into the proper form, and duly submitted to the ceremonies of consecration, will answer the purposes. "If any man swears to a falsehood upon a pickaxe properly consecrated," said the Thugs, "we will consent to be hanged if he survive the time appointed. Appoint one, two, or three days, when he swears, and we pledge ourselves that he does not live a moment beyond the time: he will die a horrid death; his head will turn round, his face towards the back; and he will writhe in torture till he dies." The infliction of this miserable fate, some, even of the most intelligent of the Thug fraternity, declared that they had often seen. The pickaxe is, in short, the standard, round which all the gloomy family of Thug superstitions rally: it is regarded as the great source of security and prosperity:—the instrument of strangulation is held in esteem; but that of burial, in infinitely more—the Thugs think of it with enthusiasm. "Do we not," said one, interrogated by Captain Sleeman, "do we not worship it every seventh day? Is it not our standard? Is its sound ever heard, when digging the grave, by any but a Thug? And can any man even swear to a falsehood upon it?"—"How could we dig graves," asked another, "with any other instrument? This is the one appointed by Davy (the goddess), and consecrated; and we should never have survived the attempt

attempt to use any other."—"No man," it was added, "but a Thug, who has been a strangler, and is remarkable for his cleanliness and decorum, is permitted to carry it."

But though the pickaxe is the great symbol of their profession, and the devout object of their care, the respect in which it is held is but one of the degrading and frightful superstitions by which these murderers steel their hearts to encounter the horrors of their wretched profession.

CHAP. IV.

The authority for the mode of murder practised by the Thugs is traced, like all their other usages, to the tremendous goddess whom they serve. It seems, that, in remote ages, a demon infested the earth, and devoured mankind as soon as created. The proportions of this devouring monster were so gigantic, that the water did not reach his waist in the most unfathomable parts of the ocean; and he strode over the world unrestrained, rioting in the destruction of the human race. The world was thus kept unpeopled, until the goddess of the Thugs came to the rescue. She attacked the demon, and cut him down; but from every drop of his blood another demon arose: and though the goddess continued to cut down these rising demons with wonderful alacrity and scientific skill, fresh broods of demons sprung from their blood, as from that of their progenitors; and the diabolical race consequently multiplied with fearful rapidity. The never-ending labour of cutting down demons, whose number was only increased by this operation of pruning, at length fatigued and disheartened the goddess; she found it indis-

indispensably necessary to make a change in her tactics;—and here the tale, which is thus far universally received, becomes subject to variations. It is admitted by all Hindoos, that the demons multiplied in the manner described, until the goddess found some means of putting a stop to this "surplus population": but there is a difference of belief as to the mode. The orthodox opinion is, that when the goddess found the drops of blood thus rapidly passing into demons—a fact which, with all her divine attributes, it seems she only learned by experience—she hit upon a very happy expedient to prevent the blood reaching the earth, where the demoniacal conversion took place. Being furnished with a tongue of extraordinary dimensions, she, after every blow, promptly and carefully licked the blood away. A "preventive check" being thus placed upon the further propagation of demons, the goddess was enabled to destroy those previously existing, at her leisure:—such is the commonly-received account of the goddess's dexterity and address. That of the Thugs is varied, for the purpose of affording a superhuman sanction to their mode of assassination. According to Thug mythology, the goddess, when she became embarrassed by the constant reinforcements of the demon army which accrued from her labours, relinquished all personal efforts for their suppression, and formed two men from the perspiration brushed from

from her arms. To each of these men she gave a handkerchief; how fabricated, at a time when reels and looms were not, is a question open to the discussion of the learned. With these handkerchiefs, the goddess's two lieutenants were commanded to put all the demons to death, without shedding a drop of blood. It does not appear why the goddess might not thus have plied the handkerchief herself: it may be presumed that she was too much exhausted by her previous exertions. Her commands, however, were faithfully executed; and the demons were all strangled without delay.

There is some difficulty in understanding how demons so powerful succumbed thus readily to two agents, who, though sprung from an exudation of the goddess's arms, were, as appears by the sequel of the tale, merely children of mortality: but the difficulty never seems to have occurred to the Thugs, whose faith, like that of the mass of their countrymen, is of a very unscrupulous character. The story is wound up with such poetical justice as might be expected in a Hindoo legend. The champions, having vanquished all the demons, offered, like honest men, to return the handkerchiefs; but their patroness, in the spirit of a grateful goddess, desired that they would retain them, not merely as memorials of their heroism, but as the implements of a lucrative trade in which their descendants were to labour and thrive. They were not only permitted,

permitted, but commanded, to strangle men, as they had strangled demons. They forebore, indeed, to exercise this privilege for a long period: so say the Thugs. Several generations passed before Thuggee became practised as a profession. Whether this forbearance was founded on the principle according to which a sportsman suffers game to accumulate, is not stated. The privilege slept; but though dormant, it was not lost; and in due time it was abundantly exercised. The lapse between the grant of the patent and the use of it might tend to raise a presumption against its having been granted; but Hindoo casuists are not accustomed to scrutinize evidence with the severity which prevails in Westminster Hall.

Thus, according to the creed of the Thugs, did their order arise; and thus originated their mode of operation. The assistance once afforded by the goddess in removing the bodies, and the means by which this favour was forfeited, have already been noticed.

It has been mentioned, that the high office of a strangler is not attained until after a noviciate of considerable length. When the disciple has been sufficiently prepared, or at least when he believes that the conquest of natural feeling is so far complete as to enable him to perform without shrinking that which he has learned to contemplate without horror, he applies to one of the most experienced

and

and respected of the gang to become his *gooroo*. This word appears to be derived from the *goor*, or "coarse sugar," which forms an important ingredient in the ceremonies of initiation; and the office of the person honoured with this title is, to introduce the aspirant to the actual exercise of his profession; to instruct him in the science of hangmanship; and to preside over the rites by which the pupil is to be consecrated to his diabolical work. Precautions are taken that the young beginner may not be embarrassed by difficulties. A victim is selected for his first essay in guilt, whose strength is below the average; and the chosen period of operation is at the moment when the senses of the traveller are bewildered by being suddenly roused from sleep. While the latter is reposing himself, the preparation takes place. The gooroo takes the pupil into a field, accompanied by three or four of the older members of the gang. The ceremonies commence by the whole party facing in the direction in which they intend to move. The gooroo then proceeds to take the auspices. Having invoked a favourable sign from the goddess, half an hour is allowed for the fulfilment of their wishes. If, in the course of that time, the required sign is obtained, all is well, and the goddess is believed to regard the attempt of the young Thug with benignity; but if no sign is obtained, or if it is of an unfavourable nature, the ambition of the novice is for that time disappointed, and

and the destined victim must fall by hands already practised in the murderous work.

If the sanction of the goddess be indicated, the group retire, in high spirits, to the place where the sleeping traveller awaits his death. The gooroo then, turning to the west, takes a handkerchief, and ties at one end a knot, in which he encloses a rupee. This knot is of a peculiar description, and the privilege of tying it confined to those who have been regularly introduced to their occupation. The clumsy intruder, who has not participated in the advantages derived from a regular apprenticeship to the art, leaves the end of the *roomal* exposed: the more accomplished practitioner manifests his science and elegance by concealing the end within the knot. This is the mark of his regular induction, and the ribbon of the order to which he has the honour to belong.

The knot being duly tied by the gooroo, the roomal is delivered to the incipient strangler, who receives it with all the reverence due to so precious a gift, bestowed by such venerated hands. The interest of the scene now increases. The executioner, attended by a *ghumgeea*, or holder of hands, stands before his victim, whose tranquil state is but an emblem of that deeper sleep which is about to seal his eyes for ever. His last earthly slumber is gradually interrupted—the victim is roused for slaughter—the fatal noose is cast over

his

his neck by the hand of the youthful assassin, and, with the aid of the attendant ruffian, the work is soon completed. One human being has passed into eternity;—another has taken the last step in guilt and infamy!

The horrible work is over; and, so far from being actuated by any sensations of pity or remorse, the wretch, who has attested the strength of his nerves and the weakness of his moral perceptions, knows no feeling but that of delight flowing from gratified ambition. To his instructor, guide, and priest, his gratitude is boundless: he bows before his gooroo, and touches his feet with both hands, in token of the deepest and most affectionate respect. But his gratitude, if confined to the person of his preceptor, would be felt to be inadequate and niggardly: the relations and friends of the reverend man are entitled to share the warm feelings of the now-accomplished assassin; and to them he tenders the same homage which he has previously paid to his father in crime.

The *thibaoo*, or happy auspice, is once more anxiously looked for; and as soon as it is afforded, the newly-admitted strangler opens the knot tied in the handkerchief by the hands of his tutor, and takes out the rupee which had been placed within it. This coin, with all the other silver which he has, the pupil presents to the preceptor: the latter adds his own stock of money to the offering, and,

after

after setting apart one rupee and a quarter to the purchase of *goor* (coarse sugar) for the Tapoonee, the remainder is expended in sweatmeats.

The Tapoonee is a solemn sacrifice, performed after every murder. The goor (sugar) is placed upon a blanket or sheet, spread upon a clean spot. On the cloth near the goor is deposited the consecrated pickaxe, and a piece of silver for an offering. The Thug whose reputation for professional learning stands the highest, and who is supposed to enjoy the largest share of the favour of the goddess, also takes his place on the cloth, with his face to the west: the most accomplished and scientific stranglers are associated with him in this place of honour. The number of this select body must be an even one; but its extent is limited only by the size of the cloth. Those of the higher grade, who are unable to find accommodation among their brethren, and the vulgar herd who have no claim to distinction, arrange themselves around the covering which bears the sacrifice, and those who preside over it. The leader then makes a hole in the ground, and, having poured into it a little of the goor, clasps his hands in the attitude of fervent devotion, and, raising them in harmony with his up-turned eyes to heaven, gives utterance to the following prayer:—"Great goddess! as you vouchsafed one lac and sixty thousand rupees to Joora Naig and Koduck Bunwanee in their need, so we pray thee fulfil our desires!" The

enumera-

enumeration of the precise number of thousands bestowed by the goddess upon her favourites is not very poetical; but the petition is so entirely accordant with Thug feeling, that no doubt can be entertained as to the sincerity with which it is offered. All the assembled followers repeat the prayer after the leader; and the latter, after sprinkling water on the pit and pickaxe, puts a little of the goor upon the head of each Thug who has been so fortunate as to obtain a seat upon the carpet. The signal for strangling is now given, as if a murder were actually about to be committed; and the Thugs who have received the portions of goor, eat them in solemn silence. The most perfect stillness prevails, till these privileged persons have swallowed the precious morsels distributed to them, and diluted the repast by drinking some water. The goor is now given to all whose rank entitles them to partake of it; the greatest care being taken that no part shall fall to the ground. If, in spite of watchfulness, such a mischance should occur, the fallen fragments are punctiliously collected, and put into the pit. The misfortune is alleviated, as far as human prudence can go, by at least preserving the hapless relics of the sugar consecrated to murder, from contamination by the foot of man.

The sacred goor is not imparted to all Thugs indiscriminately: two conditions are necessary, to qualify

qualify them for a share of it. The participant must be in a state of freedom—servitude barring his admission to the privilege: the only remaining disqualification is found in innocence of murder, either actual or comparative. None but the practical assassin can be allowed to partake of the sacred goor: no one but he whose hands have performed the office of strangling is thought worthy of the food which derives its sanctity from the prayers of stranglers, aided, it is to be supposed, by the deglutition of the privileged, to which a portion of it has been submitted. For those who cannot boast the name of freemen, or whom youth or fear or ill-fortune has withheld from performing on any of their fellow men the honourable act of strangulation, some sugar is set apart, before it acquires its holy character. This the excluded eat, at the time when their more-favoured associates are gratified by the taste of the sanctified article.

On the performance of this ceremony, after the maiden effort of a newly-admitted strangler, the proselyte of course takes his place among the select, and receives his share of consecrated sugar. The sweetmeats which have been provided are distributed among the gang generally.

The expedition being closed, and the members of the community having retired to their quarters, the happy individual, who has passed from a state of pupilage into the maturity of a practised assassin,

assassin, entertains his gooroo at a feast as magnificent as his circumstances will afford. If he have the means of defraying the expense, not only the immediate members of the gooroo's family, but all his relations, are invited, and the grateful murderer equips his tutor, from head to foot, with a complete array of new vestments: the same compliment is paid to the gooroo's lady, and sometimes to all his relatives. The hospitality of the gooroo is exercised, in return, by inviting his pupil to a future meeting. The connexion between them is henceforward indissoluble; and the most intimate and sacred relations of nature are considered as nothing, in comparison with it. A Thug will rather betray his father, than the gooroo by whom he has been introduced to the honours of his profession.

The dignity and sanctity with which murder is invested by the creed of the Thugs—and a mode of murder, too, marked by cowardice and meanness no less than the blackest atrocity—afford lamentable proof of the inseparable connexion subsisting between the corruption of religion and the corruption of morals. To obliterate all religious feeling from the heart of man is a difficult, if not an impossible task: to substitute superstitious belief for reasonable faith, is, unhappily, a very easy one; and sound morals invariably disappear with sound religion. Indeed, between false religion and false morals there is a mutual action and re-action.

 The

The wayward desires of man lead him to indulge in that which true religion forbids: he therefore seeks shelter in a false one. Again, superstition sanctions, and even commands, practices, against which pure morality revolts: hence the moral judgment is depraved, the restraints of conscience abolished, and that feeling, which should conduct men to all that is good and pure and excellent, becomes the pilot to every vice, and the prompter of the most horrible crimes.

The effect of the consecrated sugar or goor is believed to be irresistible. Captain Sleeman, having reproached some of the fraternity on account of a murder marked by many ferocious and unmanly features, one of the party replied: "We all feel pity sometimes; but the goor of the Tuponee changes our nature: it would change the nature of a horse. Let any man once taste of that goor, and he will be a Thug, though he know all the trades and have all the wealth in the world. I never wanted food: my mother's family was opulent—her relations high in office. I have been high in office myself; and became so great a favourite wherever I went, that I was sure of promotion; yet I was always miserable when absent from my gang, and obliged to return to Thuggee. My father made me taste of that fatal goor when I was yet a mere boy: and if I were to live a thousand years, I should never be able to follow any other trade."

The

The Tuponee is not the only sacrifice offered by the Thugs to their patroness. Throughout India, another feast is observed; but to which, in Hindostan, no peculiar name appears to be allotted; it being called *Kurhae kurna*, or *Kurhahee dena*—terms indiscriminately applied, by all classes of persons, to a feast of any kind. In the Deccan it is honoured by the especial name of *Kote*. The requisites for the due celebration of this festival are goats—for the feast must be graced by an animal sacrifice—rice, ghee (butter), spices, and spirits. These being collected, the parties assemble in a room, the doors and windows of which must be so closed as to exclude all observation from without. The floor must be carefully cleaned, and then covered with an incrustation of cow-dung. In the centre, a square is drawn, with a mixture of turmeric and lime. Upon this square is spread a white sheet; and upon the sheet, the rice, after being boiled, is deposited. Upon the rice is placed the half of a cocoa-nut, filled with ghee; in which is inserted two wicks, lying across each other, each lighted at both ends, so as to afford four lights. If a cocoa-nut cannot be found, a vessel of dough of the same form will answer. This kind of lamp is occasionally made by all classes of people, and is called *chou mukh*: it is only in the Deccan, however, that the form of the lamp is an object of attention. In Hindostan they are less particular:

 and

and there also the drawing of the square is omitted.

Upon the white sheet is now placed the consecrated pickaxe and the knife of the gang, with all the spirits brought for the feast. The selection of the goats is the next point; more than will be required are provided, in order that the goddess may have the advantage of a pick. Two are selected, black, and perfect in all their parts. They are bathed, washed, and made to face the west: and if they shake themselves lustily, to throw off the moisture from their bodies, this makes the Thugs happy, and seals the fate of the goats—they are immediately sacrificed, as having been accepted by Davy. If one only shakes himself, the omen is sufficient, and both are sacrificed—if neither of them, it is a sign that Davy has rejected both; and the party eat the rice and drink the spirits, but postpone the sacrifice to another day, regarding the feast in the light of a simple meal. This they do if any other bad omen is observed on that day, considering the goddess to be displeased with something.

The mode of sacrificing the goats varies; and the variations are not, like those affecting the square, and the form of the lamp, governed by locality: the custom is determined by the peculiar creed which the party of Thugs happen to profess. Mahometans cut the throats of the animals, during the

the repetition of a certain form of devotion: Hindoos strike off their heads. It has been mentioned, that the fate of these animals depends upon the receipt of a propitious sign from the goddess; and the duration of life in the rejected animals is involved in the same chance. If the desired sign be obtained by the honoured beasts shaking themselves with good will, not only are they sacrificed, but all the other goats purchased for the occasion, albeit unworthy of being devoted to the goddess, share the fate of their more illustrious fellows. They do not die with equal honour: the chosen pair ministers to the glory of the goddess of Destruction: the remainder die, but it is only to gratify the appetites of the Thug fraternity, by whom they are forthwith eaten. The withholding of the required sign, however, operates as a reprieve for the lives of all; and the meaner, as well as the nobler and more perfect animals, are permitted to live till a future day.

If the feast take place, a pit is dug, into which is thrown the skins, bones, and offal; for nothing brought in for this sacred feast must be seen by any living thing but a Thug eligible to partake of it. So important is care upon this point, and so fearful are the results which follow unfavourable omens at this sacrifice, that every part of the proceeding is watched with the most intense anxiety. If any man not a Thug see the lamps, or any part of the

the preparations; or if fire falls on the white sheet, and burns any part of it; or any animal touches the bones or offal; the leader of the gang must die within the year, and all the members be involved in some great calamity.

Secrecy is indispensable: when they are on an expedition, the Thugs must conceal themselves and their ceremonies by means of curtains, if they have not walls. After feasting, they must all wash their hands and faces over the pit, and then fill it up securely.

The expenses of this feast are defrayed commonly by subscription, when it is called the *Punchaetee Kote.* It is not confined to any particular season, but is most common during the Hooly or Dusera festivals, at which time it may take place on any day of the week; at other times, it is confined to Tuesdays and Fridays. Sometimes the feast is given by the leader or any individual member of a gang. No Thug is eligible to partake of it, in any part of India, till he has attained the rank of a Strangler; unless his family have been Thugs for at least two generations. The existence of contamination in the camp prevents its celebration at all.

The superstitions of the Thugs are all of Hindoo origin: yet Mahometans adopt them with a belief equally implicit, and a devotion equally ardent. The greater number of the Thugs in the South of India

India are said to be Mahometans: not only do they profess to embrace the creed of Mecca, but, to a considerable extent, they follow it consistently. They marry, inherit, eat, and drink, according to the Koran: their devotions are statedly performed as the rule of Mahometan orthodoxy prescribes; and the Paradise to which their hopes are directed, is that pourtrayed by the cold, unspiritual, and sensual imagination of the false prophet to whom they profess allegiance: yet they pay divine honours to the impersonation of Destruction, which, in the eyes of all sound Mahometans, must be idolatry—a crime severely denounced in the Koran, and held by all good Mussulmans in abhorrence. These inconsistencies they find it hard to reconcile: sometimes they deny the worship of the goddess—the fact, however, is indisputable. At other times they seek to identify the patroness of the Thugs with a heroine of their own creed, to the great scandal of their brethren not initiated in the mysteries of Thuggee. Their mode of escaping the difficulties, in which they are involved by the inconsistency of their creed with their practice, is illustrated by a conversation held by Captain Sleeman with some Mahometan Thugs.

Q. (by Capt. S.) "Has Bhowanee (the goddess) been anywhere named in the Koran?"

Sahib. "No where."

Here

Here (says Captain S.) a Mussulman Thug from Hindostan interposed; and said, he thought Bhowanee, and Fatima, the daughter of Mahommed, and wife of Alee, were one and the same person; and that it was Fatima who invented the use of the roomal, to strangle the great demon Rukut-beej-dana: which led to a discussion between him and some of my Mussulman native officers, who did not like to find the amiable Fatima made a goddess of Thuggee—an "Iphigenia in Tauris." The Thug was a sturdy wrangler; and, in the estimation of his associate Thugs, had, I think, the best of the argument.

Q. "Then has Bhowanee any thing to do with your Paradise?"

Sahib. "Nothing."

Q. "She has no influence upon your future state?"

Sahib. "None."

Q. "Does Mahommed, your prophet, anywhere sanction crimes like yours;—the murder in cold blood of your fellow-creatures, for the sake of their money?"

Sahib. "No."

Q. "Does he not say that such crimes will be punished by God in the next world?"

Sahib. "Yes."

Q. "Then do you never feel any dread of punishment hereafter."

Sahib.

Sahib. "Never: we never murder unless the omens are favourable: and we consider favourable omens as the mandates of the deity."

Q. "What deity?"

Sahib. "Bhowanee."

Q. "But Bhowanee, you say, has no influence upon the welfare, or otherwise, of your soul hereafter?"

Sahib. "None, we believe; but she influences our fates in this world; and what she orders in this world, we believe that God will not punish in the next."

The conjoint adoration of the deities of different and discordant creeds is neither new nor uncommon in the East. In the Old Testament, various instances are recorded, in which nations, as well as individuals, paid a divided homage to the True God and to a multiplicity of idols: and in various parts of India, the Mahometans, from having long been surrounded by a Hindoo population, have been led to adopt many of their opinions and practices. The principle, indeed, upon which this approximation is formed, is not peculiar to the East. Everywhere, time not only abates the fervour both of religious and sectarian zeal, but causes many of the distinctive marks of original difference to disappear, and tinges the entire mass with the colour of the party which, either from numbers or activity, acquires an ascendant. The natural tendency of man to superstition

stition gives to that gloomy power, in any form, an extraordinary facility of access to his heart. The weak and the wicked alike flee to it for a refuge: the former, from a morbid apprehension of undefined evil; the latter, from the upbraidings of conscious guilt. To the one class, superstition presents the alluring prospect of perfect assurance, in place of the humble faith and hope which are the characteristics of genuine piety: to the other, she holds out the offer of peace of mind upon easier terms than true Religion proposes. It is not a subject for surprise, then, that, at all periods, the votaries of Superstition, in its multiform ramifications, should have far outnumbered the faithful adherents of Religious Truth: the errors of the understanding, and the depravity of the will, are continually furnishing their recruits to swell the myriad ranks of the army of Superstition.

The principle which assigns the distribution of good and evil, in this world, to an inferior divinity is not very dissimilar from one which, in Christian countries, has been maintained by grave writers;—which excludes the Superior Being from the ordinary course of human affairs, leaving them to chance and accident, and human passion; and confines His providence to an occasional interference in what are considered great emergencies in this life, and to the final retribution of good and evil in the life to come.

CHAP. V.

THE movements of the followers of Thuggee are invariably governed by omens, with which they believe their goddess favours them, for the guidance of their course. Nothing is undertaken without a careful consultation of these sources of knowledge; and the occurrence of an accidental and unlooked-for sign is, in some cases, sufficient to derange the most fixed plans, and even to lead to the abandonment of the richest booty, though almost in possession. These omens are numerous; and the learning of the Thugs consists in an acquaintance with them.

The manifestation of the auspice or omen on the right hand is called *Thibaoo;* on the left, *Pilhahoo.* If the Pilhaoo promises good, according to their rules of augury, it is always the better from being followed by the Thibaoo soon after. If it threatens evil, that evil is mitigated by the Thibaoo. Different casts and clans of Thugs have, in some few instances, different rules for interpreting these sounds and appearances; and what is considered to threaten evil by some, is thought to promise good

good by others. If members of sects, holding conflicting opinions, act in concert, they follow the rules of the leader who opens the expedition, or who leads the greatest number of the Thugs engaged. The Pilhaoo, or omen on the left, must be observed first, on opening an expedition; and it must be followed by the Thibaoo immediately after, or the expedition cannot be entered upon. The Pilhaoo perceived on leaving any stage during the expedition, or on preparing to leave it, promises good. The Thibaoo threatens evil, and the gang halts. On reaching the end of any stage, the Pilhaoo threatens evil, and the party must move on without resting. The Thibaoo promises good, and they rest securely. There are some few exceptions to the general rule, that, for the Pilhaoo, the omen must be on the left. Some animals must be heard or seen on the right to constitute the Pilhaoo, and *vice versâ;* but these are very few. These are a few of the general rules of augury.

When preparing for an expedition, the auspices are solemnly taken. The most learned Pundit that can be procured is seated on a blanket with the leader, and four of the Thugs the most respectable in their vocation from birth and character: the rest of the gang sit around, outside. They then place before the Pundit, as an offering, a brass plate (*thalee*), with some rice, wheat, and two copper coins upon it. The leader asks the Pundit, respect-

respectfully, what day will be proper to open the expedition; and he, after due search and ceremony, pronounces the day, the hour, and the direction. Thus far the preliminaries. On the day appointed, they fill a brass jug with water; which the leader holds in his right hand, suspended by the mouth, at his side. In a clean white handkerchief they tie up five knots of turmeric, two copper coins, one silver coin, and the indispensable pickaxe. This pickaxe the leader holds upon his breast, with his left hand. He now turns in the direction indicated by the priest, and moves on slowly, followed by his gang, to a field or garden outside the village. On reaching the spot thought best adapted for the purpose, he stands with his face still in the direction indicated, his left hand on his breast, his right, with the jug, by his side; and, with his eyes lifted towards heaven, he says, "Great goddess! universal mother! if this our meditated expedition be fitting in thy sight, vouchsafe us help, and the signs of thy approbation!" All the Thugs present repeat this prayer after the leader, and join in the praises and worship of the goddess. If within half an hour they hear or see the Pilhaoo (or auspice on the left), it signifies that the deity has taken them by the left hand, to lead them on. If the Thibaoo (or omen on the right) follow, it signifies that the deity has vouchsafed to take them by the right hand also. The leader then puts the jug on the ground, and

and sits down with his face in the same direction. He keeps the silver and copper pice and turmeric during the whole expedition, and usually gives them, on his return, as an offering to some poor Brahman; but if the expedition has been very prosperous, he keeps them, to use again in opening others.

The leader remains seated, in the same spot, seven hours; while his followers bring him food, and make all necessary preparations for their journey. When all is ready, they advance a few paces, in the precise direction indicated; but afterwards they may turn to the right or left, as impediments or incentives present themselves. On arriving at the first stage, they must hear or see the Thibaoo first; and the omen is improved by the Pilhaoo afterwards. Having had the auspices favourable thus far, they proceed next morning to the nearest water; and there eat the goor and the dal, which the leader takes with him. Any bad omen after this can be averted by the usual sacrifices, offerings, and observance; but any bad omen before it, involves the necessity of returning, and opening the expedition anew. If the jug should drop from the Jemadar's hand, he must, they think, die within that or the following year, inevitably. If they hear any one weeping for the dead on leaving the village, it threatens great evil. If they meet the corpse of any one belonging to the village, it is a very bad omen: or if they meet an oil-vender,. a carpenter,

a potter,

a potter, a dancing-master, a blind or lame man, a fakeer with a brown waistband, or a jogee with long-traced hair—all threaten evil.

If, after eating the goor and dal, they get the Thibaoo, it assures them a rich booty within a month and a half. It is good, also, to see a fair in any village, but their own, on the road. A corpse from any village but their own is a good omen: so, also, is it good to see a party of friends weeping round a woman taking leave of her parental roof to go to that of her husband.

They must not open an expedition in July, September, nor December; nor on a Wednesday or Thursday.

But, however happily business may have been commenced, success is liable to be postponed by a multiplicity of ominous appearances; some of which are fatal, while others may be got over by sacrifices. The turban, being a covering of great honour, is invested in the catalogue of omens, with a due degree of importance. A Thug, except in Bengal, never moves out without his turban. If a turban is set on fire, it threatens great evil; and the gang must, if near home, return, and wait seven days: if at a distance, an offering of goor is made; and the individual, to whom the turban belonged, alone returns home. If the turban fall off, it is an omen almost as bad, and requires the same sacrifices.

It is a bad omen to meet, on the first day of an expedition,

expedition, any person who has lost a limb; and, happily for the maimed, it is equally bad to murder them. To sneeze is a fearful thing at setting out on an expedition; and the nasal enormity must be expiated by sacrifice. Bad as the omen is to the Thugs, it is unquestionably good for their intended victims. Sneezing entitles all the travellers within the gripe of the assassins to the privilege of an escape; and no one dare to put them to death.

If a party, on leaving home to enter on an expedition, meet a woman bearing a pitcher full of water on her head, it promises a prosperous journey and a safe return: the omen is still better if the female be in a state of pregnancy: but if the pitcher which she carries be empty, the tide of fate is reversed, and the indication is one of misfortune and calamity. An empty pitcher is, indeed, under any circumstances, regarded by Thugs with as much aversion as by tipplers.

Several practices, which among certain classes of Thugs are observed, in order to secure the favour of Fortune, are neglected by others. The Thugs of the Jumaldehee and Lodáha clans always make the youngest Thug kick the body of the first person they murder on an expedition, five times, on the back, thinking that it will bring them good luck. The Moteeas do the same; but the practice does not appear to be general.

The brute creation afford a vast fund of instruction

struction upon every point of proceeding; and the Thugs are assiduous in consulting, and availing themselves of it. The ass is an adviser, to whom extraordinary deference is paid. The Thugs deem the omen of the ass the most important of all, whether it threatens evil or promises good. "*Sou puk, heroo ek Dunteroo*—The ass is equal to a hundred birds," is a maxim in augury. The omen of the ass is also superior to that of all quadrupeds. If they hear one bray on the left (Pilhaoo), on opening an expedition, and it is soon after repeated on the right (Thibaoo), they believe that nothing on earth can prevent their success during that expedition, though it should last for years. In the progress of an expedition, the ass is still a most valuable and respected guide. If, on reaching any stage, or while halting at any stage, it is heard on the left, the party must leave the place and go on: for such situations the omen is good on the right. If the ass approaches the gang, braying from the front, it is a very bad omen, and is called *Mathaphore*, "the head-breaker."

The jackal plays a great part in the code of signals in use for communicating the intentions of the goddess to her followers. A pair of jackals crossing the road in front of the gang, either from the right or from the left, is a very bad omen, indicating imprisonment and chains; but a single jackal, passing from right to left, promises good fortune. The Thugs have

 a proa proverb, "*Bacan Geedee Sona Leedee*—A jackal crossing from right to left, brings gold." If, however, the beast passes from left to right, the omen is somewhat untoward, but is not much regarded. The cries of the jackals afford a variety of omens. First, there is the ordinary cry of a single jackal, which they call *Bhalee*, or *Barhohee*; secondly, the general clamour of a number, termed *Raureen*; thirdly, the *Ekareea*, or short call of the jackal, in the attempt to make which he seems as if suddenly checked. Any one of these calls, heard during the day, threatens great evil; and the gang quit the country in which they hear it, leaving untouched any persons they have inveigled, however wealthy. The first, when heard by night, must be interpreted according to the ordinary rules for the Thibaoo and Pilhaoo—right and left. The second, heard at night, is good on the left, and of little or no importance on the right, except on the day of opening the expedition. Heard then on the right, it threatens evil; and the expedition must be suspended. The third is invariably bad, whether heard by night or day. The noise of jackals fighting, called *Dant,hee*, is also a very bad omen, and involves the necessity of leaving the part of the country in which the gang hears it. The following, which appears to be an extract from a journal kept by Captain Sleeman, shews, not only the influence which a belief in augury has over these people,

people, but also how tenaciously they cling to their old faith, even when engaged in capturing their former associates.—"25th May, 1835, I had ordered a party of Sepahees, with some approvers, to proceed this morning towards Gwalior, in search of some Thugs who have lately found an asylum there. About nine o'clock last night, one of the native officers came to tell me that they could not move till afternoon to-day, as they had heard a bad omen. I have just been to the jail, and discovered that this bad omen was the Ekareea, heard about eight o'clock last night. Nunhooa, one of the approvers, declared, that on leaving Saugor, about three months ago, for Indore, he heard the Ekareea; and not attending to it, he got the wound, which he received from a sword, in arresting a noted Thug Bhyroo, the son of Himmut, between Indore and Baroda. These men never go out to arrest their associates, or to take up the bodies of wounded travellers, without taking the auspices; though they rarely tell us of it."

The wolf might be considered a not inappropriate pilot to guide the Thugs in their dark career. He does not, however, enjoy the reputation of being very friendly to his human brethren. If any of these animals cross their path from left to right, it is commonly admitted to be a bad omen; if from right to left, there seems to be some doubt whether it be good or bad—an unfortunate circumstance,

 but

but not particularly discreditable to Thug learning, seeing that in almost all sciences there are disputable points to exercise the talents of the ingenious. The call of the wolf is, on the whole, an awkward symptom: if heard during the day, it is very bad, and the gang must immediately quit the country. If between midnight and day-light, it is also bad: if between evening and midnight, indifferent: between midday and sunset, it is not so bad as between sunrise and midday. They call it the weeping (*Chimmama*) of the wolf, and consider the sound mournful. A single wolf portends more than a pair, furnishing one of their most important omens.

The deer contributes his quota of telegraphic communication. If a single small deer crosses their road from right to left, it threatens evil. If from left to right, it promises good; but neither its promises nor threats are considered very important. A herd of small deer, at all times, and under all circumstances, promises a meeting with other Thugs, and is considered good. The Deccan Thugs consider the crossing of a single deer, either from left to right, or right to left, a bad omen.

The movements and cries of the hare are not unnoticed. The passing of a hare across the road in front of the gang is a bad omen, either from right to left, or left to right. The call of this animal at night, on the left, is a good omen: on the right, it it is a bad one, and the Thugs, on hearing it, suffer all travellers to escape: if they kill any one whom they have with them at the time, they will find no booty on him, or what they find will tend to their ruin. This is not all: it is perfectly well established, that they will perish in the jungles after hearing the fatal signal, and that the hare will drink water out of their sculls if they do not avert this awful fate by sacrifice.

The elegant antelope seems out of place when brought into association with Thugs; but he has, nevertheless, been pressed into the service. If either a single antelope, or a pair, are seen crossing the road from left to right, it is a good omen; if from right to the left, very bad.

The dog enjoys the prerogative of putting a veto on the proceedings of the Thugs; and the shaking of his head is fraught with more meaning than that of Lord Burleigh's. On witnessing this expression of canine dissent, the Thugs evince their deference to the sagacious beast who affords it, by abandoning the design in hand, whatever it may be.

The fighting of cats is a matter which receives especial regard; and as these miniature tigers are tolerably pugnacious, they furnish abundant food for observation. If the music, by which the combats of these animals is enlivened, be heard during the first watch of the night, it promises good; if after the first watch, it is called "*Kalee kee Maunj*," and

and threatens evil; but the evil may be averted in the morning, by gargling the mouth with a little sour milk, and then squirting it out. The fighting of cats during the day is a very bad omen, and threatens great evil: if the cats fall down from a height while fighting, it is still worse. These ills are beyond the healing influence of sour milk, and call for nothing less than sacrifice.

Birds, no less than the four-footed creation, figure in the mysteries of Thug augury: and the owl occupies a chief place; to which, indeed, it is justly entitled, by its proverbial gravity and wisdom. The loud full call of the large owl is interpreted according to the ordinary rules of right and left. A reciprocation of the cry, between two of these intelligent birds, is however a bad omen. This, by the Deccan Thugs, is termed *Raja* or *Mahee;* and by those of Hindostan, *Thakur*. To both it is a signal of ill; and to their intended victims, a passport of safety. The low gurgling sound made by the large owl, which resembles the bubbling of a huka or goorgooree, always threatens evil. If the Thugs hear it on first setting out, they must suspend their journey for some days. If they hear it on the left, after the expedition has been opened, they must advance far and fast, for danger pursues in the rear: if on the right, they must halt, as danger lies in front. The loud and continued chirping or calling of the small owl, if made by the bird while sitting, promises

good;

good; if while flying, it threatens evil. The chatter or call, when sitting, is interpreted according to the rules of the Thibaoo or Pilhaoo. A low call of the small owl, called *Chireya,* always threatens evil.

The cry of the kite also affords tokens of good or ill fortune. Heard in the day-time, it is of little importance, and is interpreted according to their rules for the right and left hand signs; but heard during the *Kootub,* or interval between the first watch and day-break, it is called the *Kootub agasee,* a dreadful omen. If in camp, they get up and fly immediately, leaving untouched any person they may have inveigled, however wealthy. If they hear it after dark, but before the end of the first watch, they are not alarmed, as they consider the threatened evil to pass away in their sleep: in their own language, the "omen gets suffocated under their sides, as they turn in their sleep." It is the same with almost all bad omens that take place between evening and the end of the first watch.

The voice of the large mountain-crow is interpreted with some peculiarity. Contrary to the ordinary rules of augury, the Pilhaoo, in this omen, is the croaking on the right; and the Thibaoo the croaking on the left. If he croak from a tree either on the right or the left, it promises good; and if water be in sight, it is better. If heard from a tree while the gang are in camp, it promises a rich traveller on that spot; and the gang waits for him.

him. If he croak while on the back of a pig or buffalo, or from any dead body or skeleton, the omen is bad. If from the back of a cow, some Thugs think it a good, others a bad, omen. "Doctors differ" on this, as on many other points.

In this country, the partridge is of use only to afford amusement to the sportsman, and food to the epicure. The Thugs find in its cry an intimation of coming events. If heard while they are travelling, the call on the left promises good, and on the right threatens evil. If they are halting at the time, the call on the right is good; that on the left, bad. The Thugs have a proverb, and which gives the cry of the partridge another condition—"*Ratee bolee Teetura, Din ko bolee seear, Tuj chulee wa deysra, nuheen puree achanuk Dhar*—If the partridge call at night, or the jackal during the day, quit that country, or you will be seized."

The blue jay is also a soothsayer, but of a minor order. If seen to the right, or crossing from the left to right, it promises good: if to the left, or crossing from the right to left, it promises no good, but threatens no evil; it is "a chip in porridge." The cry of the jay is altogether disregarded.

Meaner animals than either birds or quadrupeds are also instruments of auguring. If a snake crosses the road before or behind the gang it is a bad omen; and they dare not go on, unless they can

can kill it. If they see it in any situation, it involves a sacrifice, unless killed.

With regard to the lizard, his voice is much more acceptable than his personal visitation. At whatever time and place Thugs hear the call of the lizard, they consider it a good omen; but the fall of a lizard upon a Thug, is a very bad one; and if it fall upon any garment, that garment must be given away in charity: if it fall upon the ground, it threatens nothing.

A careful attention to these and similar omens is regarded as indispensable to success. There are various rules, also, which no regular and consistent Thugs neglect. During the first seven days of an expedition, the families of those engaged in one expedition admit, or should admit, no visits from the families of Thugs who are absent on another expedition, lest the travellers destined for the one should go over to the other gang; neither should they eat any thing that has belonged to the families of such other Thugs. The Thugs engaged, ought not, till the seventh day, to dress any food in ghee, nor eat any animal food except fish. But abstinence alone is not sufficient to propitiate the favour of the goddess: habits of neatness and cleanliness must be, for the time, observed; and the indulgence of benevolent feeling is a deadly offence. At this period, the Thugs must not shave, nor allow their clothes to be washed by a dhoby,

nor

nor give in charity. Even charity to the brute creation, a prime virtue in the code of Eastern ethics, is suspended; for it is forbidden to bestow any food upon a dog, cat, or jackal. None of the party must bathe, nor eat sugar, except what the leader may have brought with him on setting out. Formerly, they never ate any salt or turmeric; but this regulation is obsolete. After this preparatory mortification, they, on the seventh day, indulge in a good meal; but it is necessary that greens of some kind should be a component part of it. During the whole time the expedition lasts, if within one year, they must take no milk, nor clean their teeth with a brush.

If the *Sonrka*, or first murder, takes place within the first seven days, or *Satha*, they consider themselves relieved from all restraints. They ought not to murder, as the Sonrka (or first victim), any Brahman or Syad, nor any very poor man, nor any man with gold upon him, nor any man who has a quadruped with him, nor a dhobee, nor a sweeper, nor a teylee (oil-vender), nor a bhaut (bard), nor a kaet (a writer), nor a blind man, nor maimed persons, nor a leper, nor a dancing-woman, nor a pilgrim or devotee. Some of these descriptions of persons ought not, indeed, to be murdered at all; and none but the incorrigibly heterodox would think of opening an expedition by a professional operation upon any of them: but all sects recede from their first

first principles. Some classes and individuals neglect these rules; and their misfortunes are attributed, principally, to this cause.

Captain Sleeman says, "Even the most sensible approvers, who have been with me for many years, as well Mussulmans as Hindoos, believe that their good or ill success always depended upon the skill with which the omens were discovered and interpreted, and the strictness with which they were observed and obeyed. One of the old Sindouse stock told me, in presence of twelve others from Hydrabad, Behar, the Dooab, Oude, Rajpootana, and Bundelcund, that had they not attended to these omens they could never have thrived as they did; and that, in ordinary cases of murder, a man seldom escaped after one of them; while they and their families had, for ten generations, thrived, though they had murdered hundreds of people. 'This,' said he, 'could never have been the case, had we not attended to omens, and had not omens been intended for us. There were always signs around us, to guide us to rich booty, and warn us of danger, had we been always wise enough to discern them, and religious enough to attend to them.'—Every Thug present concurred with him, from his soul."

The following colloquy, also contributed by Capt. Sleeman, will illustrate the opinions entertained by Thugs generally, as to the danger of associating with

with those who have not been regularly educated, the importance of attending to rules and omens, and the value and excellence of Thug learning.

Q. "You consider that a Borka (a leader) is capable of forming a gang, in any part of India to which he may be obliged to flee?"

Sahib and *Nasir.* "Certainly; in any part that we have seen of it."

Q. "Do you know any instance of it?"

Sahib and *Nasir.* "A great number. Mudee Khan was from the old Sindouse stock, and was obliged to emigrate after the attack upon that place. Many years afterwards, we met him in the Deccan; and he had then a gang of fifty Thugs, of all castes and descriptions. I asked him who they were: he told me that they were weavers, braziers, bracelet-makers, and all kinds of ragamuffins, whom he had scraped together about his new abode on the banks of the Herun and Nurbudda rivers, in the districts of Jebulpore and Nursingpore. He was a Mussulman; and so were Lal Khan, Kalee Khan, who formed gangs, after the Sindouse dispersion, along the same rivers."

Q. "Did they find the same patrons among the landholders and other heads of villages?"

Sahib and *Nasir.* "They everywhere made friends, by the same means; and without patrons they could not have thrived. They were obliged, of of course, to give them a liberal share of the booty."

Q. "But these men have all been punished; which does not indicate the protection of Davy?"

Sahib and *Nasir.* "It indicates the danger of scraping together such a set of fellows for Thuggee. They killed all people indiscriminately, women and men, of all castes and professions; and knew so little about omens, that they entered upon their expeditions, and killed people, in spite of such as the most ignorant ought to have known were prohibitive. They were punished in consequence, as we all knew that they would be; and we always used to think it dangerous to be associated with them, for even a few days. Ask many of them who are now here—Kureem Khan, Sheikh Kureem, Rumzanee, and others, whether this is not true; and whether they ever let go even a sweeper, if he appeared to have a rupee about him."

Q. "And you think, that if they had been well instructed in the signs and rules, and attended to them, they would have thrived?"

Sahib and *Nasir.* "Undoubtedly! so should we all."

Q. "You think that a Kuboola, or tyro, could not anywhere form a gang of Thugs of himself?"

Sahib and *Nasir.* "Never: he could know nothing of our rules of augury, or proceedings; and how could he possibly succeed? Does not all our success

success depend upon knowing and observing omens and rules?"

Q. "It would therefore never be very dangerous to release such a man as a Kuboola?"

Sahib and *Nasir*. "Never; unless he could join men better instructed than himself. Every one must be convinced, that it is by knowing and attending to omens and rules that Thuggee has thrived."

Q. "I am not convinced, nor are any of the native officers present: on the contrary, we do all we can to put down what you call an institution of the deity, and without dreading at all the effects of her resentment?"

Sahib and *Nasir*. "They may say so; but they all know that no man's family can survive a murder committed in any other way; and yet Thugs have thrived through a long series of generations. We have all children, like other men; and we are never visited by any extraordinary affliction."

In another interview, one of the approvers was asked—"And do you never feel sympathy for the persons murdered—never pity or compunction?"

Sahib. "Never."

Q. "How can you murder old men and young children without some emotions of pity—calmly and deliberately as they sit with you and converse with you,—and tell you of their private affairs—

of

of their hopes and fears—and of the wives and children they are going to meet, after years of absence, toil, and suffering?"

Sahib. "From the time that the omens have been favourable, we consider them as victims thrown into our hands by the deity to be killed, and that we are the mere instrument in her hands to destroy them: that if we do not kill them, she will never be again propitious to us, and we and our families will be involved in misery and want."

Q. "And you can sleep as soundly, by the bodies or over the graves of those you have murdered, and eat your meals with as much appetite, as ever?"

Sahib. "Just the same: we sleep and eat just the same, unless we are afraid of being discovered."

Q. "And when you see or hear a bad omen, you think it is the order of the deity not to kill the travellers you have with you, or are in pursuit of?"

Sahib. "Yes: it is the order not to kill them, and we dare not disobey."

This last point of doctrine, like the rest, is universally received; but some knotty questions arise as to occurrences which present a conjunction of a very poor victim and a very good omen. Some Thugs let the traveller escape, in the hopes of finding better game: others hold, that "a bird in the hand is worth two in the bush"; and regard forbearance, in such a case, as an act of abominable impiety.

impiety. A further extract will shew the respective views of these conflicting sects, and the reasoning by which they are supported.

Q. "When you have a poor traveller with you, or a party of travellers who appear to have little property about them, and you hear or see a very good omen, do you not let them go, in the hope that the return of the omen will guide you to better prey?"

Dorgha (Mussulman). "Let them go! Never, never!—*Kubhee nuheen, kubhee nuneen.*"

Nasir (Mussulman, of Telingana). "How could we let them go? Is not the good omen the order from Heaven to kill them? and would it not be disobedience to let them go? If we did not kill them, should we ever get any more travellers?"

Feringeea (Brahmin). "I have known the experiment tried with good effect. I have known travellers, who promised little, let go; and the virtue of the omen brought better."

Inaent (Mussulman). "Yes; the virtue of the omen remains; and the traveller who has little should be let go; for you are sure to get a better."

Sahib Khan (of Telingana). "Never, never! This is one of your Hindostanee heresies. You could never let him go, without losing all the fruits of your expedition: you might get property, but it could never do you any good. No success could result from your disobedience."

Morlee

Morlee (Rajpoot). "Certainly not: the travellers who are in our hands, when we have a good omen, must never be let go, whether they promise little or much: the omen is unquestionably the order, as Nasir says."

Nasir. "The idea of securing the good-will of Davy by disobeying her order, is quite monstrous. We Deccan Thugs do not understand how you got hold of it. Our ancestors never were guilty of such folly."

Feringeea. "You do not mean to say, that we of Murnae and Sindouse were not as well instructed as you of Telingana?"

Nasir and *Sahib Khan.* "We only mean to say, that you have clearly mistaken the nature of a good omen in this case. It is the order of Davy to take what she has put in our way; at least, so we in the Deccan understand it."

Although there are some differences in the interpretation of omens and of rules, all are agreed that the neglect of either is followed by the most fearful consequences. To this dereliction they attribute all the reverses which have of late years befallen them.—Thus, in the recent indulgence of the practice of killing females and maimed persons:—

Q. "And you think killing women has been one of the chief causes of your misfortunes?"

Feringeea. "Yes."

 Q. "And

Q. "And of our success against you?"

Kulean Sing. "Yes; I and my gang were arrested after the murder of Newul Sing and his daughters, at Biseynee, in 1820."

Q. "But Newul Sing had lost an arm; and you before told me that you suffered because you there infringed a good old rule, and murdered a maimed person?"

Kuleean. "Yes; it was partly that: but was not the greăt gang seized by Mr. Molony after the murder of Monshee Bunda Alee, and his wife and daughter, at Lucknadown, three years after?"

In another conversation, the same opinions were advanced. The Behar and Doali Thugs having vehemently disclaimed any participation in the murder of women, Captain Sleeman said—

"But you Bundelcund men murdered abundance."

Zolfukar. "Yes; and was not the greater part of Feringeea's and my gang seized, after we had murdered the two women and little girl at Manora, in 1830, near Saugor? And were we not ourselves both seized soon after? How could we survive things like that? Our ancestors never did such things."

Feringeea. "We had no sooner buried their bodies, than I heard the *chireya;* and on leaving the ground, we saw the *loharburheya:* these were signs that Davy was displeased; and we gave ourselves up for lost."

Again,

Again, at a subsequent period, the murder of a girl being adverted to, the following dialogue occurred:—

Q. "I thought Hindoos never strangled women. How came Punchum to strangle this girl?"

Feringeea. "Punchum was my mother's brother, and he never strangled her."

Q. "Who did?"

Feringeea. "I have heard that it was Bhugwan Kachee, a slave or disciple of his."

Punna. "But is not the act of the slave the act of the master? And did not Bhugwan strangle her by Punchum's order?"

Feringeea. "Well, but how was Punchum punished! Did he not die before he could reach home? And was not his son Bughola hung the November following, with twenty others whom Jacob Sahib strung up at Kalapahavee in Gwalior? And was not Bhugwan hung with him? And what a horrid death did Himmut die! He was eaten alive by worms."

This view of the subject was continually recurring in the conversations held by Captain Sleeman with the approvers.

Q. "And you think that much of your misfortunes have arisen from the murder of women?"

Lalmun. "We all knew that they would come

upon

upon us some day, for this and other great sins. We were often admonished; but we did not take warning; and we deserve our fates."

Similar visitations, according to the Thug creed, attend those who oppose or punish these ruffians. No opinion appears more deeply seated in their minds than this, which was repeatedly advanced by those with whom Captain Sleeman conversed.

Q. "Above the Nurbudda, Chiefs have never had the same dread of punishing Thugs as below it; have they?"

Feringeea. "They had formerly; and have still, in many parts."

Q. "Why should they fear? Have there been any instances of suffering from it?"

Feringeea. "A great many. Was not Nanha, the Rajah of Jhalone, made leprous by Davy for putting to death Bodhoo and his brother Khumolee, two of the most noted Thugs of their day. He had them trampled under the feet of elephants; but the leprosy broke out upon his body the very next day."

Q. "Did he believe that this punishment was inflicted by Davy for putting them to death?"

Dorgha Mussulman. "He was quite sensible of it."

Q. "Did he do any thing to appease her?"

Dorgha. "Every thing. Bodhoo had begun a well

well in Jhalone; the Rajah built it up in a magnificent style: he had a chubootra (tomb) raised to their name, fed Brahmins, and consecrated it; had worship instituted upon it;—but all in vain; the disease was incurable, and the Rajah died, in a few months, a miserable death. The tomb and well are both kept up, and visited by hundreds to this day; and no one doubts that the Rajah was punished for putting these two Thugs to death."

Q. "But Bodhoo had his nose and hands cut off before, and could have been no favourite of Davy's?"

Feringeea. "But he was a Thug of great repute: for sagacity we have never seen his equal: people who had been robbed used to go to him as an oracle."

Q. "But he had turned informer; and was sent to Jhalone, by Mr. Stockwell, to arrest his associates."

Dorgha. "He went to Mr. Stockwell in a passion; his heart was not fully turned away from us then."

Q. "Have you any other instances?"

Inaent. "Hundreds! When Madhajee Scindheea caused seventy Thugs to be executed at Muthura, was he not warned in a dream, by Davy, that he should release them? and did he not the very day after their execution begin to spit blood? and did he not die within three months?

Feringeea.

Feringeea. "When Dureear the Rathore, and Komere and Patore, the Kuchwaha Rajpoots, Zemindars, arrested eighty of the Thugs who had settled at Nodha after the murder of Lieutenant Monsell, they had many warnings to let them go; but they persisted, and kept them till some thirty died. They collected fourteen thousand rupees, at the rate of one hundred and twenty-five rupees from every Thug. What became of their families? Have they not all perished? They have not a child left. Rae Sing Havildar, the Gwalior Subah of Nodha, took the money; but that very day his only son, *and the best horse in his stable,* died; and he was himself taken ill; and died soon after, a miserable death."

Nasir. "Ah, Davy took care of you, then! And why? Was it not because you were more attentive to her orders?"

Zolfukar. "Yes; we had then some regard for *religion.* We have lost it since. All kinds of men have been made Thugs, and all classes of people murdered without distinction; and little attention has been paid to omens. How, after this, could we expect to escape?"

Nasir. "Be assured that Davy never forsook us, till we neglected her."

Q. "Do you know of any instance of her punishing a man for annoying Thugs in the Deccan?"

Sahib

Sahib Khan. " A great many. The Rajah of Kundul, some ninety cose east from Hydrabad, arrested all the Thugs in his Raj for some murders they had committed. For three successive nights the voice of Davy was heard from the top of every temple in the capital, warning the Rajah to release them. The whole town heard her, and urged the Rajah to comply. He was obstinate; and the third night, the bed on which he and his Ranee were sleeping was taken up by Davy and dashed violently against the ground."

Q. " Were they killed?"

Nasir. " They were not killed, but they were dreadfully bruised; and had they not released the Thugs, they would certainly have been killed the next night."

Q. " Were any of you present?"

Sahib Khan. "Our fathers were; and we heard it from them. It occurred sixty years ago."

Q. " And do you think the Chiefs have still the same dread of punishing Thugs, in all parts of India?"

Sahib. "Certainly not in all parts; because, in many, they have been suffered to punish them with impunity, on account of their neglect of rules and omens."

Morlee. " There is no fear now. They are everywhere seized and punished with impunity; there is no risisting your *ikbal* (good fortune)."

Dorgha.

Dorgha. "The Company's *ikbal* is such, that before the sound of your drums, sorcerers, witches, and demons take flight· and how can Thuggee stand?"

Davey Deen. "Thuggee! why, it is gone! there are not fifty Aseel Thugs (Thugs of good birth) left between the Ganges and Jumna."

Chotee Brahman. "And not more than that number of our old clans of Gwalior and Bundelcund; but the Sooseeas of Rajpootana have been untouched, and much is to be done about Delhi and Puteeala."

Q. "But Nasir and Sahib Khan think that it can never be suppressed in the Deccan?"

Nasir. "I think it never can."

Sahib Khan. "I do not say it never can. I say only, that the country is very large; that in every one of the five districts there are hundreds of Aseel Thugs, who are staunch to their oath, and attentive to their usages; that the country is everywhere intersected by the jurisdiction of Native Chiefs, who cannot be easily persuaded to assist."

Nasir. "Assist! why, when we go into their districts after a Thug, we are every instant in danger of our lives. I got nearly killed, with all the guard, lately, when close upon the heels of a gang: and when I complained to Captain Reynolds, he told me that we must consent to bear these drubbings on account of the Company, or I could

could be of no use to him in such a country as that."

Q. "And you think that all these obstacles are not to be overcome?"

Nasir. "I think not."

Q. "That is, you think an institution formed by Davy, the goddess, cannot be suppressed by the hand of man?"

Nasir. "Certainly, I think so."

Q. "But you think that no man is killed by man's killing—'*Admeeke marne se koee murta nuheen*'; that all who are strangled are strangled, in effect, by God."

Nasir. "Certainly."

Q. "Then by whose killing have all the Thugs, who have been hung at Saugor and Jubulpore, been killed?"

Nasir. "God's, of course."

Q. "You think that we could never have caught and executed them, but by the aid of God?"

Nasir. "Certainly not."

Q. "Then you think, that so far we have been assisted by God in what we have done?"

Nasir. "Yes."

Q. "And you are satisfied that we should not have ventured to do what we have done, unless we were assured that our God was working with us; or rather, that we were the mere instruments in His hands?"

Nasir.

Nasir. "Yes, I am."

Q. "Then do you not think that we may go on with the same assurance, till the work we have in hand is done; till, in short, the system of Thuggee is suppressed?"

Nasir. "God is almighty."

Q. "And there is but one God?"

Nasir. "One God above all gods."

Q. "And if that God above all gods supports us, we shall succeed?"

Nasir. "Certainly."

Q. "Then we are all satisfied that He is assisting us; and therefore hope to succeed, even in the Deccan?"

Nasir. "God only knows."

Sahib Khan. "If God assists, you will succeed; but the country is large and favourable, and the gangs are numerous and well organized."

Q. "So was the country we have already gone over. How many Thug leaders from Sindouse, after Mr. Halhed and Mr. Stockwell's attacks, came and settled in the Saugor and Nurbudda districts?"

Sheikh Inayat. "My father, Hinga Jemadar, and his three sons, two of whom were hung at Saugor the year before last, came to Lowa, a village between Dhamonee and Khimlassa in Saugor: my younger brother, Dhurum Khan, was born after my father's death; his mother could not, and my wife nursed him. We were joined by Monowur Mussulman,

sulman, Niddee and Mungoa Brahmans, Lulloo, and his sons." [Here followed the names of sixty-one Thugs of note, that came from the great Sindouse stock, and settled in different parts of these territories, and formed new gangs.]

Q. "And how many of these noted Thugs, and the gangs they formed, are still at large?"

Sheikh Inayat. "Since I was taken in 1829, these have all been seized, and have been hung or transported, or are now in jail. Two of my brothers have been hung. My youngest is now here. The men whom they made Thugs have also all be taken; and there are only five or six, that we know of. There are, Bahadur Chabukaswur, Kuseea Kirar, and Bodhooa, son of another Bahadur: these are new Thugs, but they proved themselves good ones. There are, Kadir and Poosoo, adopted sons of Imamee, the son of Mirja Mussulman. These Thugs are at large in the district of Seonee or Nursingpore. We know of no others."

Q. "Do you not think, that, if we persevere, we shall be able to do in the Deccan what we have done here, and in the Dooab?"

Inaent. "No doubt."

Sahib Khan. "It will be a work of greater difficulty. Half or three-quarters of these gangs were Kuboolas. In the Deccan, they are almost all composed entirely of *Burkas*—men well born, staunch and able, above all the men of Arcot."

Feringeea.

Feringeea. "And the Hindoo Thugs of Talghat upon the Krishna river?"

Sahib Khan. "Yes: they are extraordinary men."

The subject was renewed in other conversations, and the same impressions avowed by the Thug approvers. They appear, however, to have regarded themselves as exempt from the penalties which ordinarily followed any act of hostility to the Thugs. Indeed, from the low state of moral feeling, and the imperfect developement of the reasoning powers in the East, much consistency could hardly be expected.

Q. "If Davy's displeasure visits all who punish Thugs, how is it that you all escape so well?"

Moradun. "Davy's anger visited us, when we were seized. That was the effect of her resentment: she cast us off then, and takes no notice of us now."

Q. "And if you were to return to Thuggee, she would still guide and protect you?"

Moradun. "Yes; but what gang would now receive us?"

Q. "And you are not afraid to assist in suppressing Thuggee?"

Moradun. "No; we see God is assisting you, and that Davy has withdrawn her protection on account of our transgressions. We have sadly neglected her worship. God knows in what it will end!"

Q. "True!

Q. "True! God only knows; but we hope it will end in the entire suppression of this wicked and foolish system; and in the conviction, on your part, that Davy has really had nothing to do with it."

Nasir. "That Davy instituted Thuggee, and supported it, as long as we attended to her omens, and observed the rules framed by the wisdom of our ancestors, nothing in the world can ever make us doubt."

The conviction of the divine origin of Thuggee is strengthened in the minds of its followers by the belief that its mysteries are exhibited in the Caves of Ellora. These gigantic witnesses to human infatuation and folly are confidently appealed to, as affording proof, not only of the antiquity of the practice, but of the divine sanction and operation.

Q. "You told Mr. Johnstone the traveller, while he was at Saugor, that the operations of your trade were to be seen in the Caves of Ellora?"

Feringeea. "All! Every one of the operations is to be seen there. In one place, you see men strangling: in another, burying the bodies: in another, carrying them off to the graves There is not an operation in Thuggee that is not exhibited in the Caves of Ellora."

Dorgha. "In those caves are to be seen the operations of every trade in the world."

Chotee.

Chotee. "Whenever we passed near, we used to go and see these caves. Every man will there find his trade described, however secret he may think it; and they were all made in one night."

Q. "Does any person beside yourselves consider that any of these figures represent Thugs?"

Feringeea. "Nobody else; but all Thugs know that they do. We never told any body else what we thought about them. Every body there can see the secret operations of his trade, but he does not tell others of them; and no other person can understand what they mean. They are the works of God. No human hands were employed upon them. That every body admits."

Q. "What particular operations are there described in figures?"

Sahib Khan. "I have seen the Sotha (inveigler) sitting upon the same carpet with the traveller, and in close conversation with him, just as we are when we are worming out their secrets. In another place, the strangler has got his roomal over his neck, and is strangling him; while another, the Chumochee, is holding him by the legs. These are the only two operations that I have seen described."

Nasir. "These I have also seen; and there is no mistaking them. The Chumochee has close hold of the legs, and is pulling at them *thus;* while the Bhurtote is tightening the roomal round his neck, *thus!*"

Q. "Have

Q. "Have you seen no others?"

Feringeea. "I have seen these two; and also the Lughas carrying away the bodies to the grave, in this manner, and the sextons digging the grave with the sacred pickaxe: all is done just as if we had ourselves done it; nothing could be more exact."

Q. "And who do you think could have executed this work?"

Feringeea. "It could not have been done by Thugs, because they would never have exposed the secret of their trade; and no other human being could have done it. It must be the work of the gods: human hands could never have performed it."

Q. "And supposing so, you go and worship it?"

Sahib Khan. "No. We go to gratify curiosity, and not to worship: we look upon it as a Mausoleum, a collection of curious figures, cut by some demons, who knew the secrets of all mankind, and amused themselves here in describing them."

Hurnagur. "We Hindoos go for the same purpose. We never go to worship. We consider it as a Pantheon of unknown gods."

The word "Pantheon" is, perhaps, rather a free translation of that used by the Thug witness; and the assertion that the Hindoos visit it only from motives of curiosity seems consistent neither with the belief of its being a temple of the gods, nor with

with former reports upon the subject; nor probably do the Mussulmans, notwithstanding their assertions, regard the mysterious hieroglyphics of Ellora with as much indifference as they represent. They have adopted no small share of the customs and superstitions of the Hindoos; and the Thug formula of fraternization seems to have obliterated most of the distinctive marks which remained.

"In the Caves of Ellora," says one approver, "are to be seen the operations of every trade in the world." "Every man," says another, "will there find his trade discovered, however secret he may think it." "Every body," adds a third, in confirmation, "can there see the secret operations of his trade;"—and Thuggee is held to be a trade as regular and lawful as any other.

The Gentleman, by whom the conversation just quoted is reported, relates another, in which a Thug leader, who is stated to have been possessed of most polished manners and great eloquence, being asked by a native whether he never felt compunction in murdering innocent people, answered with a smile, "Does any man feel compunction in following his trade? and are not all our trades assigned us by Providence?" The Native Gentleman said, "How many people have you, in the course of your life, killed with your own hands, at a rough guess?" "I have killed none!"—"Have you not been just describing to me a numa number of murders?" "Yes; but do you suppose I could have committed them? Is any man killed from man's killing? *Admeeke marne se koee murta.* Is it not the hand of God that kills him? and are we not mere instruments in the hand of God?"

Fatalism is a prominent dogma of the creed of the Thugs. The old lady's doctrine, that "what is to be, shall be," is theirs; and they consider themselves, in the exercise of their trade, to be as exempt from moral responsibility, as the saw or the axe employed in cutting down a tree. Yet, in attention to omens, or in neglect of these instructions, they strangely enough appear to regard themselves as free-agents, who may expect reward for obedience, and punishment for the want of it. In their view, to commit murder is inevitable, and of necessity: to murder according to rule, is an act of choice; and to choose aright, is meritorious!

But the belief in fatalism is not peculiar to the Thugs: it is a doctrine pretty current in the East. One very extraordinary instance of its effects is related in the conversation of the Thug approvers:—

"Bura Sahib Jemadar, of Madura," said the narrator, "had several hundred followers; and used to make valuable presents to Nawab Dollee Khan, who knew how he got them, and offered him a high post, with rent-free lands, if he would leave off the trade. He would not."

 Q. "What

Q. " What became of him at last ?"

Sahib and *Nasir.* " There was a great Decoit leader of the same name, who had committed great ravages; and orders were sent by the Nawab, to the local officers, to blow him away from a gun, as soon as they could seize him. They seized Sahib Khan Thug; and blew him away by mistake, before the Nawab got information of the arrest. In a few hours after his death a message came from the Nawab, to say that he feared there might be a mistake; and when he heard that Sahib Khan Thug had been blown away, he was much grieved, but said that God must have ordained it, and the fault was not his."

This mode of settling the matter would have afforded small consolation to the man blown from the gun, could his last moments have been gratified by a communication of it; but it was amply sufficient to satisfy the conscience of the Nawab, and thus answered its purpose.

CHAP. VI

THE outline which has been given of the general character and habits of the Thugs will now be best illustrated by reference to some of the details elicited by the inquiries of the European Authorities.

In 1833, several Thugs were put on trial, and convicted, before the Zillah Court in Benares.

The following are extracts from the report of the Session Judge to the Court of Nizamut Adawlut:—

"The prisoners are Thugs, and were concerned in three expeditions, during the month of Jeit 1240 Fuslee; corresponding to part of June and July, 1833, in which six persons were murdered.

"The Thanadar of Juggut Gunge, with the Foujdaree Nazis, and the spies Goplah and Bhuggoo, went to Rajah-ka-Tullao, described as a halting-place of the prisoners and others, who were proved to have purchased various articles of food from the grocers' shops, and to have slept there. Towards morning they took their departure, accompanied by

 a Mussula Mussulman traveller, and, leaving the high road at Sarai Mohun to the right, followed a pathway for about a mile, where, having found a convenient place, they strangled the traveller, and threw his body into a well. The Thanadar and his party proceeded to the well which was pointed out; and on examining the Goraits of the neighbouring village, it appeared that there had been a body taken out in the month of Jeit, which had been concealed by the Zemindar's orders all day in some sugar-canes, and at night thrown into the Sambhar Nullah: some bones were found in the nullah, which were declared to be human, and supposed to be those of the murdered traveller.

"The second Thuggee expedition occurred in the jurisdiction of the Kilia-Khonah Thannah. The shopkeepers there sold spices, &c. to some of the Thugs who passed the night at the Dhurm Salah of Bukt-Pooree at Kupuldhara. There were about five-and-twenty Thugs, and two Mussulmen travellers with them, with three bullocks. They all left before day-break; and having proceeded about a mile towards the Ganges, the two travellers were strangled, and their bodies thrown into the river.

"The third Thuggee excursion took place in Hurooah Thannah's jurisdiction. Three persons were strangled, and the bodies thrown into Hurdoo Dhobey's well; in searching which, three sculls, several

several human bones, and a pair of shoes, the latter evidently a sepoy's, were discovered.

"As the atrocious crime of Phansigare, or Thuggee, is fortunately very uncommon in this district, and no instance has occurred during the periods I have been resident at Benares, I shall submit, for the Court's consideration, the evidence of two of the witnesses, and likewise the confession of the prisoner Shumsherah; which last was given before the magistrate, and affords, perhaps, a clearer insight into their proceedings.

"The first witness to the fact, in each of these cases, is Bhuggoo: his evidence, however, is so contradictory, and agrees so baldly with the deposition given before the magistrate, that I prefer sending the examination of the second witness, Kadir Khan, a Patan, son of Jumum Khan, inhabitant of Moujah Punnah, purgunah Moneah, Zillah Patna, aged forty-three years, formerly a cultivator, but for the last twenty-one years a Thug by profession.

"'In the month of Aghun, 1240, he says, Fuslee, Shumsherah, Oozerah, Moradun, Bukus, Asmut, Mehar Ali, and myself, went on a Thuggee expedition to the westward, and reached the Oude territory. At Chand Pertaubpoor we met Chuta Thug, in company with a traveller who was afterwards strangled, and eleven rupees with two or four cloths found on him. We journeyed onto Allahabad, and

thence

thence eastward. Near Burount we met Goplah Beekah, and nine other Thugs, and they accompanied us to Mirza Morad's Serai. There we found Mohur Singh, a Jemadar of Thugs, with ten others, whose names I do not remember. We all went on together, and rested at night near the temple at Rajah-ka-Tullao. On the road we met a traveller, whom Mohur Singh entered into conversation with, and persuaded to join our party. At the last quarter of the night we renewed our march, and, quitting the high road near Serai, Mohur followed a pathway for about half a cose, and strangled the traveller. Seven rupees, with two or four cloths, were taken, and Goury and Mehar Ali threw the corpse into a well.

" ' After walking some distance in the direction of Benares, we overtook two Mussulmen travellers with three bullocks. They went in with us to our halting-place, the Dhurm Salah, at Kupuldharah. Towards daybreak we departed; and about a mile off, near the banks of the Ganges, Mohur Singh and Goury strangled the travellers. We found on them five rupees, a sword, and two or three pieces of cloths. Mohur Singh took all, and drove the bullocks on before us. Our people threw the bodies into the river. After taking some refreshment, we proceeded to Sydpoor: there Salaroo, a Burkundaz, recognised Mohur Singh, who, in consequence, gave him five rupees. The three bullocks

bullocks were sent by Mohur Singh to his home. From Sydpoor we went to Kytee; and the next day to Rajghât. Very early the following morning we proceeded towards the west: it was then the month of Jeit, and the period of the Ghazymeean festival. When we reached a tank, we found two Sepoys and a Bearer sitting there. We drank toddy with them; and all went on together. Mohur Singh asked them where they came from, and whither they were going. They replied, "From the east towards the west." Mohur Singh said, "I am also going towards the west." In the evening, we halted at the Hurooah Bazar. When one quarter of the night only remained, we continued our journey, and went two miles on the Punch Cossy road, where there is a pucka well, with two mangoe-trees near it: there Moma and Imam Bux strangled the travellers; I standing by. Thirty rupees, ten pieces of cloths, and two brass pots, were found on them: there was also a horse and a mare. We were then twenty-five persons. Some of us threw the bodies into the well. My share was a doputta, and a rupee eight annas: the other Thugs had their proportion. I took the mare, and Mohur Singh the horse. From thence my companions and myself separated from the gang, and went home: the other Thugs likewise travelled in the direction of their homes. After being at home for some days, the Tomandar and Foujdaree Nazir of the

the city of Patna apprehended me. I was never taken up before, during the twenty-one years I have practised Thuggee. I have been in many excursions, in Oude and to the eastward; but excepting the three expeditions above alluded to, I have never done any thing in the Benares division. I have spent all my share of the plunder. The mare was taken from my house to the Patna Adawlut. There are only eight men connected with me in this business. Their names are, Moradhun, Bukus of Siveree, Shumsherah, Oozerah, Imam Bux of Khutary, Asmut, and Hunoman, a Brahmin of Jurrowah. Of these eight, Moradhun and myself are Sirdars. Mohur Singh has twenty-five men, and is a Sirdar. All the men were in these expeditions; but I cannot remember their names. We do not go armed: perhaps two may be armed. We strangle our victims generally; and never use a weapon, excepting in case of necessity. No wounds were inflicted on any of the victims of this district. Those who strangle receive an additional rupee.'

"The third witness, Goplah, son of Dyar, of the Lode caste, inhabitant of Muteepurwa, Zillah Cawnpore, aged twenty-six years said:—'A year ago, I left home alone, on a Thuggee expedition towards the east. When I reached Bhaugur Mow, in the Oude country, I met Kisseree Singh with twenty-five Thugs, and Bekram and Muhadut Jemadars with

with Mukdoom Bux and others. After travelling fifteen cose, we fell in with three travellers, whom Bekram, Mukdoom and Chudu strangled, and took their property. The bodies were thrown into a well. I had my share. Going by Meean Gunge and Hussun Gunge to Noel Gunge, we strangled five travellers. On arriving on Burount near Choby Bazar, Moradhun, Kadir, and Mohur Singh, Jemadars of Thugs, joined us with twenty-five men. Bekram and the other Oude Thugs returned thence. On the road from Mirza Mourad to Rajah-ka-Tullao, we met a Mussulman, who went with us to the latter place, where we rested at the Buneah's house near the temple, and, after taking some food, passed the night there. When the night was nearly over, we resumed our march towards Benares; and leaving the high road in a northern direction, struck into a pathway for a mile, until we came on a plain at some distance from a village. Mohur Singh strangled the traveller, and I and another threw the body into a well: we found on him seven rupees, a sword, two or four brass pots, and four or five cloths. In the division, my share was a turban. The cloths and pots were divided amongst us, and the rupees soon spent. We then came to Benares, and passed a day at the Serai Aurungabad. We crossed the Sepoy lines, and entered the Orderly Bazar, where we met two travellers with three bullocks. We inquired whence they came, and where

where they were going. They said from Hansy to Gorruckpore. Mohur Singh said, " I am on my way to Gorruckpore; come with us." We proceeded to Kupuldara, and put up at the Dhurm Salah for the evening. At the sixth hour of the night we renewed our journey. When we reached the Ganges east from Kupuldara, some of us seized the hands, and others the feet, of the travellers, whom Chutu and Imam Bux strangled: we then threw them into the river. Five rupees, a lotah, a sword, and a pair of pyjamahs, were taken. Mohur Singh took the three bullocks. We travelled afterwards to Sydpore, Kytee, and Rajghât, putting up at the Luckah Serai. The next day we went towards Sheopore; and stopping at Shunkur Talao, we drank some toddy. We saw two Sepoys and a Bearer sitting there; whom Mohur Singh asked where they were going, and whence they came. Their reply was, from Cuttack, and their destination Lucknow. We all went on to Sheopore; and from that place to Hurooah, where we rested at a Buneah's shop. In the latter part of the night we continued our march; and after walking a mile on the Punch Cossy road, Beeka, Bheegoo, and Moradhun, threw the travellers down, when Imam Bux, Mohur Singh, and Goury, strangled them. The others remained on the watch. Twenty-five rupees, a gold mohur, fifteen pieces of cloths, and twenty brass pots, were gained. Six men and a Jemadar

Jemadar threw the bodies into a well. In the division of the plunder, a lotah, a merzai, and a rupee, were my share.'—The witness mentioned, that all the prisoners were Thugs, and concerned in the three expeditions that took place in the Benares division, with the exception of Asmut.

"The prisoner, Shumsherah, is an inhabitant of Purneah, Pergunnah Moneah, Zillah Patna, twenty-five years of age, of the weaver caste. Moradhun supported and protected him whilst a child: and whenever he went on a Thuggee excursion, the prisoner accompanied him.

"The deposition before the magistrate is as follows:—'In the month of Aghun, 1240 Fuslee, Moradhun, Kader Khan, Bukus, Oozerah, Meher Ali, Asmut, Imam Bux, and myself, proceeded on a Thuggee expedition. We strangled several persons in Oude, remaining there until the month of Maug; and then went to Allahabad, from whence we travelled, in an eastern direction, until we came to Burount. We found Goplah and Beeka there; and further on the road, Mohur Singh, with four other Thugs. We met a traveller as we proceeded. Mohur Sing, and his party, went on with him. We rested in the evening at Hunoman Chokey. When the night was nearly spent, we went on, and Huna strangled the traveller. Seventeen rupees, some cloths, and brass pots, were found on him, and the body was thrown into a well. I being the adopted pupil

pupil of Moradhun, he took my share. He gave me food only, and I was his follower. Proceeding on our march, we met a Mussulman travelling: Imam Bux attached himself to him. We halted for the night at Rajah-ka-Tullao; and towards morning recommenced our journey. Leaving the high road at Serai Mohun to the right, we followed a small pathway. After walking a mile, we came near a garden, where Imam Bux strangled the traveller. Ten rupees, a sword, two dhotees, a lotah, and some old cloths, were the plunder. Two or three men took the corpse, and threw it into a well. Near Benares we met two travellers, with three bullocks. Moradhun, Kadir Khan, Goplah, and Beeka, joined them; and in the evening we made Kupuldhara our resting-place, stopping at the Dhurm Salah. When one quarter of the night only remained, the march was resumed; and near the banks of the Ganges, about a mile off, Beeka and Unna strangled the travellers. I do not remember what plunder was obtained. Meher Ali, Moradhun, Kader Khan, and Beeka, threw the corpses into the river. We then went to Sydpore. A Burkundaz, Salaroo, recognised Mohur Singh, who, in consequence, gave him four rupees; and Moradhun sent the three bullocks, by Bukus, to his house. We afterwards returned to the village of Bettree; and, going by Chundwuk, arrived at Rajghât. Remaining there all night, we marched very early the next

next morning, in a western direction. After leaving the city, we met two Sepoys and a Bearer. Beeka entered into conversation with them, and they came on in our company. We halted at Hurooah Bazar. Towards day-break we resumed our route; and going about two miles on the Punch Cossy road, where there is a pucka well, with two mangoe-trees, Mohur Singh, Ramsuhoy, and Selwunt Rai, strangled the three travellers. They gained thirty-two rupees, some cloths and brass pots. The bodies were thrown into the well. The travellers had a horse and a mare with them: Kadir took the first, and Goplah the latter. We afterwards went to Burogong, where we divided the plunder; and separated, going to our respective homes. I have never strangled any one, but have aided in throwing bodies into wells. Eight annas is a very good remuneration for murdering a man. We often strangle a victim who is suspected of having two pice. We are unrestrained by any fears, in pursuing our vocation. We do not sell our plunder; but, when there is a large quantity, send it to our homes.'

"Bukus once accompanied Moradhun and others on a Thuggee expedition in Oude, and was with them two years; but has never practised in the Benares district, and is unjustly accused.

"Oozerah declares that he is innocent. He once found himself with Moradhun, &c., in Oude; but

but ran away the moment he could, when he discovered his companions were Thugs.

"Meher Ali served Moradhun, as a grass-cutter, for five or six months. He acknowledged, before the magistrate at Patna, to having been his servant for the above number of years, and to having accompanied him in his Thuggee expeditions.

"Asmut was formerly called Dubery, alias Neeamut Ali, at present Asmut. He attributes his name being mentioned to a family dispute he had with the two brothers, Kadir Khan and Moradhun, with whom he is connected by marriage; and, of course, asserts his innocence. The depositions of Nanuk, Ramphul, Rujoo Singh, Balukgur, Purshad, Juggernat, Thakooree, Kudoo, Isseredyeal, Uchalall, and Matadyel, point out the halting-places of the Thugs in these expeditions; and the wells, &c. where the bones and other remains of the murdered persons were discovered."

The Court of Nizamut Adawlut sentenced four of the persons engaged in this transaction to be transported for life.

CHAP. VII.

WHAT is called the "Burwha Ghât affair," is remarkable, in many points of view. It became the subject of elaborate investigation; and it cannot be unacceptable to present a portion of the evidence.

Narooha Kumusdar, of the purgunah of Burwaha, taken on the 5th of November 1831, before Captain Sandys, Assistant to the Resident at Indore, and in charge of the Nunar district, deposed thus:—

"In the year Sumbut 1884 (on the 29th January, A.D. 1829,) three camels loaded with treasure, belonging to Dhunraj Seth of Omrowtee, came to the town of Burwaha, rested the 30th and 31st, paid the duties demandable at the Custom-house, and marched again, on the 31st January, towards Indore, by the village of Naen, which was then unoccupied and waste. On the bank of the nullah near that village, the men escorting the treasure were all killed, and the treasure taken off by robbers; and on the 3d of February 1829, Khosala Balar, of the village of Omureea, came to the guard in the evening, and reported it. It was then late, and the horsemen of the guard had gone to escort treasure to to Mundlesur; and I deferred going out till the next morning, when I, with Runa Ragonauth Singh, Zemindar of the purgunah, and Chutter Duffadar, and three foot soldiers of the guard, went towards Naen, the place where the murders had been committed. On the road, we met Golbeea, a Pardhee of the village of Nadeea, who told us that the three camels were left in the jungle; one with his legs tied, and the other two free. On coming to the nullah, at about a hundred paces distant from the road to the west, on the dry bed, we found three bodies: they were under the branches of a Golur-tree, covered with leaves, dry sand, and stones. We took them out; and found all their throats cut, apparently with swords. On one of the bodies was a black coat; and by that coat he was recognised to be Meer Futteh Alee, a merchant of Borhanpore: he often passed by Burwaha on business, and became known to the peeadas of the guard. We then went to Omureea; and asked Humtah, the Putel of that place, where the bodies were that he had reported: and he took us to a part of the nullah in which some water remained, with Girdhur Mukatee and Nanna Putwaree; and about fifty paces west from the place where we discovered the first three bodies, we saw two more bodies, lying on the ground on the edge of the water: their throats had been cut in the same manner as those of the other two, and they had been mangled by animals. From this

this place, we returned to the first three bodies, and, searching further, found two more, about ten or twelve paces from them, covered with sand, leaves, and stones, and lying one over the other: we took them up, and found their throats cut in the same manner as those of the others. There was no other wound discoverable on any one of the seven bodies. We now went in search of the camels; and about a quarter of a cose from the bodies, to the east, we found one camel down, with his legs tied. We took him up, and came on to the village of Nadeea, where we found the two other camels browsing in a field; and sent all three, without ropes or saddles, to Burwaha: and I collected the Baloes from Nadae Rampoora, and Agurwara, and Omurreea, to bury the bodies; and returned to Burwaha; and, at the Custom-house chokee, ascertained, from the books of Gunput Raw, the agent on the part of the Farmer of the Customs, that, on the 30th of January 1829, Dhunraj Seth's three camels had paid duty; and that on the same day, a Bhowanee Persaud, and others his companions, bearing arms, and residents of Bundelcund, thirty persons, with six ponies, had been entered as paying Rahadaree duties; and, on the same day, Meer Tullah Alee, the merchant, had passed on his way to Indore. After learning these particulars, I sent off in pursuit of the robbers."

Davey Singh, peeada of the guard, deposed, on

 the

the same day, to the same effect; as also did Gobind Apa, peeada of the same guard; and Chutter, dufadar of the same guard; and Rana Rugonath Sing, zemindar of the purgunah of Burwaha. The men employed for this purpose deposed to their having buried the seven bodies, by order of the Kumasdar.

Bijan Naek Nahil, of Omureea in Burwaha, said:—" In the year Sumbut 1884, three camels laden with treasure, from Dhunraj Seth, were robbed at the nullah of the village of Naean, and seven men, who escorted it, murdered. Naraba, kumasdar of the purgunah, called me, and ordered me to search for the murderers. I took three other nahils from Omureea, and two danuks from Nadeea, and Bheela Raw, a peeada of the guard of Burwaha, with me, to pursue the track (*many*) at the place where the bodies lay. We could find no trace; but, after a good deal of search, we found the *many* on the road to Key, about a cose from the village of Naean east, near the deserted village of Khoree; and from that place we followed it, through the villages of Gidwara, Jugutpoorah, Ramgolah, Chorurnudee, Khamkee, Khargee, Baroul, and Kutkote, Holkar's territories. From this place Bhula Raw returned home to Burwaha; and we took zemindars, one Dhanuk and one Bilae, to follow on the *many* or track. We found it through Ranjhunna, Gowarbar, Gureegor, Chundere

dere Gurh, Sankola, Byroogow, Kop Gowra, Beetora, up to the bowlee of the village of Portula, in the purgunah of Neemunpore, Mukoar, in the territories of Bunnear; which bowlee is situated about two hundred paces from the village: from that bowlee no trace could be found. We told the putel of that village, Dew Chund Kolee, and two other people, to carry on the trace; and if they could not, they must answer to their Government for the murders; and having told them this, we returned. On our way, we saw the people of Kutkote cutting wood, and asked about the people who had passed of late. They said they had seen, on the Nuddee, under Kutkote, twenty-five or thirty men from Bundelcund Awud, with five or seven ponies, and asked them whence they came: they said they were from Malwa, and were going to Pootula, but had lost their road. We returned, and reported all to the kumasdar of Burwaha."

Another witness, named Tejula Bular, of the village of Nadeea, purgunah of Burwaha, testified to this effect:—"In the Sumbut 1884, on a nullah in the village of Naean, in the purgunah of Burhawa, three camels laden with treasure, belonging to Dhunraj Seth, were robbed, and the men who escorted them murdered. I had been taken as a begar with a kafila of Government servants, who were going with a palkee, and other things, from Borhanpore, as far as the village of Omureea;

and

and was on my return, and warming myself at a fire left burning on the ground, which a party of Brinjaras had just quitted, near the village of Naean, when I saw a number of carrion-birds, such as vultures and others, descend from the sky, and collect on the bank of the nullah: on seeing this, I went to the village of Rampora in the above purgunah, and told Omrow Bhugwan, and other Baloes, that some animals must be lying dead in the nullah of Naean, as carrion-birds were there collected. They all accompanied me to the nullah, to see; and we found two human bodies lying in the nullah, close to the edge of the water. On seeing them, my companions returned to Rampora, and I came home. On my way, I met Heera Rajpoot, of the village of Agurwara, feeding his cattle in the grounds of Naean; and I told him that I had seen the bodies of two murdered travellers in the bed of the nullah; and, at his request, I went again, and pointed them out from a distance."

The deposition of the person thus referred to was as follows:—"I was grazing my cattle on the boundaries of Naean, when Tejula Bular, of Nadeea, came towards me from the nullah, and said some people had murdered two travellers, and thrown their bodies into the nullah; and, at my request, he went and pointed them out to me. At that time, Nana Putwaree, of Naddera, was on his way from Burwaha to Omureea; and meeting him, I men-

I mentioned the circumstance. He went on towards Omureea; and I returned to my cattle."

Nana Putwaree deposed—"That, on hearing the circumstances from Heera Rajpoot, he went to Omureea, and told Girdhur Muktee and Himota Putel; and went with them, and Bichun Nahil and Shamila Bilae, to see the bodies. After seeing the two, we returned; and I requested Shamila Bular to go and report to the guard at Burwaha; but he sent his brother Khosala to do so. Khosala deposes, that he was sent to report the circumstance to the guard at Burwaha; and reached the place towards evening, and reported accordingly."

Urzee, of Dhun Raj Seth, forwarded, through Captain Robinson of Ellichpore, the following statement:—"About thirty-three months ago, 45,000 rupees of my property, on three camels and one pony, with nine men, on their way from Bombay to Indore, were taken by twenty-nine Thugs, four cose from Alvee Bureyra, and twenty from Indore. The men were all killed, and the pony taken with the property, but the camels were let go. Behareelal and Gomanee Ram, my gomashtas, went, with Dolla Hurcara of Holkar's, in search of the Thugs; found them in Jhansee; and gave information to the Governor-General's Agent at Humeerpore, who got them seized and put in irons. They confessed that the property had been taken, and divided into a huna hundred and one shares; and the Agent sent them all to the Resident at Indore. The Resident sent them back to the Agent at Humeerpore, who made them over to the Jhansee Rajah's vakeel, with orders to recover and make good the property.

"Some time before this, gold, to the value of 22,000 rupees, in charge of four hurcaras, and another batch of gold to the value of 11,000 rupees, on their way from Poona to Jeypore, were taken by Thugs, and the people murdered. The robbery was traced to these same Thugs, some of whom were in the Gwalior, and some in the Dutteea territories: many were taken, and made over to Kishen Persaud, Holkar's vakeel, and put into his highness's fort of Alumpore. I have recovered fourteen or fifteen thousand rupees out of the whole; but my agents have, in thirty-three months, spent, in the search, fifteen or sixteen thousand.

"The officer in charge of the Jubulpore district has seized seven of the Thugs, and sent them to the Resident at Indore; and their case is not yet decided. All these Thugs reside in Jhansee and Jubulpore; and they should be made to give up my property. My gomashta at Humeerpore wanted a hurcara and a letter; but the Agent of the Governor-General would not furnish them, out of regard for the Jhansee Chief; though the Residents of Nagpoor and Gwalior and other places have written to him in my behalf."

Some

Some information on the subject was also received from Urzee, of Nanik Ram, gomashta of Dhunraj Seth, through Mr. Graeme, the Resident at Nagpore:—"About three years and four months ago, three camels and a pony were laden with 12,500 reals of silver, value 40,000 rupees, and, under the escort of seven matchlock-men, were on their way from Bombay to Indore: on the road, about six cose from Indore, twenty-nine Thugs killed all the escort, and took the pony, but left the camels. Behareelal and Gomanee Ram, my gomashtas at Indore, heard of the robbery; and informed the Court of Holkar, who sent Dolla Hurcara with them, to search for the Thugs. They found them at Jhansee; and informed the Agent at Humeerpore, who got them secured: and when they had confessed the crime, he sent them off to the Resident at Indore, with the Jhansee Rajah's hurcara. 1200 rupees and three of the reals were found upon them, and made over to the gomashtas; and the Resident, having proved the theft, sent them back to the Governor-General's Agent at Humeerpore; who made them over to the Jhansee Rajah's vakeel, with orders to request his master to make good the property.

"Some time before this, silver and gold, to the value of 33,000 rupees, were on their way, in charge of hurcaras, from Poona to Jypore; and the men were all killed by Thugs, and the property

property taken: this was made known to the Agent at Humeerpore, who discovered that the Thugs were from Gwalior. They were seized, and sent to the Resident at Gwalior; who ascertained the truth, and recovered gold to the value of 4000 rupees, and put it in deposit at Gwalior, and afterwards made it over to my gomashta. Four Thugs had been seized by the gentleman at Jubulpore, with 1400 rupees of gold upon them; and, on my representation, through the then Resident of Nagpore, Mr. Wilder, they were forwarded to Indore. The gold was there made over to my gomashta, and the Thugs sent to Humeerpore; where the Agent made them over to the Jhansee Rajah, with orders that he should satisfy me, and get my razeenameh, as he must have received a share of the booty.

"The vakeel sent them all to Jhansee, but remained himself at Humeerpore: and the Rajah detained my gomashtas a month; and then told them to go to Humeerpore, and he would send them the thieves. They went accordingly to the Agent at Humeerpore, who promised to recover the property for them; but it is not yet forthcoming. The gomashtas are reduced to despair, and have expended thousands of rupees. The Saugor gentleman is now in charge, and 320 reals have been found upon the Thugs: and as Beharcelal and Hursahee, my gomashtas, are now

now at Saugor, I pray a letter to his address, to request he will cause the Jhansee Rajah to make good my losses."

The confession of one of the principal actors in the Burwaha-ghât massacre cannot but be interesting. The adverse fates of so many of the leaders enumerated must be sufficient to shew that, of late, the occupation of a Thug is far from having been a comfortable one. The person whose confession follows was named Moklal. The deposition was taken at Saugor, before Captain Sleeman:—

"In the month of Kartick, about six years ago, I, Bukhut Jemadar, and Thukoree at large, Dhokul Meraea Pande (hung at Saugor), and Moklal approver, left our homes at Poorah in Jhansee, on an expedition to the Deccan; and after taking the auspices outside the village, we proceeded *viâ* Jhansee, Bhilsa, and Rehlee. Leaving Bhopaul on the right, we crossed the Nurbudda at Cheepanere, and encamped outside of the village, under a Bur-tree on the bank of the river, where we found a gang of fifty Thugs under the following leaders:—

"Roshun Jemadar, hung at Saugor, with ten followers.

"Khuleel ditto, hung at ditto, with ten ditto.

"Ghureeba Dhadee, hung at ditto, with seven ditto.

"Zolfukar

"Zolfukar Jemadar, hung at ditto, with seven ditto.

"Golab Khan, alias Puhara, hung at ditto, with three ditto.

"Sheikh Madaree, hung at Joura.

"Moollooa Aheer, and Kehree Lodhee, who died in the Saugor jail.

"Nunha Mussulman, Manoola, Bhowanee (son of Rostum), Mahomed Buksh, Pawn Mahomed, Sheikh Chotee, Daood, and Pawn Khan, approvers, also encamped, and we joined them: they had reached this place from their homes without committing any murder. The next morning, we all, fifty-six, set out on the road to the Deccan; and arrived at Hurda, where we passed that night. Thence we proceeded, by Singeea Deo Boregow and Asseer, to Borhanpore, and encamped outside of the town, in a grove where there was a Muth (Gosaens lodging). We halted there the next day; and about noon, a gang of fifty-six other Thugs, under the following leaders, came up from their homes, and joined our gang:—

"Purshaud Lodhee, hung at Saugor, with ten followers. Purusram Jemadar, and Sirawun his brother, at large, with fifteen. Munohur Partuk Jemadar, who lately cut his throat near Jhansee when he found the guard from Jhansee coming up with him upon the open plain, and died on the spot. Khooman Brahman, brother of ditto (at large),

large), number of followers not remembered; and Mahraj Patuck, who drowned himself in the lake at Dhamanee, on his way to Saugor under an escort, 1832.

"We all amounted to 112 persons.

"From this place we set out on the road to the Deccan. On reaching the bank of the Taptee river, we sat down; and while we were talking and smoking, two Mussulman travellers came up, on their way from Bhopaul to Aurungabad. Roshun Jemadar acted as Sothae, and won their confidence. They sat down with us, and smoked the hookah; and Roshun gave them some food to eat, as he was himself eating. After resting here some time, we went on with the travellers, and reached Tankolee, a village six cose south from Borhanpore, and encamped on the bank of the river on the north side of the village. After we had taken our dinner, about two ghurries after sunset, we sent some people of our gang to converse with the travellers; and while they were engaged in talking, they were both seized and strangled upon their beds, by Khoda Buksh Mussulman and Bukhut Brahman, both at large, assisted by others as Shumsheeas, who were sitting near them. We got from them one hundred and fifty rupees in cash, two matchlocks, one tattoo, and some other articles. In the division, we got one rupee each.

"After

"After this affair, the next morning, we proceeded on the road to the Deccan, and reached Edulabad, about ten cose south from Borhanpore; and encamped outside of the town, at a Fakeer's Tukeea under some trees. The same day, eight Rokureeas, of whom six were armed with matchlocks, and two camel-drivers, came up with Tippoo Sahee rupees (Spanish dollars), from Dunraj Seth's house at Bombay, on their way to Indore, and lodged in a shop in the bazaar. We sent Khoda Buksh (at large), and Molloo Jemadar, as tilhaes (spies), to watch them: they went and put up in one of the shops near them. The next morning the Rokureeas set out, and both our spies followed them. We conjectured that they would probably encamp at Tankolee that day; and, as we had already committed a murder there, we did not think it advisable to follow them to that place: we accordingly went on to Chaund Devee. The Rokureeas did not, however, go to Tankolee, but to Borhanpore, on the following morning. Khuleel, Mahraj Patuk, Purusram, Zalim, and Bukhut, jemadars, with fifty select Thugs from the gang, set out for Borhanpore, thinking that the Rokureeas would arrive there from Tankolee. The remainder of the gang returned from this place to Deoleea, in the Bhopaul district, having appointed to rejoin them there after perpetrating the murder of the above Rokureeas. About one watch before sunset,

sunset, our party arrived at Borhanpore, and encamped outside of the town, towards the north. Here both of the spies brought information that the Rokureeas had put up in the bazaar. On this, we sent Molloo and Ghureeba, jemadars, to make inquiries; and on reaching the bazaar, they found three other camels lodging there, but not the Rokureeas we were in search of. They returned, and reported; and we sent off Khuleel and Monohur, jemadars, and Mudara Thugs, to trace them, offering to give them one hundred rupees' reward, over and above their share of the booty. They were to proceed to Asseer, and thence on to Boregow; where we would wait for them. These three men arrived at Asseer about midnight; but could not discover the Rokureeas, although they were at the time lodged in the bazaar. The next morning we reached Asseer, without finding any trace of the Rokureeas; and sent Ashraff (at large) and Monga (who died in Saugor jail) to the bazaar, to purchase some flour, &c.; and went on to a nullah about one-half cose distant from Asseer. Soon after we had sat down at this nullah, these two men returned, and told us that they had seen the Rokureeas settling the duties at the Custom House. On learning this, we were much gratified; and leaving Moonga and Ashruff, as tilhaees, to watch their movement, we went on to Boregow. A little after our arrival there, the spies brought information,

tion, that the treasure-bearers would not pass that way, having gone to Punchpuhar. On hearing this, we immediately set out for Punchpuhar; but could not find the Rokureeas. We passed that night there; and in the morning we sent six other active Thugs, in different directions, to trace them; two to Asseer, two to Boregow, and two to Sherpore, on the Indore Road; while the main body halted at Punchpuhar. About a watch before sunset, the two men from the Sherpore came back, and told us that the Rokureeas had lodged in the bazaar at Sherpore the preceding night; had set out on the road to Indore that morning; and intended to put up at a village about eight cose from Sherpore, name not remembered. They got this information from the people at Sherpore, and it was correct. Here the four other men rejoined us also. On learning this, although we were all much tired, we immediately set out for that village, leaving Sherpore on the right: we arrived there at midnight, and encamped outside of the village, under a large Peepul-tree. The next morning, when the Rokureeas set out from this village, we followed; and about a cose from the village we were detained by the chokeedars of the Custom-chokee; and during our detention, the Rokureeas went on, out of our sight: we paid the chokeedars one rupee four annas, and went on. During this interval, the treasure-bearers had, we found, crossed the Nurbudda at

Burwaha-

Burwaha ghât, and gone on to the bazaar of Burwaha, a village the other side of the river, and put up in a shop. We followed, and crossed the Nurbudda at the same ghât, and encamped outside of the same village, under a Bur-tree, near the small reservoir. The next morning, the Darogah of the Custom-chokee detained the treasure-bearers, to settle duties on their treasure; and we were detained also by the same authority: but we did not intend to pay them till the treasure-bearers had settled, with the view of following them. The treasure-bearers had great altercations with the people of the chokee, who demanded a high rate of duty from them; when Maharaj Patuck went to the Darogah, and admonished him, and asked why he did not let the treasure-bearers go; as, in the event of any accident happening to their treasure, if they moved at a late hour, he would be responsible for it: on this, the Darogah became alarmed, and took from them whatever they had intended to pay. It was now late, and the treasure-bearers would not move that night. We advanced to a garden about two cose on the side of the road; where we cooked and ate our dinner, and passed the night. The next morning, while we were preparing to move, we saw the camels and the treasure-bearers coming on; and we immediately set out, and went on to a nullah in an extensive bamboo jungle, where there was an uninhabited village. Here we all

all sat down, after cutting some large bamboo sticks, thinking this a suitable place for murder. While we were smoking, a man on horseback, who had been the companion of the Rokureeas ever since the preceding night, came up, and sat down with us to smoke. Soon after the Rokureeas arrived, and sat down to rest. We surrounded them from every side; and seized and strangled the six matchlock-men; then the horseman; and, lastly, we pulled down the surwans from the camels, with the bamboo sticks we had cut there, and strangled them. We buried the bodies of the whole in the nullah; and instantly made Ghureeba mount on the sowar's horse, and took the treasure-camels by a bye-road through the jungle, leaving the high road to Indore on the left. Going on about two cose from the place where we had committed the murder, we sat down and took the loads off the camels, put them on our tattoos, and turned the camels loose in the jungles. Here we left the Indore road altogether; and took another, in a direction to the east. In three days we reached Sundulpore, and encamped on the bank of a tank. Here we cut the treasure khoorjees with tulwars and knives: and took out the treasure, in which we found 15,000 Tippoo Sahee rupees (Spanish dollars), silver bullion 100 rupees weight, and a small brass box stamped. When we broke open this box, we found in it four diamond rings set with jewels,

jewels, eight pearls, and one pair of gold kurras or bangles. The whole of these articles amounted to 1000 Tippoo Sahee rupees in value. From this booty, Zalim took out a handful of money, as an offering to Davy, which we intended to give to priests of Bindachul; but not finding an opportunity for doing so, it was left with Zalim. Afterwards we divided the booty, and got about 150 rupees each—Tippoo Sahee rupees (Spanish dollars). The pearls and jewels were divided according to their value, which had been then estimated. The shares of those who left our gang for the Bhopaul district, as before described, were given to their friends and relations. Hurry Singh [at large, adopted by Khoman, died in Jubulpore jail] took the horse, for ten rupees. We passed that night at Sundulpore; and afterwards returned to our homes, by regular stages. A few days after our return home, the part of our gang whom we had left behind at Doolea returned, having heard that the treasure had been robbed at Burwaha Ghât."

Few things are more difficult to a native of India than to tell the truth, under any circumstances; and the confessions of criminals, in all countries, may be expected to contain a mixture of truth and falsehood. The deposition of Moklal is not perfectly consistent with the rest; nor even with another statement by himself, made in conversation with

Captain Sleeman, and drawn forth by the question, "How did you manage the Burwaha Ghât affair?" That statement is here submitted; and the reader must choose between the narratives.

"It (Burwaha Ghât affair) gave us a great deal of trouble, as the dollars were laden on camels. They went fast, and, afraid to appear near to them in a body, we several times lost all trace of them. We first fell in with them at Borhanpore. Ours was only one of three great parties that went from Bundelcund, Gwalior, and Saugor, that year, to Kandeish; and it consisted of about one hundred and sixty Thugs, concentrating upon the treasure party. At Burwaha Ghât, on the Nurbudda river, we found them disputing with the Custom-house officers about the payment of duties, and stating the hardship of being obliged to expose the value of their charge in an unsettled country. We paid duties for ourselves and our six ponies; and, leaving a few scouts, passed over the river, and went on to the small deserted village of Naean, in the midst of a jungly waste. Here we waited till the treasure party came up; consisting of eight men, mounted on camels, and armed with matchlocks; and a merchant, by name Futteh Alee, who had joined them on the road, in the hope of being more secure in their company than alone. It was about nine o'clock in the morning when they reached the place.

place. The signal was given: we rushed in upon the camels, seized them by their bridles, and made them sit down, by beating them with sticks. The men were seized and killed; some strangled, some stabbed with spears, and some cut down with swords. Futteh Alee was pulled off his pony, and strangled. We transferred the treasure to our ponies; threw the bodies into a ravine; and went on for three days without halting any where, as we knew we should be immediately pursued. After we had got beyond danger, we rested, and divided the booty; setting aside the proper share for the Temple of Davy, at Bindachul, near Mirzapore.

"Dhun Raj Seth sent his agent, Bearee Lall, to the Resident at Indore, and the Agent of the Governor-General in Bundelcund, to recover his dollars. He got a good many of the principal Thug leaders arrested: they were sent by the Agent in Bundelcund to the Resident at Indore, who sent them back to the Agent; who made them over to the Native Chiefs in whose jurisdiction they resided, with orders to make good the money. These Chiefs told us to make good three-fourths of the money taken at Burwaha Ghât, by a general contribution. We agreed to do so, and were let go: some paid out of the fruits of former expeditions; others borrowed in anticipation of future success; and those who had neither money nor credit, pledged themselves to pay part of their future earnings.

earnings. To this, Bearee Lall agreed; and sent them on expeditions; retaining Chotee, Bukhut, and other Jemadars of great influence, about his person. He got a good deal of money by procuring the release of all the noted Thugs then in confinement at different places. He got nine thousand rupees for the release of Dhurum Khan Jemadar from Gwalior, on the pretence that he was engaged in the affair, when he had been in prison long before. He had got a great prize of jewels from some men killed near Kotah, and his family could afford to pay. Such was Dhun Raj Seth's influence, that he could get a gang released from prison in any part of India; and for some time, his agent, Bearee Lall, had always half-a-dozen of the principal Thug leaders about his person, and used to attend all our marriages and festivals. What his master got, we know not; but he got a great deal of our money."

CHAP. VIII.

A WITNESS, named Feringeea, whose evidence has been already frequently referred to, gave the following account of an exploit known as the "Dholia and Malagow affair."

"Five gangs concentrated in the village of Jokeer, between Dholia and Malagow, in Kandeish, amounting to two hundred and fifty Thugs, under myself. Makun, who was hung at Indore, 1829; Gunga Deen, who was hung at Indore, 1829; Chotee, approver; Maharaj Partuk, who drowned himself at Saugor; Sheikh Nungoo, dead; Persaud, hung at Saugor, 1832; and others.

"We left Jokeer for Malagow, with two travellers whom we had killed before daylight; and were resting at a well two cose north of Malagow, when we heard, after sunrise, the *Chim mama* on the right. I proposed, according to all the recognised rules of augury, to go back to Jokeer immediately. To this proposal they would not consent; and we went on to Malagow, where I proposed that we should

should halt, and avert the threatened evil by a sacrifice. This was overruled by a party who supposed that it might be as well averted by quitting the high road to Kopurgow, and diverging to the right, upon that of Chandore. I went on with them four cose, to a village whose name I forget; but at night determined to obey the omen, and came back, with my gang of twenty-five Thugs, to Malagow, where I found a gang of one hundred Thugs, under the following leaders: Omrow, hung at Indore, 1829; Bhimmee, approver; Buduloo, hung at Saugor, 1832; Bukut, approver; Kunhey Aheer, killed in Joudpore, 1833; Hinder Benguna, approver.

"They had with them four treasure-bearers from Poona, on their way from Indore, whom they intended to kill on the way to Dholeea. I joined them; and we went on to the village of Jokeer; and were joined on the way by three other travellers, whom we could not shake off. Hinder Benguna's son, Chiddee, had quarrelled with his father; and gone off to join Chotee's party, on the Chandore road, with Gurhoo, who went to see two of his brothers who were with them: and they having let out the secret of the treasure-bearers, Chotee came off, as fast as he could, with Maharaj and a party of forty, and joined us, during the night, at Jokeer.

"Omrow's party was composed chiefly of Kuboolas,

boolas, fellows of all castes; whom he had scraped together, to make up a gang for this expedition; and we insisted upon his sending thirty of the rawest of them in advance from Jokeer, in the afternoon. There were at least two hundred men that night at Jokeer, on their way back from Hindostan to their regiments; but we watched the treasure-bearers closely; and when they set out, we followed; and at a bowlee, a mile or two on, we closed in upon them, and put them to death. We had not been able to shake off the other three travellers; and were, in consequence, obliged to put them to death also: some of the bodies were thrown into the bowlee, and the others were slightly buried in a field close by.

"Chotee claimed a share for that part of their gangs which had gone on to Chandore, as well as for that which had come with him; and Omrow claimed an equal share for all the thirty Kuboolas whom he had consented to send on in advance, that they might not, by their blunders, frustrate our designs upon the treasure-bearers. After a good deal of dispute, it was settled, that those who were actually present should all share alike, without distinction of rank or office; and that those who belonged to absent parties might share what they got with them, or not, as they pleased. According to this arrangement, each man got, of gold, one hundred and twenty-five rupees' worth. Omrow's seventy

seventy men afterwards shared with the thirty Kuboolas; and Chotee's party went and shared what they got with the men at Chandore."

The bones of these persons were subsequently found: but the discovery seems to have been regarded, by the Native Officers, with a great deal of coolness. One of them, Oda Putel, deposed, on the occasion, as follows:—"The Mamlutdar at Malagow asked whether I had gone, upon Dusrut Bheel's report, to search for bodies. I said, that on the 7th March, on Saturday, Dusrut Bheel, of Jhorka, came to me, and said, that in the Gya-Pokar field were dead bodies. Papa Bheel told me the same thing. I told the ——; and he, I, and Raghoo Putel and Meerab Kulkarnee, and four others, went; and I saw, in a hollow place, bodies with stones over them: animals had devoured part of the flesh: we uncovered, and took out bones, and two or three sculls. About ten cubits from this pit we found bones of two or three other people; but the skeletons were not entire. The hair on the head was about a cubit long; and part being cut off, shewed they were men. We reported to the Court at Malagow."

Dusrut Putel deposed thus:—"Papa Bheel of Dharureea, on Thursday, came to Maujee Naig while we were together, and said he had seen dead bodies in the field of Gya Pokar, the day before, while

while hunting. I sent Gurha Bheel with him. He saw them, and returned. I next day, with Dusrut Shikdar, and Oda Putel, and three or four others, went and saw bodies, under stones, in a ditch. There was little flesh upon the bones. At another place, twenty cubits distant, were the bones of two or three people; but the skeletons were not entire, and we could not see the wounds. We came to Malagow Kutcheree, and reported."

Krishna Putel said:—"On the 22d of Cheyt, Saturday, Bhika Bheel, on returning from Aumee to Jhorka, smelt a bad smell; and came to Shikdar, and reported. I and Oda Putel were sitting with him. He said there was a bad smell in the bowlee, and it should be searched. We went; and were joined by Shukaram and Luchmun from Poona, who had just come from Dholia in search of three men who had been sent with money from Poona to Indore. Having arrived at the bowlee, we perceived the smell; and, looking down, saw the body of a man under stones. He had on a white ungarka, with blood about the collar of it. We threw it in again, after looking at it. There was long hair on the head. We concluded he had been murdered by Thugs. We returned home, and reported. Next day, further search was made; but no more were found in the bowlee. Some time before, five or six bodies had been dug up, about five hundred paces from the bowlee, on the Purola road."

CHAP. IX.

On the 6th February 1829, a robbery of large extent, accompanied, according to invariable practice, by murder, was perpetrated in the Dholeebaree Pass of the Sathpoora Hills. The circumstances of the narrative, as far as they could then be ascertained, together with the steps taken by Government for bringing the criminals to justice, were detailed in a letter from Captain Hodges, acting magistrate, to the Secretary to the Government of Bombay; from which the following is an extract:—

"The persons robbed and murdered were six men; who, together with a seventh, had been entrusted with twenty-seven packages of pearls, a small package of cloth, and a few rupees, by four mercantile houses at Bombay, on whose account they were to have been conveyed to Jeypore. At Malegaon and Parolah, the persons entrusted with these commodities, the value of which is stated by the Gomashtas of the several houses to be, rupees 72,322, took under their charge some gold mohurs and

and Venetian ducats; and it is not improbable, that, from this circumstance, it became known to the gang, by whom they were plundered, that they had such valuable property under their charge.

"The first intimation of the robbery was conveyed to the Mamlutdar of Chofrah, on the day after it was committed, by Dusrut, the Bheel Naig of the Dholeebaree Pass; who stated, by letter, that, at about eight o'clock in the morning of the preceding day, seven Beemawallas, of the designation of the persons robbed, had passed by Dholeebaree; and represented, in reply to his inquiries on the subject, that they were come from Bombay, and were going to Indore; and had no property of value in their possession. He added, that they were followed shortly after by twenty-two men, with five tattoos; who had among them two swords, and a dagger; and who stated, that they had been in the service of the British Government, from which they had received their discharge, and were proceeding to Cawnpore.

"The circumstance of the robbery became known to Dusrut Naig, in consequence of one of the Beemawallas having proceeded in advance of his companions as far as Gudurghât, about four cose from Dholeebaree; where he waited for his companions during that day and night; and afterwards, finding he was not followed by them, returned to Dholeebaree.

"On

"On his way to Dholeebaree, this person was informed, by a traveller whom he met on the road, that he had seen the body of a murdered man in a nullah near the road; and proceeding himself to the spot where it was reported to have been seen, he recognised it to be the body of one of his companions. From that spot he proceeded to Dholeebaree; and obtaining some of Dusrut Naig's people to accompany him, he returned to the nullah, where the bodies of his other five companions were also found: on one of them, concealed in his clothes, a bag of pearls was found; and on another, a rupee and a half.

"Dusrut Naig shortly afterwards joined his followers at the nullah where the bodies had been found; and traced the footsteps of men and horses as far as a deserted village on the way to a deserted part of country, between two ranges of the Sathpoora Hills, called the Pall Tuppa. From thence, he states, some footsteps were traced in the direction of a village called Chinahpanee, in the Arraward purgunah; but the footsteps of the horses, and the greater part of the gang, were traced to a village named Dhegaum, in the Yawull purgunah. It being, by this time, late in the evening, no further traces could be discovered; and the Naig came to me at Yawull.

"The following morning, every Sowar, whose services were available for the purpose, and several of of the Mamlutdar's hurcarahs, mounted on tattoos, were sent out in quest of intelligence of the robbers.

"Three Sowars, and one of the hurcarahs, having obtained intelligence, on the road, that some persons, answering to the description of the robbers given by Dusrut Naig, had been seen at a village called Nahnee, in the Yawull pergunah, proceeded to that village; and one of the horsemen, being in advance of the others, entered the village by himself, and, standing near a Buneeah's shop, met a man, who, on inquiry, described himself to be a Sepoy of the 4th regiment. Upon being asked if he had any companions with him, he said he had two, who were preparing their food at a well near the village. Afterwards, the person addressed accompanied him to the gate of the village, near which he pointed out two persons, whom he stated to be his companions. These two persons, on being called to, stopped, in the first instance; but, after accompanying the horsemen a little distance, ran off. The horsemen gave the man whom he had first accosted in charge to a Sebundy, and went in pursuit of the others; who, he says, ran towards a place called Martunachee Warra; and he observed they were preceded by five other persons, all of whom were running away. The Sowar came up with five of the party, who stood on their defence against him, one of them drawing a sword for the purpose: and, in the end, by the assistance of other

other persons, the whole five were apprehended. The Sowar stated, that the other two were apprehended also at Fyzpoor, to which place he followed them; but there is not yet sufficient evidence that the two persons who were apprehended there are the same he had seen at Nahnee.

"The prisoners, six in number, who were taken at this place (Nahnee), all describe themselves to be persons without employment or connexions in the country; and most of them state, that they have recently come from Hindostan. They all agree that they came to Nahnee together; but give different accounts of the time and place of their first meeting each other; some of them saying it was Dholia, others at Maligaum, and others between these two places; and, notwithstanding they acknowledge they had been travelling together for some days past, they generally professed an ignorance of each other's names.

"A short time after they were apprehended, a Chowdry of the village of Nahnee observed a sword and some other things, without any person near them, in the place called Martunchawarra. He communicated the circumstance to another Chowdry of the village; who, taking a dirk with him, brought the things found there to a Sheikhdar who was in the village; and, upon examining one of the things found, it was discovered to contain two sealed bags, which proved to be two of the bags of of pearls of which the murdered Beemawallas were robbed.

"I cannot obtain any clear and certain evidence that the persons apprehended had been seen in the place where the stolen property was found; but all the circumstances under which they were apprehended, point them out as the persons in whose possession it had been: and their guilt is further established by the important circumstance of two of them being recognised by one of the followers of Dusrut Naig, as two of the party that passed Dhooleebaree immediately after the Beemawallas; by which party, there can be no doubt, the murder and robbery were committed.

"The party of Sowars, whose operations have been described, proceeded from Yawull; and another party of five proceeded from Russoolpoor in the Rewair purgunah, and went to Borhanpore in quest of the robbers. They there learnt, that some strangers, with tattoos, had just arrived, and alighted in a garden near the city. They proceeded to the spot, and found three men together; two of whom were in the act of unloading their tattoos, and the third was standing near them with a sword under his arm. Other two were observed at some little distance from them; who, when they found the Sowars questioning the three men, ran off, and made their escape. The three men were secured by the Sowars. The sword of the man

man described to have been standing unemployed, was, on examination, found to be stained with blood, from the point to the hilt. Suspended to the neck of the same man was a tobacco-pouch, containing some rupees, gold mohurs, and Venetians;—the latter, the exact number that had been in charge of the Beemawallas. On examining the baggage that had been taken from the tattoos, four of the bags of pearls that had been plundered were discovered.

"The evidence against these three persons appears to be quite conclusive. They themselves, however, deny their guilt; assert that all the Sowars have sworn to is false, and that they know nothing about things pretended to have been found with them. There is not the slightest reason to doubt the truth of the Sowars' statements, which are perfectly clear and consistent; and, in confirmation of them, one of the three persons is recognised to have been with the party of twenty-two persons who followed the Beemawallas at Dholeebaree.

"On the same day, and about the same time that the three persons were apprehended as above mentioned, other four were stopped by some persons employed in the Collection of the Zukat near Borhanpore, and detained until some of the party that had been in quest of the robbers arrived. The four persons are stated to have been going towards the garden where the other three

were

were apprehended. They had with them two swords, and two tattoos. Both the swords were stained with blood, and one of them considerably so. The loads on the tattoos were not examined on the spot; but taken to a place where the Sowars were, and there examined. Nothing of value was found with the baggage of these persons: but two brass vessels were found with it, which are recognised, by the Beemawalla that escaped, to have belonged to one of his murdered companions. Of the two tattoos taken with these prisoners, one of them was seen at Dholeebaree, by a follower of Dusrut Naig, in possession of the party of two and twenty men that followed the Beemawallas, and is recognised by him. Two of the prisoners are said to have been seated on the tattoos when the party was stopped by the Zakat Collectors; but, unfortunately, these last cannot point out which of the prisoners were so seated; nor can I ascertain, on satisfactory evidence, from which of them the swords were taken. One man only can swear to one of the swords being taken from one of the prisoners in particular.

"Three of the prisoners acknowledge that the four had been travelling in company together, before they were apprehended; but give discordant accounts as to the time and place of their first meeting. One of the prisoners denies that he had previously been in company with the other three before he was apprehended; and alleges, that they were merely following him on the road, unconnected with him. One of the swords is stated by the prisoners to have been in the possession of one of his companions; but that companion denies that he had any sword in his possession. The other sword none of the prisoners will acknowledge. One of the tattoos, but not the one which was recognised at Dholeebaree, is acknowledged by one of the prisoners to have been in his possession; but the other tattoos none of them will acknowledge.

"Such is the evidence against the prisoners who have been apprehended on suspicion of having been engaged in this atrocious robbery and murder. I regret, with regard to some of them, it is not so perfect as could be desired; although it appears to me that there is sufficient to warrant the committal of thirteen of them, and to leave little doubt of their guilt. I have in vain endeavoured, by every proper means, to induce some of them, against whom the evidence is least perfect, to turn King's evidence, and merit pardon by a full confession and disclosure of all the circumstances connected with the robbery."

The thirteen persons referred to were brought to trial. Three were acquitted. One is stated to have been released; but the grounds of the release are not mentioned in the document from which this account

account is taken. One was sentenced to be imprisoned for the remainder of his life, which, however, was protracted for only a few months; six, to be transported beyond seas; and two to be hanged. One only of them suffered the penalty of the law; —the other having evaded it, by becoming his own executioner.

Feringeea, who was an actor in this, as in so many other tragedies of a similar description, gave the following account of it to Captain Sleeman:—

"We were a gang of about 150 Thugs from Hindostan, in the month of January 1829, near Chopra, on the bank of the Tuptee river—under Khoseeala, alias Rynwo, executed afterwards, at Dholia in Kandeish; Bhujjoo, executed at Saugor in 1832; and Perraud Mussulvu, executed at Indore in 1829—when the seven treasure-bearers came up, on their way from Bombay to Indore. We followed them, with a select party from all the gangs, on to Dhoree; and thence through the Dholeebaree Pass, where they spoke with Dusrut Naig, the officer of the police-guard stationed at that pass. While they rested here, one of the seven, without our scouts perceiving it, went on in advance towards Godurghât, which is about four cose distant. When they had left the guard, we continued to follow; and, on passing the guard, we were questioned by Dusrut Naig; and we told him that we were

Govern-

Government servants, on our way home, on furlough. About half way between this pass and Godurghât, we came up with the treasure-bearers, and strangled them; but, to our surprise, we found only six, instead of seven. Heera and three others were instantly sent on after the other; but they could not find him; and we hastily threw the bodies into a nullah, and made off with the booty.

"The man who had gone on in advance, finding that his companions did not come up so soon as he expected, returned to look after them; and met a traveller, who told him that he had seen some dead bodies in a nullah by the side of the road. Going to the place described, he found that they were the bodies of his companions; and reported the circumstance to Dusrut Naig, who sent information to Captain Hodges, the acting magistrate in Kandeish, and set out with all his men in pursuit of us. Captain Hodges, with his mounted police, succeeded in seizing thirteen or fourteen of our party, who had separated and lost their road in the jungles. They had with them the greater part of the booty, which we in consequence lost. Of these men, four contrived to get released; and the rest were either hung at Dholia, or sent to the black water. Only three of the bags of pearls were brought off: one by Purumma, who honestly shared it, on his return, with the rest of the gang who escaped; and two by Bhujjoo, alias Sooper Singh

Singh and Rae Singh, who were lately hung at Saugor, and who could never be prevailed upon to give up any share."

Thus it appears that "honour" is sometimes wanting, even "amongst thieves."

CHAP. X.

In 1816, an act of Thuggee, upon rather a large scale, was perpetrated at Shikarpore. It is thus related, in the records of the Nagpore Residency:—

"This day, Bukshee Chitara, the vakeel of the Punah Rajah, came and presented an Urzee, stating that twenty-five persons had been murdered on their way from Jubulpore, by fifty robbers, near the Pass of Shikarpore, in the Punah Rajah's territory; and that six or seven of them had been wounded, and four taken by the people of Row Burjore Singh, a relation of the Rajah's. The vakeel stated, that Omrow Zemindar of Bumhoree was present, and would be able to give further information; and his deposition has accordingly been taken;—and, as it may lead to the discovery of their associates, the four robbers arrested are to be demanded from the Rajah, who will also be desired to take care of the property for the heirs of the murdered people. The Rajah is at the same time to be thanked for his exertions on this occasion: and as these robbers may pass through these territories, the following Chiefs are to be written to, and conjoin to aid in in their arrest:—Gwalior, Bijawur, Tehree, Jhansee, Dutteea, Kour, Sonee Sa, and Kour Purtab Singh."

The following is the Urzee of Bukshee Chitara referred to:—"Row Burjore Singh, a Jemadar of my master, in the purgunah of Powae, writes to me, that near Shikarpore, about five cose south of Powae, near the pass, in the middle of Phagun, twenty-five travellers, on their way from Jubulpore, a district of the Nagpore Government, were murdered by fifty robbers, and their property taken off. That, after the murder, the robbers came to Powae, and purchased food at the Buneeas' shops; but, without sitting down, went on. The Buneeas asked who they were, from whence and whither going; and they said they were from the Deccan, on their way to Banda: saying this, they went on. That, contrary to their professed design, they took the road to the west, and rested at the village of Chowmooka, in my master's territory; and left the place again at midnight, for Tighurra, in the Jytpore territory. As soon as Row Burjore Singh heard these circumstances, he sent on twenty-five of his soldiers after them; and they came up with them within the boundary of Tighurra; and, unable to prevail upon them to surrender, they wounded six or seven of them, and took four out of the number into custody. They secured seven ponies; and brought them, with other things, to Burjore Singh. Unable to stand against

against the sepahees, the robbers sought shelter in Tighurra; and the villagers came to their support, and escorted them to Simareea in Jytpore; and the holder of that village entertained them one day, and the next dismissed them, but took from them all their property; first understanding that it amounted to ten or twelve thousand rupees. Burjore Singh wrote to the Simareea man, and desired him to keep them in custody; but he would not."

A deposition was, at the same time, made by Omrow, Zemindar of Bumhoree:—"I heard that twenty-seven persons, male and female, had been killed, on their way from Jubulpore to Chutterpore, by fifty or sixty decoits, and all their property taken off;—that they had gone, after the murders, to Powae, and thence to Tighurra in Jytpore;—and that Row Burjore Singh had sent after them twenty-five of his followers; who seized four, and two more that had been wounded, and brought them, with seven ponies, to Powae, to the Row, who still has them. An action took place between the Row's people and robbers at Tighurra; but the people of that place came to the aid of the robbers; and, as night came on, they effected their purpose, and escorted them to Simareea. Burjore Singh's people sent a message to the Thanadar of Simareea, by the Zemindar of Pourneea, to say that the Tighurra people had sent the robbers to him, and he must

must secure them. The robbers remained there all night, till noon the next day, and then took the road to Deoree in Huttah. I heard that all the property they had with them was taken by the Zemindar of Simareea in Jytpore. I hear that the four taken confess they are from Gwalior; and that the robbers had with them twenty-five matchlocks, and the rest had bows and arrows, and were all dressed differently, and talked like people from the West."

The Superintendant, Mr. Wauchope, subsequently recorded this minute:—"On the 7th March, a Purwana was addressed to Burjore Singh, to require the arrested robbers, by whose gang the twenty-seven persons had been murdered at the Pass of Shikarpore. This day (18th April 1816), Bukshee Chitura, the Punna vakeel, has presented a Hindoo letter from him in reply, with a list of property, and stated that the four arrested men are present—Husun Khan, Imam Buksh, Shumshera, and Bahadur. These men have been examined; and they declare that they were not concerned in the murders, and state that they were innocent travellers. The vakeel states, that the men who took them have not come with them, but are with their masters at Powae;—that among the things taken from them was a phansee or noose, and one of the Row's sepahees took it to draw water from a well;—that Bahadur, one of the four taken, had confessed that

that they murdered the people in the nullah; but Shumshera, who calls himself also Kuramut, forbade him, and said he would get hung if he confessed; and he remained silent. Although they deny the crime, still it is clear that they are men of bad character, and the suspicion is very strong against them. They are to be sent to the magistrate, with the rest of the Thugs taken with them; and Burjore Singh is to be thanked for his meritorious conduct, and to be requested to send the other evidence required."

Nothing appears to have been then done towards punishing any of the apprehended persons; but some of them were, at a later period, hanged.

Two distinct confessions, by an accomplice, were taken several years afterwards by Captain Sleeman. As each contains some particulars not found in the other, both are here appended. One of them proceeds thus:—

"About fifteen years ago, in the year when Mr. Jenkins, the Resident, went from Nagpore to Banda, I was with a gang of one hundred and twenty-five Thugs, under Nathea, Noor Khan, Bhudae, Gholab Khan, Hyput, Jemadars, at Sehora, in the district of Jubulpore. We heard of Mr. Jenkins's approach from Jubulpore, and waited a day for his party; and when they came up to Sehora, we joined them, and made acquaintance with the travellers. Some pretended

pretended to be on their way home from service, others to belong to the Resident's camp. They went on to Cowreea; and we continued with them, and went on the second day with them to Belhree, where we inveigled, to join us, twenty-seven of the party, including five women, and two boys about three years of age each. We persuaded them that they suffered much loss and inconvenience by travelling with so large a camp—that food was much dearer, and often not to be got for money—that the water was always scarce and muddy—and that we should escape all this, by leaving the camp, and taking the road by Powae. To all this they agreed and assented; and the next morning we left the camp, which was going by way of Lohargong, and took the road through Powae. We reached Shikarpore, in Punna, which is three cose on this side of Powae, and encamped in the grove; and in the afternoon, we sent on Kurhaea and Mutholee, to select a place for the murder of this party. They chose a place on the bank of a river between Powae and Shikarpore, where the jungle is thick and extensive; and about midnight we set out with this party. As soon as we reached the appointed place, we recommended them to sit down and rest themselves, as a good deal of the night still remained. About half of them sat down, and the other half remained standing: and the signal being given, twenty-five of the party were strangled.

Jowahir

Jowahir took one boy: and the other boy was taken by Kehree. The bodies were thrown into a dry pit in the nullah; and some stones and branches of trees thrown in upon them, to conceal them. The boy whom Jowahir had taken, on seeing the bodies thrown into the pit, cried loudly; and Jowahir dashed him against a stone, and killed him. We concealed the bodies of all, but that of the boy, which we forgot to throw in upon the rest: and it lay by the stone, exposed. We went on to Powae, and purchased five rupees'-worth of goor; which we took on with us to a village whose name I forget. In the morning, a bearer going to the river to fish, saw the body of the boy, and gave information to Burjore Singh, the Thakur of Powae: and he went to the place with his people, opened the pit, and took out the bodies; and proceeded in search of the murderers. He searched all day and the following night in vain: and the next day he came up with us, at a river where we were washing our hands and faces, after having left the small village, where we had eaten our goor. He had before him two matchlock-men; and, suspecting his design, we formed into a close body, and proceeded on our road. They ran upon us; but we kept waiting, with our matchlocks ready, and pointed towards them: but they had some horsemen with them, and they charged in upon our body; and they wounded Hyput, with a spear, in the breast; and Bhugwan

Bhugwan on the face, with a sword: and, finding it vain to attempt resisting any longer, we dispersed and fled. They each seized his man; and, after possessing themselves of what property they found upon them, let them all go, except Hossein Khan alias Kunheya, Roshun, Khoosalee, and Kureema, whom they sent to Bandah; where they were kept in confinement four years, and then released.

"The boy's name who was saved was Gunesh: and he was taken by Kehree Patuk, who brought him up as a Thug; and he died about three years ago.

"Our gang consisted of 125 Thugs; under Noor Khan, hung this year at Jubulpore; Bhudae, lately arrested at Kotah; Gholab Khan, hung at Saugor, 1832; and Hyput, approver.

"Other Jemadars and myself were encamped in the grove near the town of Sehora, in this the Jubulpore district, in March 1816, when the Resident of Nagpore passed on his way from Nagpore to Bundelcund*. We had heard of his approach with a large escort, and determined to join his party, in the hope of picking up some travellers; as in the time of the Pindaries, travellers of respectability generally took advantage of such opportunities to travel with greater security. Our gang separated into small parties; who mixed themselves up with the

* This was Major Close, on his way from Poona to Gwalior, to take charge of his office as Resident, in 1816.

the Resident's parties at different places along the road, without appearing to know any thing of each other; and pretended to be, like others, glad of the occasion to travel securely. When the Resident reached Belehree, some of our parties stated, that, as the Resident was going the western road by Rewah, they had better go the northern by Powae, as there was no longer any danger from Pindaries; and, by separating from so large an escort, they should get provisions much cheaper;—that water was now becoming scarce on the western road, and was always made dirty by the elephants and camels. Other parties pretended to argue against this, but at last to yield to the strong reasons assigned. We had by this time become very intimate with a party of travellers from Nagpore, consisting of eighteen men, seven women, and two boys. They heard our discussions, and declared in favour of the plan of separating from the Resident's party, and going the northern road, through Shikarpore and Powae.

"On reaching Shikarpore, three cose this side of Powae, we sent on Kunhee and Mutholee, to select a place for the murder: and they chose one on the bank of the river, in an extensive jungle that lay between us and Powae. We contrived to make the party move off about midnight, persuading them it was near morning; and, on reaching the place appointed, they were advised to sit down and rest themselves. All our parties pretended to be as much

much deceived as themselves with regard to the time; but not more than half of the travellers could be prevailed upon to sit down and rest in such a solitude. The signal was given; and all, except the two boys, were seized and strangled by the people who had been appointed for the purpose, and were now at their posts ready for action. The boys were taken by Jowahir and Kehree, who intended to adopt them as their sons; and the bodies of the twenty-five persons were all thrown into a ditch, and covered over with earth and bushes. On seeing the bodies thrown into the ditch, Jowahir's boy began to cry bitterly; and finding it impossible to pacify him or to keep him quiet, Jowahir took him by the legs, dashed out his brains against a stone, and left him lying on the ground, while the rest were busily occupied in collecting the booty. Going on to Powae, we purchased five rupees' worth of sugar, to celebrate this event; and, without halting, we went on to the village of Choumooka, in Punna. After resting till midnight, we went on to Tighurra in Jytpore, where we ate the sugar, and then set out the same day for Huttah.

"A fisherman going to the river to fish, soon after we had left the scene of the murders, found the body of the boy lying by the stone against which his head had been beaten; and he gave information to Thakur Burjore Singh of Powae, who proceeded

proceeded to the place with some of his followers, and discovered all the other bodies lying in the ditch. He collected all the men he could; and following our traces, which were still fresh, he came up with us as we were washing ourselves in a stream within the boundaries of the village of Tighurra. We formed ourselves into a compact body, and retired upon the village of Tighurra. The Thakur repeatedly charged in upon us; and seeing Hyput Jemadar pierced through the chest with a spear, and Bhugwan receive a sabre cut in the face, we dispersed, and made for the village of Tighurra in the best way we could. The villagers all came to our support, and defended us against the Thakur; but he had already secured Hossein Khan, who afterwards died at home; Imam Buksh, alias Kosula, who was hung in Kandeish in 1829; Shumshera, who was hung at Saugor in 1832; and Bahadur, who is now in service at Hingolee.

" The Tighurra people, tempted by the promise of part of our booty, protected us all that day and night; and in the morning escorted us to Simareea, where a promise of all the booty that we had left secured us a safe retreat till the pursuit was over, in spite of all that the Thakur could say or do.

" The Thakur took all his prisoners to the Governor-General's Agent, Mr. Wauchope; before whom Bahadur confessed, and stated all the circumstances as they occurred: but being afterwards told

told that it was the practice of the English to hang all who confessed, and to release all who denied, he soon denied stoutly all that he had said, and pretended to know nothing at all about the murders: and being made over to the magistrate, they were all released, for want of evidence. Ram Buksh Tumbolee came from Nagpore to the Agent, Mr. Wauchope, in the hope of recovering his child, who was the boy that was killed by Jowahir."

Jowahir appears to have been a Brahman, who was hung at Saugor in 1832: he had settled on the Nurbudda river. Kehree was the father of Sewa, approver; and he was hung at Jubulpore in 1831. He, it is stated, named the boy Gunesha, and kept him at home to look after his cattle. "Bahadur," said the accomplice, "was, about ten years ago, a sepahee in the 1st battalion of a brigade of five Bahulwas, at Ourangabad: he had given up Thuggee, and never, that we know of, returned to it; but he was still our friend."

CHAP. XI.

An atrocious act of Thuggee, which took place either in 1809 or 1810, excited at the time great sensation; but, like many others resembling it in enormity, it gradually almost ceased to be recollected, and no definite information on the subject was obtained until the year 1834. An accomplice then made the following deposition:—

"In 1810 or 1809, we were 200 Thugs, at a village near Suhajie in Nagpore; when we met forty persons, some from Ellichpore, and some from Gwalior, and Jhalna, and Aurungabad. We came on with them seven stages; and, in a jungle between Choree and Sutrunju, we killed them all, and buried their bodies under stones in the bed of the river: one was a subahdar, a Brahmin, belonging to the regiment of Sulabut Khan and Behlal Khan, Newabs: one was a Brahmin Tewaree, with two daughters; he was going home, to get married: they were murdered with their mother and father. There was another Tewaree Brahmin, with an old woman, his wife, and a young daughter. The old woman was killed; but the daughter was preserved, and

and married to Hunce Rao, nephew of Kasal, subahdar of Thugs; she had two or three children by him, but they are dead: all three were residents of the Purdesee Mahulla, in Ellichpore; and they were going to the provinces on the Ganges."

The female referred to, deposed, at the same period, to the following effect. The colouring of passion is not looked for in a law paper; but, after making all allowance for this fact, it must be admitted, that the coolness with which the depónent relates the murder of her relations and her own captivity, and their consequences, does great credit to her philosophy.

"My mother and father resided in some town in the Deccan; but their names I do not recollect, as I was only three or four years of age when my uncle and mother took me with them on a journey towards the Ganges. On the road, my mother and uncle were killed, by Thugs, with many other travellers. Kasal Singh Putuck Jemadar preserved my life, and took me with him to Pahlun in Gwalior, where he brought me up; and when I became of age, he married me to his son, Hunce Rao, who is now dead. As long as he lived, I lived with him; but he has been dead several years, and I have since lived with his mother, and earned my subsistence by my labour. Your sepahees found me out, and have brought me into Saugor. I had

 two

two sons by Hunce Rao: the first died when fifteen months old; the other is eight or nine years of age, and is named Buksh; he is in Khyrawa in Jhansee, with his grandmother. I was the only person out of the party saved. There is now no Thug left in the family of Hunce Rao, who can provide for me. If you will maintain me, I shall be glad to remain here; but I have never heard whether my parents have any surviving relations or not. I was in advance of the party, when they were killed. The other two girls who were killed were not related to me; but our parents resided at the same place, and we used to call each other sisters. I had no other relation killed but my uncle and mother."

The witness whose deposition was first quoted gives, at another period, a fuller relation of the facts.

He said:—"The roads from the Deccan, across the Nurbudda, had become so unsafe, from the Pindaries, that all travellers from Poona, Hyderabad, and Nagpore, going towards the Ganges, went by way of Surgooja and Sumbulpore; and several of our gangs, that went from Bundelcund and the Dooab to that road, came back with immense booty, for several years. In the rains preceding this affair, it was determined that all the gangs should take that direction; and we accordingly set out. There were more than forty Jemadars of note: among them

them, Bukshee Jemadar, whose head Dr. Spry sent to England; and Ghassee Subahdar; and many others of equal note. We set out from our respective homes, after the Dushera, in October 1806; passed through Mirzapore, in order to make our votive offerings at the Temple of Davy, at Bindachul; and rendezvoused at Ruttunpore in the Surgooja district, where we were assembled above 600 Thugs. From Ruttunpore we went to Tukutpore; where we murdered a good many travellers, who took up their quarters in our several places of encampment. All pretended to have been on furlough; and to be returning from Hindostan to different armies in the Deccan; with some of our relations and friends, as young recruits. On the third day, a female of rank came up. Her husband had been an officer in the Nagpore service; and being left a widow by his death at Nagpore, she was on her way home to his friends, with her deceased husband's brother. She occupied a tent; and was accompanied by a slave girl, and had twelve armed men as a guard. She left Tukutpore the morning after her arrival; and was followed by a detachment from every one of our gangs, making a party of 160 Thugs, under some of our best leaders. For several days they followed them, without finding a convenient opportunity of disposing of them; till they reached the village of Choora, between which place and the village of Sutrunja the road passed

through

through an extensive jungle, without a village on either side for many miles. Leaving this place in the morning, they put the whole party to death, and buried their bodies in a nullah.—I did not go with this party.

"When they set out after the widow, we all proceeded towards Nagpore: and on reaching Lahnjee, a party of sixty Thugs remained there, while the rest went on towards Nagpore. I remained with the sixty at Lahnjee; and, two days after the main body had left us, a party of forty travellers came up, on their way to the Ganges—thirty-one men, seven women, and two girls. The greater part of these people were from Ellichpore; the rest from Nagpore. Our Jemadars soon became intimate with the principal men of this party, pretended to be going to the same parts of India, and won their confidence; and the next day we set out with them; and in four days reached Ruttunpore, where we met the party of 160 Thugs returning after the murder of the widow and her party. They did not, however, appear to be known to us. Soon after, two hundred of the main body, who had gone on towards Nagpore from Lahnjee, came up, having heard of the forty travellers soon after they left us; and all pretended to be going the same road, without appearing to have any acquaintance with each other. It was, however, agreed that sixty of the 160 should go on, and rejoin the party

who

who had proceeded to Nagpore ; leaving 360 to dispose of this party.

"From Ruttunpore we proceeded with the party of travellers to the village of Choora, whence we sent on people to select a proper place for the murder. They chose one not far from that in which the widow and her party had been put to death. Durroo and Sheera were sent on to the village of Sutrunja, to see that all was clear in front; and about a watch-and-a-half before daylight we set out with the travellers ; leaving scouts behind, to see that we were not interrupted from the rear. By the time we reached the appointed place, the Bhurtotes and Shumseeas had all, on some pretext or other, got close by the side of the persons whom they were appointed to strangle ; and on reaching the spot, the signal was given in several places at the same time, and thirty-eight out of forty were seized and strangled. The daughter of Gunga Tewarree was a very handsome young woman ; and Punchum, one of our Jemadars, wished to preserve her, as a wife to his son, Bukholee. But when she saw her mother and father strangled, she screamed, and beat her head against the stony ground, and tried to kill herself. Punchum tried in vain to quiet her, and promised to take great care of her, and marry her to his own son, who would be a great Chief; but all was in vain. She continued to scream; and at last Punchum put the roomal round her neck, and strangled her. The widow of Alfie's brother

brother was strangled; but her daughter, a girl about three years of age, was preserved by Kosul Jemadar, who married her to his own son, Hunce Rao Brahmin; by whom she had two sons, one of whom is still living, and about ten or eleven years of age. Since the death of Kosul and Hunce Rao, she has lived with her husband's mother.

"We buried all the bodies in a nullah; and got property to the value of about 17,000 rupees, which we took on with us, and divided at Sutrunja. After this affair we returned home, through Rewah and Chitterkote, the place where we had murdered the sixty persons at one time, about two years before. The widow of Hunce Rao often heard, after she grew up, of the Chaleesrooh affair, in which her mother and uncle were strangled; and she has herself told you all that she knows about it."

The fate of one of the principal actors in this dark scene, and that of his family, is edifying.—"Punchum, on his return, died before we reached home. Of his five sons—Chunderbhan died on a Thug expedition; Bhugholee was hung at Gwalior, by Jacob Sahib; Jowahir died in Gwalior; Odeebhan was hung in Kandeish, in 1829; and Molloo died in the Nursingpore jail. The children of another worthy, Kosul Subahdar, were not more fortunate. One of them, Ajeeta, was transported from Saugor in 1832; and Rawut Rao died in the Saugor jail."

CHAP. XII.

Many years have elapsed since the occurrence of the barbarous acts of Thuggee now about to be related; but very circumstantial accounts of them were given by the approvers examined in 1833. One of them is that which follows:—

"About twenty years ago, I was with a gang of 350 Thugs, under Ghasee Subahdar, Noor Khan, and other leaders, at Jubulpore. Some of us were at Gopaulpore; and some encamped at Adhartal, and some in the bazaar. We remained there three days; and on the third day, Gholab Khan, the Killadar of Gawilgur in Nagpore, with Kadher Khan, and a party of sixty persons, including seven women and a boy, came up, and encamped on the bank of the Gopaulpore tank, in a grove of Mangoe-trees. Ghasee Khan Subahdar went to them, as our Sothae; and told them that he was a subahdar in the service of Rughoojee the Rajah of Nagpore, and on his way home, on leave, with a number of the men of his regiment. Gholab Khan said, he had been the Killadar of Gawilgur; and, having been deprived of the command of that fortress, was now on on his way home. Ghasee said, he and his friend should be glad to travel in his company; and finding the Killadar pleased with his proposal, he returned to us. The Killadar remained the next day, and we remained also; and the following day went to Punnagurh, and thence to Sehora: from this place we quitted the high road through Belehree, and took that through Rewah; and encamped at a village whose name I forget. We sent on people to choose a place for the murder, but no suitable one could be found; and we went on in this manner for eight days, searching every day in vain for a convenient place for the murder. On the eighth day we reached a village, called, from a large Bur-tree, the Burwala village, five cose from Birsingpore, and encamped under trees; and sent on men to search for a Bele. At a place two and a half cose distant between this village and Chitterkote, they found a place suited to our purpose, on the bank of a nullah; and about a watch before daylight we set out with the party of travellers; and contrived, as we went along, to put a Bhurtote (strangler) and a Shumseea (holder of hands) by every traveller's side. On reaching the spot chosen, Ghasee Subahdar gave the signal; and the travellers were seized by the men placed by their sides for the purpose, and strangled. Their bodies were buried in the sand in the bed of the nullah; and we got from them 19,000 rupees in money, and 7000 or or 8000 rupees' worth of other property, which we took on to Chitterkote. From thence we sent back men to bury the bodies deeper; and they found one body exposed, which they buried; but the rest had been all washed down by the flood arising from some heavy rain that fell: alarmed at this, we all dispersed, and returned to our homes.

"The boy was preserved by Mungul and Laljoo, brothers and Brahmins of Sindouse. He was a Brahmin, and transported in 1834 for murder.

"We passed through Rewah, and Simereea and Chandeeah also; and another town, a few cose from Bundoogur."

This substantially agrees with the subjoined statement, made on another occasion; though there is some difference as to names.

"After the capture of Gwalior by General Wellesley (Duke of Wellington), it was restored to the Nagpore Rajah, who appointed Ghureeb Singh to the command of the fortress. Anxious to get some good soldiers from Hindostan to garrison it, he sent his younger brother, Ghyan Singh, with a number of followers, and a large sum of money, to raise them, in the Oude country, and districts between the Ganges and Jumna rivers.

"Ghyan Singh and his party passed through Nagpore; and came to Jubulpore in the month of June,

June, while we were there concentrated from the different parts into which we had extended our expeditions that season. His party consisted of fifty-two men, seven women, and a Brahman boy then about four years of age. Some of our gangs lodged in the town; some in the cantonments among the troops; and some were encamped at the Tank of Adhar, two or three miles from the town, on the road to Mirzapore. As soon as we heard of the arrival of this party from the Deccan, every party of Thugs deputed some of its most respectable members to mix with them in the town, and win their confidence. At first, they tried to separate them into different parties, to proceed by different roads: but though they had collected together at different places on the road, it was found impossible to separate any part of them from Ghyan Singh; and we agreed to unite all our gangs, and to lead the party by the most unfrequented roads, till we might find a place convenient for the murder of the whole at once.

"On reaching Sehora, we persuaded them to quit the high road through Belehree and Myhere, and take that through Chundeea and the old Fort of Bundoogur, which leads through very extensive tracts of jungle and uninhabited country. We went with them through all this country, however, without finding what we considered a fitting time and place; and reached Rewah, winning more and more upon

upon their confidence every day. From Rewah we went to Simareea; and from that place to a small village half way to Chitterkote; called by us the Burwala Gow, from a large Bur-tree that stood near it. Thence we sent on people, as usual, to select a place for the murder; and they found one about two cose and a half distant, in a very extensive jungle, without a human habitation for many miles on either side. We persuaded the party to set out soon after midnight; and as they went along, we managed to take our appointed places, two Thugs by every traveller, and the rest in parties of reserve at different intervals along the line; every two managing to keep the person, whom they were appointed to kill, in conversation. On reaching the place chosen, the signal was given at several different places, beginning with the rear party, and passing on to that in front; and all were seized and strangled, except the boy. It was now near morning, and too late to admit of the bodies being securely buried: we made a temporary grave for them in the bed of the river, covered them over with sand, and went on with the boy and the booty to Chitterkote, intending to send back a large party the next night, and have the bodies securely buried. The rains had begun to set in; and, after the murders, it rained very heavily all the day. The party, however, went back, but found that the river had risen and washed away all the bodies, except two or three,

three, which they found exposed, and pushed into the stream to follow the rest. The boy was brought up by Mungul Brahmin, the brother of Laljoo; and, having taken to the trade of Thuggee, he was last year sent to the black water, from Saugor. Mungul and Laljoo both died in a village in Bhopaul, where they had settled.

CHAP. XIII.

"THE Dhosa affair," as it is called, lives in the confessions of two of the murderers, Kaem Khan, and Rustum Khan. That of the former runs thus:—

"We were on our way from Madhoorajpore to Gwalior—a gang of about forty Thugs—in the month of March, ten years ago; when we fell in with Bunseelal, the son of Bhujunlal, the Cotwal of Sopur. He was a lad of about seventeen years of age; and had with him two Brahmins, one Rajpoot sepahee, and a servant of the Jat cast; and was going to Rewaree, to fetch his bride. One of the Brahmins had come from Rewaree, to accompany him. They came and took up their quarters in the same Serai with us, and we pretended to be going the same road. The next morning we went on with them to Lolsont; where we again lodged together, in the Serai of Kosul Bhuteeara. The following day we went on to Ramgur with them: and thence Bhikka Jemadar went on, to select a place for the murder; but he came back without finding one that pleased him; and the day after we went

went on together to Dhosa. We had now become very intimate with the boy and his party, who told us all their secrets. The boy lodged in the shop of a Buneea who had been long in league with us, while we lodged in the Serai at Dhosa; and in the afternoon, Bhikka went on again, to select a Bele. He chose one in the bed of a nullah a cose and a half distant; and the five stranglers having been appointed, we set out with the boy and his party long before daylight the next morning. On reaching the place appointed, they were persuaded to sit down and rest themselves. The boy sat with one of the Brahmans, upon a carpet that we had spread for him; and the other three attendants sat down upon the sand at a little distance from them. A Shumseea took his seat by the side of each of the five; and the Bhurtotes stood each behind his intended victim. The signal was given by Rustum Khan; and all five were immediately strangled; the boy himself by Bhikka Jemadar, who is still at large, while his hands were held by his brother Chunda. The bodies were buried in the bed of the nullah. While they were strangling them, the fine mare on which the youth rode ran off; and while we were engaged in recovering her, Chunda made off with a purse of gold mohurs, which he found in the boy's waistband."

The witness was asked; "Did you not return to Dhosa soon after, and heard of the boy's friends searching

searching for him?" He answered: "Yes; we came back to Dhosa some time after, and heard from our friends the shopkeepers that the bodies had been dug up by jackals, and that the friends of the murdered youth were then at Dhosa, inquiring about him. Going to the Serai, we found the uncle of the youth sitting on a Chubootra, in front of the door, weeping and lamenting the loss of his nephew."—Being questioned whether the father did not die of grief soon after, he said: "Yes; he could never be persuaded to eat any thing after he learnt the fate of his only son, and soon died. This we afterwards learned from the people of Seopore, who still recollect the circumstance of the loss of the son, and death of the old Cotwal."

Rustum Khan's testimony is to the same effect:—

"In Jet, about six years ago, I was with a gang under Nuthee Khan (lately hung at Saugor), Bhurjee, Bhikka, and Saadut, Jemadars, and a gang of forty Thugs, on our way from Madhorajpore: we reached Mularna Dongerka in Jypore, and lodged in the Serai. A little before dark, the son of the Cotwal of Seopore came up, with four companions, on their way from Seopore to their homes in Rewaree, and lodged in the same Serai. Nuthee Khan went to the young man, who was about fifteen years of age, and won his confidence. He agreed to travel with us; and we set out the next morning, and reached

 Lalsont,

Lalsont, and lodged in the Serai of Khosal Bhuteeara: next day we reached Ramgur in Jypore, four cose distant, and lodged in some shops. Thence we sent on Bhikka Jemadar, to select a place for the murder; but he could not find one, and returned in despair. The next day we went on to Dhosa in Jypore, which place we reached about noon; and we lodged the boy and his companions in a shop, while we went to the Serai. The shopkeepers in whose shop they lodged were three, Nanuk, Sewlall, and another, whose name I forgot. We were all well known to these three shopkeepers, and they had shared liberally in our booty; and their shop was near the Serai in which we lodged. Four ghuries before night, we sent on Bhikka again to look for a Bela; and he chose one on the bank of a river, a cose and a half distant; and at night reported his success. Nuthee Khan, Bhikka, Kureema, Incha, and Ramla a Sooseea Thug, were chosen as stranglers, and others appointed to assist them; and a watch and a half before daylight we set out; and on reaching the place chosen, in the bed of the river, which was then dry, they were persuaded to sit down to their ablutions. A carpet was spread for them; and the son of the Cotwal, with one of his companions, sat upon it, and the other three sat at a little distance. The Shumseeas sat near them, and the Bhurtotes (stranglers) stood behind them. I was appointed to to give the signal; and I did it by saying, "If the lads are all come, give them tobacco;" and instantly the Bhurtotes threw their angochas over their necks, and strangled them. Their bodies were buried in two graves—two in one, and three in the other—in the sand, in the bed of the river. Bhikka Jemadar (still at large) strangled the boy; and the four other Bhurtotes strangled the others. We got from them a mare, a pair of ear-rings with two large pearls in each, and other things worth 250 rupees. Bhikka Jemadar states, there was a bag of gold mohurs found upon them, which we had no opportunity of counting: he found them upon the boy whom he himself strangled. Bhikka's brother, Chunda, held the boy's hands while he strangled him; and took off his kummurbund as soon as he was dead, and put it round his own waist. At this moment the mare ran off; and several Thugs ran after her, and brought her back: but, before their return, Chunda had made off with the waistband, and gone home: Bhikka, however, pretended that his brother had lost the road. We went to Seopore in Jypore, and divided the booty; but not the Seopore whence the party had come from. We got five rupees each: and Nuthee Khan took the mare at a valuation of forty rupees, and sold her to the Thakur of Puchawur in Jypore, for sixty rupees. Three days after the murder, the bodies were dug out by the animals of the

 jungle,

jungle, as we learnt from the Bhuteearas and shopkeepers, who requested us to keep away from Dhosa, in consequence. The Cotwal wrote to his home, to announce the departure of his son: and as he did not reach home, his uncle and another man came out to search for him, and came to the shop where he had lodged him at Dhosa. We returned to the place twenty days after; and found the uncle on a Chubootra in front of the shop, weeping, and saying that he could trace his nephew thus far and no further. We concealed the property we got, after hearing this; but we have none of it now."

The Report of the Aumil of Seopore confirms the evidences, to a certain extent:—

"Lalla Bhujun Lal, in the time of John Baptiste, was stationed at Seopore, on the part of Chutter Bhoje Dewan. He had his family with him. He sent his son, Bunsee Lal, towards Rewaree, to bring back his bride. He had with him Pirthee, Brahmin of Seopore, and Jogul, Brahmin of Rewaree, Heera Singh Sepahee, and Govinda Jat: they had a horse with them. They set out on the 27th of Cheyt, 1885 Sumbut, towards Rewaree: and after three months, a letter arrived, stating that he had never reached home. Bhujun Lal sent people in search of him; and found, that on the other

other side of Madhoopore, and the other side of the Bimas River, a half cose from the Bower Bowlee, they had been all killed. Bhujun Lal died soon after, of grief for the loss of his son.

CHAP. XIV.

Men, even of rank and consequence, disappear, from the mysterious operation of Thuggee; and, after a little excitement and a little inquiry, the matter passes over, and is no more recollected, till some fresh atrocity or some unlooked-for discovery again calls attention to it. Sheikh Inaent, an approver, in answer to an inquiry by Captain Sleeman, how often he had been at Thuggee before he saw a murder, gave the following relation:—

"It was on my return from the first expedition which I made with my father to the Deccan, when I was fifteen years of age, and about thirty-five years ago. We were a gang of about eighty or ninety Thugs, under my father Hinga; and some of the Deccan Chiefs lodged in the Mausoleum, outside of the town of Ellichpore. Two of our leaders, Gumboo and Laljoo, on getting into the bazaar, fell in with the grooms of the Nawab Subzee Khan, the uncle of the Nawab of Bhopaul, Huzeer Mahommed Khan; who told them, that their master had been, with his son and his 200 horse, in the service of the Nizam at Hydrabad; and

and having had a quarrel with his son, he was now on his way home to Bhopaul. They came back and reported; and Dulele Khan and Khuleel Khan, and other leaders of fame, went and introduced themselves to the Nawab, pretending that they had been to the Deccan with horses for sale, and were now on their way back to Hindostan. He was pleased with their address and appearance, and invited them to return the next day, which they did; and the following day he set out with as many of our gang as it was thought safe to exhibit. He had two grooms, two troopers, and a slave-girl, two horses, a mare with a wound in the neck, and a pony. The slave-girl's duty was to prepare for him his daily portion of subzee; and he told us that he had got the name of Subzee Khan from the quantity of that drug which he was accustomed to drink.

"We came on together three stages; and during the fourth stage we came to an extensive jungle this side of Dhoba, and in the Baitool district; and on reaching a nullah, about nine o'clock, Khuleel said: 'Khan Sahib, we have had a fatiguing journey, and we had better rest here and take some refreshment.'—'By all means,' said the Nawab; 'I feel a little fatigued, and will take my subzee here.' He dismounted, laid his sword and shield upon the ground, spread his carpet, and sat down. Dulele and Khuleel sat down by his side,

side, while the girl was preparing his potion; of which he invited these two men, as our supposed chiefs, to partake; while the grooms were engaged with the horses, and the troopers were smoking their pipes, at a distance. It had been determined that the Nawab should be first secured; for he was a powerful man, and, if he had a moment's warning, would certainly have cut down some of the gang, before they could secure him. Laljoo also went and sat near him; while Gomanee stood behind, and seemed to be much interested in the conversation. All being now ready, the signal was given; and the Nawab was strangled by Gomanee, while Laljoo and Dulele held his legs. As soon as the others saw the Nawab secured, they fell upon his attendants; and all were strangled, and their bodies buried in the bed of the water-course. On going back to Ellichpore, Gomanee sold the Nawab's shield for eight rupees; but it was worth so much more, that the people suspected him, and came to our camp to search for him. Our spies brought us timely notice, and we concealed him under the housings of our horses."

The witness being asked, "What was the cause of the quarrel between Subzee Khan and his son?" answered, "The son, in a passion, had drawn his sword, and cut the Nawab's favourite mare over the neck. A quarrel ensued; and he left his son in charge of the squadron of horse, to return to Bhopaul.

Bhopaul.—This," he added, "was the first murder I ever witnessed, and it made a great impression upon my mind. You may rely upon the correctness of what I state regarding it."

On another occasion, the witness added the following particulars :—

"The bodies were all buried under stones in the nullah ; but I did not see the graves ; nor could they be now found, after so long a time. We got from them two horses, a mare, and a pony ; a gold bracelet, twenty-five gold coins, and fifty rupees; some cloths, and a very handsome bird-cage. Khuleel Khan got one of the horses ; Dulele and Gungoo got the mare ; my father got a horse ; and Gomanee and Laljoo the pony. Dulele sold the mare at Omrowtee ; and my father his horse, at Borhanpore. Khuleel sent his horse home ; and Gomanee kept the pony for many years. Gomanee got also a valuable shield, which he sold at Ellichpore for eight rupees ; and the people said that it was sold too cheaply to have been honestly obtained. Gomanee, hearing this, made off without taking the money, and came to us : the people pursued him, but we concealed him under some housings. As soon as the search was over, we made off : and afterwards, on coming to Ellichpore, we heard that great search was being made for the Nawab Subzee Khan, and left that part of the country."

The

The statement of the witness was corroborated by inquiries at the Court at Bhopaul. Mirza Amjud Beg, the Vakeel of Bhopaul, thus addressed Mr. Wilkinson, Political Agent :—

" On receipt of your order to me, to ascertain whether any such persons, as are stated to have been killed in the deposition of Sheikh Inaent of the 3d of July before Captain Sleeman, disappeared about that time, I wrote to Rajah Khoshwukt Raё, the Bhopaul Minister; who has forwarded to me the deposition of Sultan Khan Afghan, an old resident of Bhopaul;—from which it appears, that, about thirty-five years ago, Subzee Khan, the man named, was the son of Shere Khan, who was a near relation of Nawab Wuzeer Mahommed Khan, the late Nawab of Bhopaul, and Resident of Bhopaul. He was called Subzee Khan, as stated by Inaent, in consequence of the quantity of subzee, or inebriating drug, he drank. He was in service at Hydrabad, with Gholaum Hyder Khan, his son: he became annoyed with his son; and left Hydrabad, on his return home, with some followers, and property laden upon ponies; and on the road was murdered by Thugs. When his son came home, and found that his father, who had set out long before him, had not returned home, he got 200 rupees, and, with four attendants, set out in search of him. He went to Nagpore and Ellichpore; and found traces of of his father to the last place, but could find no trace of him beyond it."

Another witness deposed thus:—"Thirty-five years ago, or more, Gholaum Hyder Khan, and his father Subzee Khan, were in service at Hydrabad: and when Hyder Khan came back, he stated that his father had left Hydrabad six months before, in anger with him; and apprehended that his anger had prevented his returning home, and induced him to remain in service on the road. He got 200 rupees, and set out in search of his father, with four attendants: he found traces of him to Ellichpore, and no further."

Question.—"Did he use much subzee or Bhung?" *Answer:* "Subzee Khan used a great deal of that drug, and he got the name in consequence; and I never knew him by any other." *Q.* "Was he related to the Nawab?" *A.* "He was the uncle of Nawab Wuzeer Mahommed, but not the brother of his mother or father." *Q.* "Did the son mention the names of the people who accompanied his father, or the property he took with him?" *A.* "He did not. Twelve years ago, when I was in service there, I saw Gholaum Hyder Khan at Ellichpore, with his mother. Where he is now, I know not."

CHAP. XV.

At Dhoma, on one occasion, twenty-seven persons were sacrificed together, as is related in the following deposition of Zalfukar Jemadar, one of the perpetrators taken at Saugor by Captain Sleeman, some years after the occurrence of the facts.

"About twenty-one years ago, at the time of Mohurrum, I, with the following leaders and their gangs, in all about 300 men, were assembled at Chooree in Chupara, with intention of proceeding on a Thug expedition: — Bodhoo Jemadar, who was afterwards trod to death under the feet of an elephant at Jhalone—Hingah Jemadar, father of Sheikh Inaent, approver, who died on a Thug expedition twelve years ago, near Bhurtpore—Khan Sahib, alias Noor Khan, hung at Jubulpore, 1835—Khuleel, hung at Pothoreea in Saugor, eighteen years ago, a year after being released from Nagpore—Kurreem, alias Kurondee, hung at Saugor—Dhurum Khan, the stutterer, hung at Saugor—Mohun Brahmin, Purasur (dead), at Dumah—Sheikh Nuggoo, hung at Saugor, 1835—Mahasookh, approver—Muchul, who died at home, thirteen years ago—Rajah

Rajah Khan, alias Rajale, uncle of Zalfukar, hung at Jawra—his son, Nizamut, at large—Sheikh Inaent, approver—Hur Singh Rae Patuck, who died at home, in Sumter, ten years ago—Hur Singh Rae Tuhungooreea, still at large—Bhudae, at large, arrested 1835—Puhar, who died at home, seven years ago—his son lately transported from Saugor—Laljoo Sookul, who died at home seventeen years ago—Sumadha Brahmin, dead—Adhar Jemadar, hung at Saugor, 1833.

"We encamped two days at this place. The second day, while we were sitting down, after performing the concluding ceremonies of the Mohurrum, twenty-seven travellers came up, (they were decoits,) on their return from the Deccan to the west, and lodged in the bazaar. Dhurum Khan brought this intelligence to us; and said that they had four tattoos laden with cash, besides much other rich property.

"The next morning the above travellers set out for Chupara, where they lodged in the bazaar: we followed them, and encamped outside of the town. From Chupara they proceeded to Lucknadown; and we again followed, and all lodged in the bazaar. Boodhoo Jemadar, Mussulman, called himself by the name of Kour Khuluck Singh; and went to the shops where the travellers were put up; opened a conversation with them; and won their confidence, by saying that the road was very dangerous, and

we

we all had better travel together till we could pass through the jungles. They agreed to do so. The next morning, the following leaders, with about 125 Thugs, followed the travellers; while the remainder of our party proceeded towards Nutwara, in the valley of the Nerbudda, where the detached party was directed to rejoin them, after effecting the murder:—Bodhoo Jemadar—Noor Khan, hung at Jubulpore, 1835—Hingah Jemadar, father of Sheikh Inaent, approver—Khuleel Khan, hung at Saugor, 1832—Deponent—Inaent—Hur Singh Rae—Lolmun, approver.

"When the detached party, with the travellers, reached the spot where there are two trees in which people tie pieces of cloths (called Chitureea Peer and Kunkureea Peer), the whole of the travellers were murdered: sixteen of them were strangled, and eleven were cut down with tulwars. Their bodies were thrown a little off the road; and we came on with the booty we obtained from them, and reached Nutwara. The whole of the booty amounted to about 13,500 rupees.*

"From Nutwara we went to Kutungee, where we divided the booty. On division, we received forty

* "*List of the Property we obtained from them:*

Gold ....worth 3000 rupees.
Cloths ....1500.
Ready Cash ....8500 or 9000 rupees."

forty rupees each. We sent 100 Thugs with money for our families; and of the rest, some proceeded to the east, and others in different directions. The undermentioned took the route to Jubulpore: — Bodhoo Jemadar — Hinga Jemadar — Subhan Jemadar, who died sixteen years ago at home—Kurrondee Jemadar—Khuleel Khan Jemadar — Noor Khan Jemadar — Mahasook, approver—with about eighty other Thugs. I went to my home.—The intelligence of the above murder reached Jubulpore previous to the arrival of our party; and on their arrival, the Pundit manager of Jubulpore confined them all on suspicion. Khuleel Jemadar had a young lad adopted by him. The Pundit Komasdar called this lad to him, and asked him who they really were; and on his denial, the Pundit ordered him to be tied up to a Bur-tree, and flogged with the zerbund. Upon this, Khuleel Jemadar represented to the Pundit, 'that there was no use in his punishing the boy; and that he had better send for some tulwars, and have us all cut down.' On hearing this, the Pundit called Khuleel to him, and he confessed all our crimes before him. Bodhoo Jemadar offered to give 10,000 rupees to the Pundit, as a bribe, if he would release them. The Pundit accepted their offer; but, as they were unable to procure the money, he kept the following Thugs in confinement for six months, inside the Fort:—Bodhoo Jemadar,

Mr.

Mr. Stockwell's approver, who got his nose and hands cut off, three years after, at Seronge—Hinga Jemadar, father of Inaent, deponent —Subhan, ditto—Murdan ditto, who died after his nose and hands had been cut off at Seronge—Kurrondee, hung at Saugor. Two lads, and the under-mentioned Thugs, were kept in confinement in a building called by the name of Beaharka Havelee, at Jubulpore.

"After six months, we determined to attempt our escape; and seven Thugs jumped the Fort wall. Hingah had his back broken; Murdan was severely hurt in his legs; and the other five got off. The sepahees of the Fort-guard came and took away both the wounded men, and confined them again in the Fort.

"After the escape of the above five Thugs, the Pundit sent Khuleel and Murdan to Nagpore; and Hingah was removed from the building to the Fort. Noor Khan Jemadar, with some of his party, obtained some instruments from Newul Singh Byde a Thug, cut the irons, and broke open one of the windows of the building; and while it was raining slightly, they effected their escape.

"When the whole of our party had escaped, the Rajah of Nagpore released Khuleel, Murdan, Hingah, and the others who had been sent to him. The bodies of the twenty-seven victims were eaten by the animals of the jungle.

"Gyan

"Gyan Singh, late a prisoner in the Saugor jail, released after fourteen years' imprisonment, was saying, while here, that some of his relations had been murdered by the Thugs, among a party of twenty-seven at Dhooma; and these must have been the men.

"A Pundit also saw the bodies, while passing by that way from Nagpore.

"The following are the approvers who were concerned in the above affair: The deponent; Inaent; Lallmun; Peer; Mahomed; Sahoo; Imamee, son of Joomun; Mahasookh; Punchee; Kunhae, son of Laljoo; Mungul Brahmin.

"Most of the Thugs who were concerned in this affair have died, and the others been disposed of. Should there be any in the Saugor jail, I can point them out.

"Many of the Nujeebs are acquainted with this affair."

Another actor gave the following account:—

"There were a good many gangs, both from Hindostan and the Deccan. We had concentrated at Choorae, in the Geonee district, between this and Nagpore; and were at least 300 Thugs; and had just performed the concluding ceremonies of the festival of the Mohurrum, when a party of about twenty-seven persons, decoits I believe, came up, on their way from the Deccan to Hindostan.

 They

They had four ponies laden with rich booty, which they had acquired in an expedition to the South. The following day they came on to Chupara, and we followed. They lodged in the town; we, outside. Bodhoo Jemadar Mussulman, calling himself Kour Khuluck Singh, and pretending to be a Hindoo of rank, went to the party, and told them that the road from Chupara passed through an extensive and very dangerous jungle; and begged that, for security, we might unite our parties, as we were merchants and Government servants, and not very well armed. They agreed; and the next morning, 125 of our gang went on with them, while the rest came by another road; all agreeing to rendezvous at Nutwara, in the valley of the Nurbudda.

"I was with the 125; and on reaching two trees in the jungle sacred to the two saints, Chittureea and Kunkureea, and on which people tie pieces of cloth as votive offerings, the signal was given, and sixteen of the decoits were strangled, and eleven cut down with our swords. We took the bodies into the jungle near the road, and, without burying them, made off with the booty, and rejoined our friends at Nutwara. The booty consisted of gold, silver, and cloths, to the value of 13,000 rupees. We went on to Kutungee, divided the booty, and separated. The Deccan Thugs returned home; and we came, with a party of eighty, to Jubulpore, and

and encamped in the Beohar's grove which you see yonder, where we had a grand natch (ball).

"While engaged in our feast, we heard that the Subah of the district was sending troops to seize us, and we made off. When the signal for murder was given, a boy happened to be, unperceived, at a distance from the rest; and hearing their screams, he got up into a tree, and, as it was daylight, saw the whole affair, without our seeing him. After we had come on, he descended, came to Jubulpore, found some of our party selling some of their gold lace in the bazaar, and denounced us to the Governor. We all denied any knowledge of the affair, of course; but the Subah got hold of the adopted son of Khuleel Jemadar, tied him up to a tree, and gave him a severe flogging. Khuleel protested against this; and said he had better send for swords, and have us all cut to pieces at once. The Subah would not listen; and at last the boy confessed. The seven leaders were confined in the Fort; the others, all in the Beohar's house: but after having been made to disgorge all their property, they were all suffered to escape, except three leaders, Hinga, my father Khuleel, and Murdan: the two latter were sent to Nagpore, where the Rajah released them. My father Hinga had broken his back in jumping over the Fort wall, and Murdan sprained his ankle."

Being asked, "Were you all taken in the grove?"

 he

he answered, "No. We had got off, on the Saugor road, to Kutungee; but the Subah sent a squadron of horse after us, and we were all brought back. It was commanded by Khan Mahommed, the present Cotwal of Saugor. Nasid of Telingana was in this affair."

This was confirmed by Nasir, who said it "is all true: and I was obliged to give the chief officer at Kutungee a fine horse, and some other valuable articles that I had picked up in the expedition; as I found that he was an old acquaintance of mine, and well disposed towards us as long as he was conciliated in this way. I had got far off with my gang, before the Subah's party came up with the rest."

Inaent added: "Purumsook was then master of the Adawlut here, and all our property had to pass through his hands. He was an old friend of ours, and must recollect the circumstance well."

Capt. Sleeman observes here: "Purumsook, who is now a kind of attorney at Jubulpore, being referred to, confirms all this, but denies the friendship. He sold the property, he says, for the then Government, and not for himself or the Thugs. He was a kind of Deputy Chief-justice at the time, and in league with all these gangs."

The deposition of such a person as Purumsook cannot but be interesting; and it has fortunately been preserved. This respectable person says:—

"I

"I recollect, that about the year 1868 or 1869 Sumbut, this affair took place. I was at that time under the Rajah Rughoojee, Punj of the Adawlut. A boy, by caste a Gosaen, who had been saved from the murdered party, came to Jubulpore, and saw the Thugs who had murdered his party selling the gold and silver lace in the Jubulpore bazaar. He came to the Adawlut, and complained to Lalla Ramchund Fauj; and stated that his companions had all been killed by these men, and that the murderers were then in the town, and might be arrested. Lalla sent five or six persons to watch them; and went to report to Bulajie Pundit, the Subah of Jubulpore; who ordered Dhoneerajnana Resaldar, who is now at Laleya in this district, and Khan Mahommed Khan, now Cotwal of Saugor, to go with their Resalahs, and seize the Thugs who were then in the Beohar's grove. The Thugs at that time had assembled a party of dancing-girls, and were engaged in looking at their dancing; but hearing of the preparations for their arrest, they made off towards Kutungee. The Resaldars reached the Beohar's grove; but not finding the Thugs, they pursued them on the Kutungee road, and arrested about forty of them. The Subah confined these men in the Fort, and in the house of the Beohar: four of their principal leaders were confined in a bastion of the Fort. They leaped down from this place four or five days after; and one of them hurt his

his back-bone; and being heard, they were all four retaken. These four were kept in the Fort; the others, all in the Beohar's house. A month after, all those in the Beohar's house made their escape, by cutting through the wall; and they were searched for by the Sowars in vain. The four men confined in the Fort were sent to Nagpore, with the lad whose life had been saved. What became of them, I know not: their property, to a very large amount, was confiscated by the Subah, and the assets arising from the sale were carried to the account of the Nagpore Government. The gang of Thugs had been five or six days in the Beohar's garden, in the guise of travellers. The property confiscated was sold through me, but I never sold property for the Thugs themselves.

"The boy said, that the party belonging to him consisted of twelve Hindoos; that seven out of these were killed before his face; and the other five must have perished with the crowd of other travellers, at some distance. I did not see the bodies, nor were they brought to Jubulpore; nor was any body sent to see them, that I recollect."

The Urzee of Moohsim Ally Mootsuddee, employed in investigating the affair, is another document connected with this transaction:—

"On the 6th of April 1835, Isher Ally, Lance Naick

Naick of Nujeebs, and Uuggun Khan Nujeeb, reached the Tuhseeldaree of the village of Dhooma. The Tuhseeldar was absent, investigating some other affair; therefore we shewed our purwanah to Nobut Raee, accountant. He assembled all those from among the villagers who were most experienced; but these even could supply no information; till, at last, one Kunhie Brazier stated as follows:—'In the Sumbut 1868 or 1869, as I was coming from Jubulpore with ten or twelve others (not one of whom is now living) to my home at Lucknadown, we perceived, at the outskirts of Dhooma, and some three cose from the village on the north, four or five corpses, with the legs, heads, and arms severed from the bodies: birds and beasts were devouring them; and four pairs of shoes were lying by. Of other travellers who were passing by, I heard that twenty-two or twenty-five travellers had been there murdered by Thugs, and that their bodies were lying about that neighbourhood. This statement confirmed my own observations.'

"This man's information ended here; and it was supported by the deposition of Jowahir Singh, Putwaree or writer of the village of Khoorsee Par Purgunah Birgee, who spoke as follows:—'During the reign of Ghoosla, Rajah of Nagpore, I was in service in the Thanna of Dhooma. On my return once from leave to a visit to my home, Ramchund Pundit,

Pundit, who was then Aumil of the village, told me that twenty horse-merchants had been lately proceeding from Nagpore towards Hindostan; that they had been inveigled into junction with a body of seventy-five Thugs; and that, by these villains, of the twenty travellers nineteen had been murdered, near a Bur-tree between the villages of Dhooma and Selnee;—the twentieth escaping by the following circumstances. He had quitted his party, when he heard an outcry, as of human voices, and, in terror, climbed a tree to discover its cause. Here he beheld the Thugs, who had accompanied them, strangling the remaining nineteen of his party, and afterwards beheading them. He further saw, that, after having appropriated the cattle and effects of their victims, they took the road to Jubulpore.

"Having reached the garden of Duriao Singh Beohar, they halted. The solitary horse-merchant who had alone escaped, had in the mean time descended from the tree, and took the road to Jubulpore. On reaching the above-mentioned garden, he beheld the Thugs engaged with natches and revelry. He then repaired to the Soobah Neelkhet, and entreated him to cause their seizure; relating, at the same time, the above-detailed events.

"The Soobah Neelkhet thereupon called a Resaldar of horse; whom he directed to take with him a body of troopers, and seize the Thugs alluded to. But

But ere the horsemen could arrive, the villains had got news of their movements, and made off in the direction of Kutungee. But the Sowars pursued so promptly and so closely, that they seized them at Kutungee; and thence conveyed them back to Jubulpore, where they were confined in the house of Duriao Singh Beohar aforesaid. They alleged, that they were servants of Rughoo Jee, Rajah of Nagpore; and that they paid tribute to that sovereign, on account and from the proceeds of Thuggee. Two months, subsequently, they all escaped from their confinement, in the house of the above Beohar."

The stories of various other parties confirmed these statements.

CHAP. XVI.

THE statement that follows was given by a person called Sahib Khan, in answer to an inquiry, from Captain Sleeman, into the circumstances that made him fly from the Carnatic :—

"It was about twelve years ago that my own gang of fourteen, and another of twenty-five, under Jumal Khan, Seodeen, and Fakeer Mahommed, in an expedition between Aurungabad and Ellichpore, joined in the murder of a Subahdar, his servant, and two Rajpoots, at a bowlee near Chandae. The bodies were tied up in blankets, and thrown into the bowlee. Going on towards Jhalna, we fell in with a Marwaree, taking turbans for sale to Jhalna, and near Phaleegow we strangled him: but getting only a rupee each, we agreed to go on, and wait in the Jhalna cantonments till we could find a Bunij more worth taking. We had, however, no sooner come to this resolution, after discussing over our plans on the bank of the river, than we heard the dire Chimmama on our right. We all started up; and, with my gang, I instantly retreated. Jumal Khan, however, ventured to take

take his gang on towards Jhalna, in spite of this warning. We came on to Omrowtee, where we celebrated the Mohurrum: after which, I returned to my home at Nandair, where I heard that Jumal, on reaching Jaferabad, had got drunk in a spirit-shop, and been seized, with the Subahdar's doo-putta upon him, by some of Captain Sherriff's runners. He gave information against Sied Ally; and he against others, till fourteen of his gang were arrested. The four bodies were taken out of the bowlee; and parties were sent off to Major Parker, who commanded at Hingolee, with information against me and my gang. I kept myself well informed of all these proceedings, and continued to cultivate my fields. Eleven of Jumal Khan's gang having been hung, and seeing no longer any chance of escape at home, I fled. My wife and children, and my brother Bureea, and brother-in-law Chand Khan, were seized and taken to Major Parker, who released the women and children. I went first to my uncle Towukul Sah, a celebrated Fakeer and Thug, but not yet suspected; and fearing to implicate him, I proceeded soon after to Golburga, to my cousin Sahib Khan Jemadar. I found that he, Rusool Khan, Hyder Khan, and other Thugs of his party, had been seized and taken to Hydrabad. As soon as the women saw me, they wept bitterly; and having heard the tale of my misfortune, his wife took me the

the next day to Ochergee, eight cose distant, in the hope of finding some Thugs with whom I might serve, and earn my bread. They were absent on an expedition; and I left her, and went to Muheenkulga; where I met Lungotee Jemadar, an old follower of my father's. He made me dine with him; and, after dinner, he told me that he intended to take the auspices in a few days, and, if the omens proved favourable, should take out his gang, and me with them. I told him that I should be glad to join him; but that I would not consent to recognise him as my chief, by paying him the fees of office as Jemadar, like the other members of his gang. He said he would take me on no other conditions. I expostulated with him; and as Peer Khan, the brother of Chand Khan, was with me, I said that he must set aside both our shares before the general division; and asked him whether he had so far forgotten the obligations he owed to my father, who had initiated him, as to have the impudence to demand tokens of subjection from the son. 'Give us,' I said, 'our shares separately, and then divide the spoil with your gang, and take your fees as leader; for I will never consent to pay you any.' He said it would be a bad precedent, and lower him in the estimation of his followers; and having refused to join him on any other terms, I proceeded to Korergee, where Sahib Khan, the husband of my sister, resided, and served in the gang

gang of Nubee Sahib Jemadar. On our way, we spent one evening at Hidjgeera with the families of Baba Jemadar, and eleven other Thugs of note, who had been for some time in prison at Amba, and are now with Captain Reynolds. On reaching Korergee, we found my brother-in-law, who had been sent home by Nubee Sahib with a booty of 7000 rupees. Nubee Sahib being absent on an expedition, he recommended me to go to the great leader, Sahib Khan of Kakurmulla. I did so; and found his brother Sooltan at home. I told him the story of our misfortunes; and he consoled me, and told me, that though Thugs were getting seized all around them, *they* were as yet secure, and had still a few hundred good men for work. Sahib Khan soon after returned from market, received me very kindly, and made me dine with him. While at dinner, however, we heard the Orutputholee, which is considered a very bad omen in the South; and Sahib Khan told me that I ought immediately to return to my home, after such an omen; but that, as this was impossible, under present circumstances, I must leave his house, sleep in another village, and return in the morning. I and Peer Khan did so. We remained with him six weeks; and were so kindly treated, that we forgot all our misfortunes. He consented to comply with my conditions, and not to exact from us two his fees as leader. With a gang of sixty Thugs,

Thugs, we proceeded a cose, to the village of Dewurnatjee, where we waited eight days for favourable omens. Having got them, sixteen old men and boys were sent home, and the expedition was opened by forty-six. It is the custom in the Carnatic to take out all the old men and boys to the first stage where the auspices are taken; and when the omens are favourable, to send them back. When they get booty, they take what is necessary for the subsistence of the gang; and send all the rest to the house of the leader, where it remains till the gang returns; when it is divided, and the boys and old men who are sent back have an equal share of it with the others who go on. The same custom prevails among the Thugs from Arcot, who are said to have taken it from them.

"We proceeded to a village near Dharwar, which we reached in eight days; and there met the great Sheikh Ahmed, the Thug leader from Arcot, with his gang of fifty. Going on to Dharwar together, the two leaders divided the whole into two separate gangs; one, under these two leaders, to operate on the road to Poonah; and the other, under Nathoo, and Sirjee Khan the brother of Sheikh Ahmed, and Sooltan the brother of Sahib Khan, towards Naggur. We were all to rendezvous at Echora, at the end of a month.

After killing a good many travellers, and getting a good deal of booty—which was all sent, as taken,

to

to the house of Sahib Khan—we all re-united at the appointed place, and remained together two days; when our division took the road to Naraenpath; and the other, that to Dharwar. On the bank of the Bhimra river we got a prize of 12,000 rupees' worth of silk, from six men; and returned home. Seven days after our return, seven of the other division came, and reported, that, in a drunken brawl at Dharwar, the secret of their proceedings had been disclosed, and the division, except themselves, arrested; and, as a good many had turned King's evidences, we might soon expect a guard down upon us.

"Having heard that my cousin and his gang had been released at Hydrabad, and come with their families to Korergee, I went and joined them; and Sahib Khan left his house at Kukurmulla in charge of his brother Meean Sahib, who was not suspected, and concealed himself with an old friend in our neighbourhood. A guard came from Dharwar; seized Meean Sahib; and so maltreated him in order to make him point out his brother, that he threw himself into a well and was killed.

"Alarmed, I, and my cousin and his party, with all their families, went to Golburga; and leaving the women and children there, with a small gang went to Hydrabad, for we had now nothing to subsist upon. Near Bamnabad we found a traveller washing himself in the stream: he was strangled,

strangled, and his body left upon the sand. The rains had now set in; and going on beyond Akelee, we found a traveller waiting on the bank of a river for some one to assist him over. He was persuaded to go up the stream, a little off the road, for a better ford; and there strangled. We went to Hydrabad; and thence came back, through Akelee, to Nowta Moshturee, killing two men on the road: and here we met Sheikh Ahmed, the great Arcot leader, with a small party of twelve. He told us that Sahib Khan had been arrested, and all the booty of our late expedition taken by the Government guards. The next morning he left us for Hydrabad; and on our way to Golburga, we, for three successive days, continued to fall in with small parties of Sheikh Ahmed's gang, following each other at long intervals. My cousin and his party changed their abodes from Golburga to Ertalee in Bedur; and, taking my family, I went to Kunkee, and entered into the service of Dhurumdass, the Amil on the part of Chundoolal the Minister. He employed me to make the collections of two villages for him; and I resolved to leave off Thuggee, at least for a time. Taking the collections to Hydrabad, two years after this, I met Sheikh Ahmed, who asked me how many Thugs I had with me. I told my story; and he mentioned that our old friend Sahib Khan of Kakurmulla was confined in the Fort of Sattara; but that he would effect his release, what-

ever

ever it might cost him. He soon left me; and I could perceive that he distrusted me. One of his followers, however, Hossein Khan, told me that they had now all established themselves comfortably about Nulgonda, on the road to Masulipatam; and, in return, I bade him tell his chief that he need not fear me."

The particulars of the apprehension of Jumal Khan, mentioned in an early part of the above narrative, are recorded on the proceedings of a Court of Inquiry assembled at Jhalna in October 1823. Captain Sherriff, who was actively employed on the occasion, submitted the following statement:—

"On the 20th ultimo, I learnt, by a letter from Major Parker, commanding at Hingolie, addressed to Lieut.-Colonel Lushington, C.B., that four bodies had been discovered in a nullah near the village of Tanklee, in the Purbunnee Purgunnah. The Major's letter was accompanied with four native papers, and a small piece of yellow morocco leather, which had been found near the bodies. On translating two of these papers, I had reason to believe that a gang of Phansigars had left Hydrabad, to march for or towards Jhalna. Having obtained considerable information, in September 1821, of the habits and movements of the Phansigars, I lost no time in disposing of the police in such a manner as I thought most conducive to the apprehension of the parties; who, I concluded, from the information contained in the native papers, were moving on these roads.

"Two hurcaras were accordingly despatched to the spot where the bodies had been seen, near Tanklee; whence they were directed to make a vigilant and cautious search for the murderers. On the 22d ultimo, I learnt that five bodies had been seen in a well on the right of the Jafferabad road, and distant about seven cose from Jhalna. About this period, a respectable Brahmin, attached to the bazaar, informed me that his son and nephew had disappeared near the village of Pokery, where they had halted for one night, on their way to Jhalna, from their own village, Laorgee; the Brahmins and the Puteel of Pokery had adopted every measure and means in their power to discover the lads who were missing, but nothing could be found of them. I directed two hurcaras to accompany the Brahmins, to examine the five bodies that had been found in the well. On reaching the well, the hurcaras found four bodies floating on the water; three with their faces uppermost, and one with the face downwards. An attempt was made to take the bodies out of the well, but it failed. They had been so long in the water, that they separated, and broke to pieces on being moved. The villagers informed the Brahmins, that they were of opinion, from

from the appearance of the bodies on being first discovered in the water, that they must be Rajpoots or Marwaries, and two of them had been bound together with pieces of jungle-creepers: from this account, and the general size and appearance of the bodies, the Brahmins were satisfied that they were not the lads they had lost.

"I was now certain that the Phansigars had passed towards Berar; and sent two smart hurcaras to find them out. These hurcaras reached Jafferabad on Wednesday the 24th ult., and apprehended Jumal Khan, the leader or Muneem of the gang, and his brother-in-law, Abbas Ally, and sent them into Jhalna, with a tattoo loaded with a quantity of suspicious property. The hurcaras wrote me from Jafferabad, that they had first seen Jumal Khan in the village of Gordegaon, drinking spirits, as they passed for Jafferabad, without his observing them: he reached Jafferabad the following day. The hurcaras knew him to be a thief; as three years ago he had been apprehended in the Jhalna bazaar with suspicious property in his possession, which he had offered for sale. They inquired of him the cause of his being at Jafferabad: he answered, that he had left Jhalna that morning, and was on his way to Ellichpore.

"The hurcaras found a person called Seo Deen talking with Jumal Khan; and as they knew him to belong to the village of Nagewaree, close to

 our

our camp, they inquired the purport of his conversation with Jumal Khan. Seo Deen replied, that he knew nothing about the old man, and had only replied to some questions put to him about travelling; and that they had agreed to march together, early in the morning, for Chickly. The hurcaras supposing Seo Deen to be an honest man, warned him against travelling with Jumal Khan, and recommended his returning immediately to Jhalna: he promised to do so; and came to me on the afternoon of the 27th ult., and apprised me of the apprehension of Jumal Khan and Abbas Ally: he added, that the hurcaras had, by their diligence and arrival at Jafferabad, saved his life, as he would certainly otherwise have been murdered by Jumal Khan and his party. On the arrival of Jumal Khan, the Brahmins were sent for who had lost their sons; and the suspicious articles found upon Jumal Khan were examined. Amongst these articles they recognised a Jemboo and Churaloo, the property of the missing lads. These poor people instantly set up a most dismal yell; and requested Jumal Khan, by threats and entreaty, to divulge how he had disposed of the missing lads. Jumal Khan seemed agitated on the discovery of these articles, and partly allowed that the youths had been murdered. He was given to know, that the property found upon him, as well as the circumstance of the lads being missing, were sufficient evidence

evidence that he had been concerned in their murder; and he was again requested to point out where the lads might be found. Then he mentioned, that the Brahmins had been killed by his people, who had effected their escape when he was apprehended at Jafferabad; and that their names were, Malluk Mahommed, Fakeer Mahommed, Hossein Mahommed, and a boy, Rumzanee.

"Jumal Khan soon afterwards described the spot where the young Brahmins had been killed. The relations went out the next day, and searched all about the place mentioned, but could not discover the bodies, or the remains of them. This induced me to send Jumal Khan to shew the place. He was attended by the Cotwal; and went direct to the part of the nullah where they had perpetrated the murders; and a little further down, in a pool which had deep mud at the bottom, the bones, and two odd slippers that belonged to the lads, were found.

"The hurcaras got two more of the gang, Sied Ally and Hossein Mahommed, at Chickly. These men have made extensive and valuable confessions, which have led to the detection of Seo Deen, the man who met the hurcara at Jafferabad, and who turns out to be an old offender; and three men residing in our bazaar, upon whom property, corresponding with that found upon Sied Ally, Hossein Mahommed, and Jumal Khan, has been found. They have also detected five men, a woman,

a boy

a boy, and girl, at the village of Dioraee, who are associates of Jumal Khan, by their own free confession; and have a large quantity of articles upon them, taken from travellers whom they have minutely described, as well as the situations where they found and murdered them.—The Phansigars are present, and can be examined by the Court."

One of the gang, named Sied Ally, was then examined, and said:—"I am the son of Meer Fuzul Ally, who was a Bhala Admee (respectable man). I was born near Chota Amraotee, in the Unturgaor Sawergaor Purgunah, where my father lived under the protection of Rajah Jand Singh of Mahoon: my father died when I was very young; and having quarrelled with my brothers, I joined the Phansigars when I was a boy, without knowing at first that it was their profession to kill and rob in the way they do. Emaum Sahib initiated me into their habits, and forced me to marry his daughter, by whom I have had two children, who are dead. I am heartily tired of this bad profession; and would have quitted it after the Mohurrum, when I came to Jhalna to find better service; but failing, I had nothing for it, but to return to the Mayl, under Jumal Khan. You may inquire of this man, if I had not quarrelled with him, and if my assertions regarding my quitting the gang, then at Budnapore, with the intention of not returning, are

are not also correct. I have done much injury; and will henceforth make every atonement in my power, by discovering and pointing out every person belonging to the gang. All I require, should my life be spared, is permission to live in irons, or in any situation where I may be protected from the numerous Phansigars who inhabit the Nandair districts, as they will exert every endeavour to destroy me.

"I have already undermined all their houses, and have gone too far in my information against them to recede: no person engaged with this people has hitherto said so much, as every body knows how revengeful these Phansigars are. My wife is now at the village of Khuree: it would be conferring a great favour by letting her live with me, in confinement, or wherever I may be sent. I have nothing more to ask; but will do all I can in putting a stop to the work of my late friends, the Phansigars, as my safety now depends upon their destruction."

There is, at least, some frankness in the last avowal of the witness's readiness to secure his personal safety by the destruction of his former friends. This man, having identified a number of articles found upon the Thugs, retired;—and was followed by Bundhoo, or Bundegee, a Phansigar of Jumal Khan's gang, who voluntarily offered to point out, to the

the horsemen who escorted him into Jhalna, the names and residence of all the people who have been engaged with him. Being directed by the Court to look at the articles found upon Jumal Khan and Abboo Ally, he generally corroborated the account given by Sied Ally; but differed, in one or two instances, regarding the persons from whom the articles were taken. This difference was easily accounted for, when it is known that the gang act in parties, and scour all the parallel and cross roads on the route which they take. These parties brought in, and gave account of their respective acquisitions; after which, a fair distribution of the whole was made. Bundhoo, alias Bundegee, recognised several articles in the bundle found in the house of Abboo Mahommed, and his son-in-law Esoof, of which Sied Ally had no knowledge; and, from the open and direct mode of this man's communications, and answers to all the questions put to him, the Court had no reason to suppose that he has concealed any circumstance that could throw light upon the questions proposed.

Two horsemen of the Reformed Horse, who escorted the prisoners from Dioraee, were then called in.

They stated, that a brother of one of the Rajpoots killed by the gang and thrown into the well seven cose from Jhalna met them at Dubboree. He said that he came from Ellichpore to look for his brother,

brother, who was missing on the road between Aurungabad and Ellichpore. He entreated permission to look at the swords found upon the prisoners; and when he saw his brother's sword, he began to cry very much. The man was a Rajpoot; and his murdered brother was said to have been a Havildar, a great favourite of Major Davis, and that he was going to Ellichpore to teach the cavalry there the new drill exercise.

Bundegee and Sied Ally, being again called in and questioned regarding these Rajpoots, Sied Ally spoke to the questions proposed, as follows:—

"We, Jumal Khan's party, which was composed of Jumal Khan and his boy Rumzanee, Abbas Ally his brother-in-law, Burry Khan Puthan, a very wicked young man, Mulluck Mahommed, brother-in-law to Jumal Khan, Mahommed Hossein, Julloo, a man who occasionally lives in the bazaar, and myself. Sied Ally moved from Dharkingaum, on the road between Aurungabad and Moongy Putun, with two Brahmins, and proceeded towards Aurungabad. We killed them in a deserted village, five cose from Aurungabad. We moved into Aurungabad the same night; where we met Sahib Khan's party, and started with them the following morning, towards Jafferabad. At the village of Buroor we joined company with two Rajpoots, and marched

in

in a friendly and sociable manner with them to a shaded Chubootra at Bundgaum. Here they smoked their hookahs; and one of the Rajpoots, who said that he was going to Ellichpore to teach the sword exercise, amused them, by displaying his skill while they sat on the Chubootra.

"Jumal Khan proposed many friendly questions, and expressed his great satisfaction on having got so pleasant a companion to travel with to Ellichpore. We all marched together; and put up that night at a small village between Bundgaum and Dubbaree. We again started together from this village; and having passed by Dubbaree and Chandie, met another Rajpoot, and a boy with a tattoo going to Ellichpore. We all put up for the night in a small Khera on a village in the Jafferabad side of Chandie.

"Sahib Khan and his party followed the Rajpoot and his boy, and put up with them in the inside of the village. Jumal Khan and myself stuck by the other Rajpoot, Tucker Sahib's Orderly; who was now completely in our power, as he looked upon us as friends and fellow travellers.

"We concerted matters with Sahib Khan's party to start first in the morning; and got up when there were six ghuries of the night remaining, and persuaded the Rajpoot to march: he did so; and we killed him and his companion, tied them together, and threw them into a well one cose from the village.

Here

Here we remained, concealed in different parts of the road, until Sahib Khan's party arrived with the other Rajpoot, the boy, and a tattoo. When they arrived near the well, Sahib Khan and his man killed the Rajpoot and the boy, and threw them into the same well; and we all moved on to Donegaum, with three gold putlies, one sword, one topee, and two red cloths found upon the Rajpoot going to teach the sword exercise. On the other, we got 121 rupees, three brass vessels, and the tattoo, a mare."

The following is an extract from the Minutes of the Court:—

" From the various articles of property which have appeared before this Court, and found upon different individuals employed under the directions of Jumal Khan, the Court is of opinion, from the strong similarity of one article with another, found, as already stated, on different people, that they are parts of a whole, which must have been divided and given from a general stock; and this opinion is made very strong by the concurrent testimony of the individuals, Sied Ally, Hossein Mahommed, and Bundegee, who assert, in the most solemn manner, that they were present, and assisted in the destruction of the persons from whom the articles were taken.

" Captain Sherriff, Sub-assistant Commissary General,

General, has represented to the Court, that he is greatly indebted to the information furnished by the prisoners Sied Ally and Hossein Mahommed; which enabled him to get hold of Seo Deen, an old and active Phansigar, who has, from his being a Hindoo, been peculiarly successful in the art of deception, and has led many Hindoos, Marwaries, and Brahmins to their destruction. The above-mentioned individuals have also divulged the practices of three individuals, Abboo Mahommed, his son Julloo, and son-in-law Esoof, who have had a hut for the last ten months in rear of the General Bazaar in this camp. Julloo has been present for a long period with the gang, and occasionally comes in here with plunder that cannot be disposed of at other places. Abboo Mahommed, by the evidence of Sied Ally and Hossein Mahommed, served with the gang when he resided in the neighbourhood of Nandair; and his son-in-law served with them, until he was obliged to quit, from rheumatism in the knees. These men had in their house a large portion of articles which appear to the Court to be exactly similar to the things found upon Jumal Khan and other acknowledged Phansigars. The Phansigar Seo Deen, after deceiving the police, and the officer commanding, before whom he was taken, on the 27th ultimo, to relate his story regarding the miraculous escape he had pretended to have made by the arrival of the hurcaras at Jafferabad,

abad, was found at the house of Abboo Mahommed: and as Seo Deen does not now pretend to deny having accompanied the Phansigars into Berar and Kandeish on several occasions, and as he describes the murders that were perpetrated there, the Court are of opinion that Abboo Mahommed, his son Julloo (who has effected his escape from Jafferabad, in company with some other individuals of the gang), and his son-in-law Esoof, must be principals, or at least accomplices in these nefarious practices.

" Though the Court are fully aware that Sied Ally and Bundegee are polluted with innumerable murders and robberies which they have freely acknowledged and confessed, and that their acknowledgments and confessions may have been in the hope of saving themselves, nevertheless, in consequence of the good which they have already done in detecting so many of the gang, some of whom are nearly related to them—added to their promises of pointing out all the people in their own country who are concerned in these fatal practices of secret murder and robbery—the Court consider it to be their duty to bring forward the services of these men, and to recommend them to the favourable consideration of their superiors.

" The horrid murders of the four Rajpoots, and two Causee Cowree Brahmins, perpetrated so close to Jhalna, and the murders of the Brahmin lads, are

are crimes of so black and destructive a nature, as to require no comment from this Court.

"The following are the individuals of the gang who have been apprehended: — Jumal Khan, leader of this gang, and brother to Nunny, a leader of the gang taken at Akoolah in 1821, and now a prisoner at Aurungabad—Abbas Ally, brother-in-law to Jumal Khan—Sied Ally—Hossein Mahommed—Abboo Mahommed—Esoof—Seo Deen—Fakeer Mahommed—Bundegee—Kurreem Khan—Payma Boodha, joined from the Hindostanee gang—Ajoorah, joined from the Hindostanee gang—Hyder, a boy.

"Lists of all the other individuals of these gangs have been sent by Captain Sherriff to Majors Parker and Seyer; and it is expected, that, with the assistance of Sied Ally and Hossein Mahommed, they will all be secured in the course of one or two months.

"From all that has appeared before them, the Court have no doubt in their minds of the guilt of the individuals enumerated above: and it would appear that these Phansigars moved round Aurungabad and Jhalna as two centres, and murdered travellers on all the principal roads leading from and to those places; extending their excursions from these centres as convenience or a chance of plunder suited, and always returning to them."

As

As the Court were about to conclude their proceedings, Rukbur Singh, the brother of one of the Rajpoots thrown into the well near this place, made his appearance; and was directed by the Court to state what he knows of his brother's death.

Rukbur Singh acccordingly deposed as follows:—"My brother Arjoon Singh, a Dufadar, served with Captain Tucker, at Aurungabad. He left at Aurungabad a Byragee who usually lived with him there, and proceeded towards Ellichpore. This Byragee started some time after my brother, and came to Ellichpore; where he informed me, that one month and five days had elapsed since my brother left Aurungabad, and he was surprised that he had not reached Ellichpore. I got leave from Major Seyer to come down this road, to look for my brother. I arrived at Chickly, and found some of the individuals of the gang there. I also met them at Jafferabad and Dubbaree. The old man, Fakeer Mahommed, asked me where I was going. I said that the Sahib log had sent me to perform a duty, which I was engaged in. I kept moving about, and returned to Jafferabad. I found the horsemen conveying the Phansigar taken at Chickly by the Jhalna hurcaras to Dioraee, to apprehend the Phansigars that lived there. They gave me a full account of my brother's murder, and his servant Khoobas' murder; and pointed out the well into which they had thrown their bodies. I went

went there, and found five sculls close to the well, and eight sculls in the bottom of the well; into which I dived repeatedly, and took up all the bones I could find. As it was impossible to distinguish my brother's scull and bones, I collected all the bones, and placed them, with the thirteen sculls, on a pile of wood, which I prepared agreeably to the rites of my caste, and burnt them all together. I made the Phansigars shew me the spot where they had buried the Mogul and his two servants, as he belonged to Major Seyer's Russalah: they pointed out the spot, which I caused to be dug up; and I found the skeletons of the Mogul and his two servants, all together, and quite perfect."

The articles found upon the individuals already mentioned were then produced; and Rukbur Singh, Mungul Singh, and Maun Singh, relations to the deceased, were directed to examine them. They recognised a considerable quantity, as having belonged to the murdered person.

The finding of the Court of Inquiry proceeds as follows:—

" From the evidence of Rukbur Singh, and the acknowledgment of the individuals of the gang who have been confronted with him, and who allow that they killed his brother and the other Rajpoots, as well as the Mogul and his servants, there is not

the

the slightest degree of doubt, in the minds of the officers composing this Court, of the guilt of all the persons taken up by the police, and implicated originally by the confession of Sied Ally, and subsequently by the articles found upon them, and recognised by Rukbur Singh.

"The prisoners have just sent, from the Cotwal's choultry, a Peon, to inform the Court that Rukbur Singh has taken more articles from the property exposed before him than were actually taken from his brother and his servant killed by them and thrown into the well near this place. They merely mention this circumstance, and leave it for the consideration of the Court. This incident has had so powerful an effect upon the minds of the Officers of this Court, that they cannot, however trifling it may appear, omit bringing it forward in these proceedings; as it corroborates, in a powerful degree, the opinion already expressed of these murders."

In a Letter subsequently written, Capt. Sherriff says:—

"In the gang lately apprehended, we have very fortunately got hold of two natives of Hindostan who served with the northern gangs under Assaulut Khan and Ghasee. They describe these gangs to be more formidable and better organized than the Deccanee *geroos* or gangs. They seldom move in less numbers than thirty or forty, and sometimes

 amount

amount to 300. In travelling, they generally have nothing but a stick, and a bundle on the end of it, over their shoulder. The Subahdar or Jemadar is always respectably dressed and mounted. The Brahmins, who are leaders, make a display of great ceremony and preparation at their meals; and they will not permit a Mahratta Brahmin, on these occasions, to come near them.

"In coming to a town, they look after all the travellers; and sometimes detach as many as four parties in four different directions, to destroy and plunder them. The tricks and wiles practised by these men, in the destruction of their own species, are as numerous and abundant as the victims which fall under their diabolical practices.

"Seo Deen, now in custody, a native of Hindostan, after solemnly asserting that he repents of his past sins and murders, states:—

"'About ten years ago (which corresponds with 1813), Assaulut Khan Jemadar, Ghasee Subahdar, and Himmut Laul Jemadar, collected from thirteen villages in the Zillah of Calpee—five of which are, Sayndoos, Murnee, Bhadwah, Degumunpore, and Rampoorah, the others I do not recollect—a gang of 300 men, who all assembled at Saugor.

"'We committed ravages along the roads, and killed many travellers and other people, horse and foot, who were decoyed from their homes by Assaulut

Assaulut Khan and Ghasee, under a promise of being employed in Bajee Row's service at Poonah. We forwarded this deception set forth by our leaders, and assured these deluded villagers that we were going to serve Bajee Row.

" 'Assaulut Khan gave some of these people money, to get their horses and baggage ready, and to defray their expenses.

" 'On the road to Poonah, the gang moved from Saugor, by Jubulpore and Ramsuck, to Nagpore, and thence to Oomrowtee. At a small village in the jungle near Oomrowtee, called Manah, the gang got seven camels, and killed the merchants that attended them.

" 'On reaching Poonah, we sold these camels. From Poonah we went to Kulleanee; and returned thence to Beergaom, where eight travellers were killed; and we carried their bandy and bullocks towards Aurungabad.

" 'A man near this place recognised the bandy; and we gave it to him, and said that it had been found, without a driver, between Aurungabad and Jhalna. We fell in with six tattoos laden with merchandize, going to Jhalna, and attended by some men. We killed the men; and carried on the tattoos and their loads, which consisted of a great variety of articles; such as, pearls, beads, combs, looking-glasses, &c.

" 'At Jhalna we put up in the tope between

 Jafferabad

Jafferabad and Chickly, and killed eight men, who had eight tattoos, and 200 rupees in money. We moved to Akoalah by Balapore. After leaving Akoalah, we went to Boregaum, and exposed for sale the articles taken between Aurungabad and Jhalna. It so occurred, that a robbery had shortly before our arrival taken place at Boregaum; and, as we offered the articles at a very low price, the Puteel looked upon us as the thieves that had plundered his bazaar: and, as he had no force at hand to apprehend so large a gang, he accompanied us to Ellichpore, where he informed Salabut Khan that we were robbers. Futty Jung Khan sent Mungul Khan, with 300 men, to apprehend our gang: 250 were secured, and the remaining fifty escaped.

" 'Futty Jung Khan put us in confinement; and having taken all our plunder and cash, which amounted to a large sum, let us depart for our own country, after being one month in prison: at this period, Captain Singh Sahib was at Ellichpore. The gang returned to Hindostan, and I remained at Oomrowtee.' "

Thus ends the confession of Seo Deen. Captain Sherriff proceeds:—

" I shall now propose the plan of operations, which has been partly suggested by the captive Phansigars, for the discovery and apprehension of all these villains; who will soon be in motion, for

and

and within his Highness the Nizam's territories. The Phansigars, like the Pindaries of old, sally forth immediately after the Dessurah.

"It is proposed to station one of those Phansigar prisoners at each of the under-mentioned places, through which those plunderers must pass. A small guard of ten horsemen, added to the local assistance to be had at the several places enumerated, will be quite sufficient to secure the prisoners that may be made.

"As the prisoners have pledged their lives to discover and detect all the Thugs and Phansigars that they may pass along these roads, the arrangement and preparation required to ensure success may be left to their own adoption and approval. A pair of loose trowsers, to conceal a light form of chains on their feet, is all that they require, with a decent-looking jacket and turban.

"They intend taking post at some of the chowkies were Customs are collected; and they can be attended by two or three horsemen on foot, who will allow the Phansigars, who may be pointed out in the first instance, to pass the chowkies, and afterwards apprehend them."

More than one person named Sahib Khan being spoken of, some confusion is likely to arise from this circumstance. The following extract is from the deposition of one of the parties bearing that appellation,

appellation, before Lieut. Elwall, at Sholapore, in September 1835. The deponent is the person described in the narrative of the first Sahib Khan, as Sahib Khan of Kabrin.

"About eight or nine months after this time, deponent and Mukhdoom Sahib, Sahib Khan Ruhmutwallah, and Mooheeodeen Jemadar, with forty followers, set out on a Thuggee expedition towards the Carnatic, and halted for the night at the village of Gornullie. On the same day, Sheikh Ahmed Arcottee Jemadar, with Guffoor Khan his brother, and Osman Khan Jemadar, with their followers, arrived at the village of Goburargee, about two cose from Gornullie: and both parties, starting in the morning, met on the road to the Carnatic, and went on together; and after four days arrived at Jubulpore in the Company's territories, where we passed the night; and, having consulted together, agreed to divide into two bodies; and it was settled, that, from my followers, Mukhdoom Sahib Jemadar, Sahib Khan Ruhmutwallah, and Mooheeodeen Jemadar, and sixteen sepoys, should accompany the Arcottees; and Sheikh Ahmed Jemadar, and sixteen Arcottee followers, accompanied me towards Poonah; while the other party went towards the Carnatic. After three days, deponent arrived at Eroor, on the Krishna river, when there was a fair. Deponent staid there; and Sheikh Ahmed went on towards Jokul, and about two cose from Eroor fell

fell in with two Hindoo jewellers who were seated on the bank of a stream, drinking water. Having found out what the travellers had with them, they strangled them, and buried the bodies carelessly. Deponent arrived while they were burying them. We got from the murdered travellers a dabba of pearls and other jewels, which were of large value; and sent them home, in charge of four of our men. We arrived ourselves in three days at Sangolee, on the Punderpore road, at the same time with four Hindoo traders with a pony load of cloth, who were going from Jhalna to Kolapore; and Sheikh Ahmed, having insinuated himself into their acquaintance, went on with them to Walmurra, where they halted, near a Hindoo Dewul. Deponent also came there, and joined Sheikh Ahmed in the evening; and we staid the night there. In the morning, Sheikh Ahmed and the others went on with the Beiparies; and about a mile from the place, in a dry nullah, strangled the travellers, and buried their bodies. I came up after the murder. We got from the travellers the following property:—thirteen embroidered doputtas; nine silk scarfs, embroidered; forty-five rupees' weight of gold thread; and 156 turbans; which we sent home with six men, and went on to Mirich Taj Gaon, when the fair of Khoja Shumna Meerun Sahib was being held. We saw the fair; and then went towards home, and arrived at a village on the Krishna river, where

where four Hindoo traders, in the service of some Saokar, with three bullocks laden with silk, had put up. We staid there; and the next morning the Jemadar Sheikh Ahmed went on with the Beiparies; and about a cose from thence, in a dry nullah, murdered and buried them; and, taking the property, went towards home. Sheikh Ahmed Jemadar took half the silks home with him to Chilmullah, in the Nizam's country; and the rest I took with me.

"The other party, which separated from us at Jaulpar, and went towards the Carnatic, having reached Anegra in the Dharwar district, halted there. At this time, in the cantonment of Hooblee, a Decoitte had taken place; and the police, seeing the Thugs there, suspected them, and they were immediately seized and taken to Dharwar. The Aumil then inquired concerning the Thugs; and one of the Arcottee followers, named Mahommed Khan, confessed, and told that Sheikh Ahmed Jemadar lived at Chilmullah, and Sahib Khan Jemadar (deponent) at Kakurmullah; and that the persons seized were the followers of the two Jemadars. I, hearing that search was making for me and Sheikh Ahmed, left my home, and went and staid at the village of Neem Nullie. In the mean time, the Sircar's people, by order of Mr. J. Munro, came to my house, and ordered my brother Meean Khan to tell where I was: he said that I had left the village.

village. They, thinking he was speaking falsely, began to kick and beat him, till he said he would tell where his brother was; and taking the police people with him outside the village, into a garden where there was a baolee, he watched his opportunity, threw himself in, and was drowned. My other followers, being frightened, fled the village, and came to me at Neem Nullie; and about fifteen days afterwards, the police, having got information of our being there, came and seized us, and took us before Mr. John Munro at Mungolee. The under-mentioned property was seized in my house, and sent in by Gobind Sobhajee Pundit, and Dewan Ramchand Rao, Moonsifdar of Koolkunundghee :—

Silk	bundles	3
Gold thread, or Kullabuttoo	ditto	4
Buttooah, weight several stones		1
Dabba with pearls		1
Horses		3
Daul		5
Swords or tulwars, &c.		14
Musquets		2
Doputtah		13
Silk scarfs, or Sowla		9
Turbans		156

The three horses were sold, and the price was given to my father and family; and afterwards Nursing Ba Resaldar was ordered by the Gentleman to give them their ornaments and brass vessels, &c., as also a quantity of grain of different sorts,

sorts, of the value of about 100 rupees: about this time, Mr. John Munro was shot at the fight at Kittoor; and the Resaldar sent myself, my brother Sheikh Dawoll, and Sona Khan, Sheikh Imam Sahib, and Sheikh Hossein, followers of Sheikh Ahmed Arcottee Jemadar (in all five persons), to Pando Rung Subahdar at Beejapore; but the jewels &c. were not sent. We were kept twenty days there; and then sent to Sattara, where we have been imprisoned for twelve years. When we had been there about three months, Aproop Khan, Mean Khan, and Gurd Sahib Khan, living at Naghnee, were seized, and sent to the Rajah by the Resaldar at Mungolee. About six years after this, Mooheeodeen, a relation of Gurd Sahib Khan, living at Naghnee, in Ulmullah, procured the release of the six others, by paying 600 rupees to the Rajah's people; and I and my brother remained in prison till we were sent here."

The great *Sheikh Ahmed*, from Arcot, is a person of too much consequence to be passed over slightly. It appears that he was obliged to leave his native province by a hot pursuit kept up by Mr. Wright, an active magistrate. Sahib Khan (the person whose narrative is the first in this chapter), says of Sheikh Ahmed:—

"Sahib Khan of Kakurmullah told me, that while he and his gang of sixty men were one day cooking

cooking their food on the bank of a river near Kukurmullah, they saw these people come down to the river to fish. They soon perceived that they understood their mystic terms, and got into conversation with them. The two Chiefs had an interview, in which Sheikh Ahmed explained how he had been obliged to leave Arcot, and seek an asylum, which he did not much like, in a village in the neighbourhood. Sahib Khan prevailed upon him and all his party, with their families, to come with him; and having introduced him to the Rajah of Shorapore Bedur, as a great Thug leader, the Rajah got them established in his neighbourhood, in the town of Chichurmulla. Sheikh Ahmed is the wisest man I know. He has great wealth, but he keeps it concealed in the woods. When danger approaches, he scatters his gang; and wanders alone, with his wife, till it is past, or till he finds another secure abode, when he transfers his wealth to the woods about it. His followers have wonderful confidence in him, such as I have never seen in the followers of any other leader."

The following Extract from the Deposition of Sheikh Sahiban, arrested at Hingolee, shews that the Arcot Thugs enjoy a great reputation:—

"The Arcottee Thugs are proverbially wary and alert among all the Thugs of the Deccan, and their rules and regulations are very strict. They do do not allow of indiscriminate strangling. The stranglers are regularly instructed in the use of the handkerchief; and no one is permitted to use it until he has practised, and until the omens which are looked for at his initiation are considered favourable. The Arcottees will not strangle women, nor shoemakers, dhers, barbers, goldsmiths, or washermen. If the first travellers met with on an expedition have a cow with them, they are spared, even if it is known they have treasure in their possession. The Hindoostanee and Deccanee Thugs, by not attending to these rules, and strangling shoemakers, barbers, and all sorts of people, have brought down retribution on the heads of all the Thugs in India. All the Arcottee Thugs, that I have met with, adopted the dress and appearance of Sepoys of the regiments of Infantry and Cavalry. They wear the chequered loongees and short jackets. like Sepoys; carry canes in their hands; and, being very fond of betel-nut and paun, every man has a small bag in his possession for holding the ingredients. They frequently represent themselves to be Sepoys, going on leave, or removed from one station to another; and even make themselves acquainted with the names of European Officers, in order to pass more easily through the country. They make themselves *knapsacks* (the word made use of by the deponent), and carry their clothes in them. The Jemadars take on themselves the semblance

blance of merchants, and pretend to make purchases of goods, or to be conveying merchandize for sale. They always have four or five of the gang in personal attendance on them, to give them the hookah, cook their victuals, and clean their ponies. These men march in company with the Jemadar; while the other Thugs move along the road in twos and threes, and only collect on the occasion of the perpetration of a murder. They can only be arrested by having parties of approvers stationed on all the great roads of the Carnatic. The police, though it is very vigilant, has not the means of preventing cases of Thuggee; and even if Thannahs of police peons are posted along the roads, the Thugs will manage to murder close to them. I will give an instance in proof of this. Sheikh Ahmed Arcottee Jemadar came into the southern Mahratta country, and strangled some treasure-carriers in charge of 16,000 rupees, at the Salpa Ghât. There is a Chowkee placed on the ghât now; and if the peons are asked, they will state the Chowkee to have been placed there in consequence of this murder. But this has not had any effect in diminishing the number of murders perpetrated at this very ghât, where I am sure a hundred sculls of murdered travellers might be dug up any day. The Thugs will be first to go out, beg the protection of the Police Chuprasses on the roads they travel on, pretending great dread of robbers, and then will perpetrate a murder

murder close to the road which the police is supposed to guard.

"The Arcottee Thugs usually start on their expeditions during the first seven days after the festival of Dewalee and Holee; and if they have had favourable omens, they have no doubt taken to the roads before this time. It is very probable that Dawuljee Jemadar of Binsee has heard of the seizures at Sholapore, and therefore will not come northward this year; and as this is his usual season of setting out, he will certainly proceed towards Bangalore and Seringapatam, or perhaps by Bellary, towards Cuddapah. When I was at Binsee, this time last year, Dawuljee and his gang were intending to make an excursion into the Mysore country. They had a short time previously been as far as Hurryhur, but had turned back in consequence of the omens being inauspicious. The Arcottee Thugs do not now come into the Deccan so much as formerly. Indeed, since the time of the arrest of my brother-in-law, Sahib Khan Jemadar, and his companions, by Mr. Munro, which is about twelve years ago, they have never made their appearance north of Dharwar. When the great arrest of Thugs took place in the zillah of Arcot, by Mr. Wright, during my youth, great numbers of Arcottee Thugs fled from that part of the country, and settled first in the Sorapoor Talooka, under the Hydrabad Government. I have heard that Sheikh Ahmed,

Ladeekur Sahib Khan, Oosman Khan, Chabriah Emaum, Hoonoorgah, and other Jemadars, who were the leaders of the party that came first to Sorapoor, agreed to pay the Sorapoor Rajah 2000 rupees a year for his protection. The party consisted of fifty or sixty Thugs, whose numbers were afterwards increased by stragglers from Arcot, and the families of the Thugs who followed them. All these Thugs remained in the Deccan until Mr. Munro commenced his seizures; when they left their habitations, under the guidance of Sheikh Ahmed Jemadar; and, passing through the Hydrabad country, settled somewhere fifteen days' journey beyond it, toward Masulipatam. They afterwards obtained, on three occasions, 14,000, 7000, and 3000 rupees of treasure, by the murder of the carriers. This is within the last eight or ten years. They then went and settled near Nundyal, in the Cuddapah district. About two years and a half ago, Emaum, the brother of Tippoo Jemadar, a relation of my own, went from Binsee, where I was at the time, to Nundyal, to see Sheikh Ahmed Jemadar. When he returned, he informed us that Sheikh Ahmed Jemadar had a short time previously been out with his gang, and had strangled four Gollah peons, carrying treasure; and that each Thug had received nine tolahs of gold, and 300 rupees, as his share of the booty. During the time of Sahib Khan Jemadar's confinement at Sattara, Tippoo

Tippoo Jemadar, brother-in-law of Sheikh Ahmed Jemadar, was also detained along with him; and Arcottee Thugs were in the habit of coming to gain intelligence regarding him and his companions; and by that means we were kept acquainted with the proceedings of the gangs to the south."

Myan Khan, alias Lungotea, Jemadar of Thugs, lately arrested, taken before Captain Reynolds, at Hingolee, on the 31st of October 1835, gave an account of the dispersion of these worthies; thus:—

"I will state the names of such of the Arcottee Jemadars of Thugs as I am acquainted with.

"Oosman Khan Jemadar, a man of robust habit of body. I met him last, upwards of four years ago, on the Kurnool road, beyond Hydrabad, with a gang of fifty Thugs. He resides at Mulhar, somewhere in the vicinity of Bellary.

"Sabih Khan Ladeekun Jemadar, a relative of Oosman Khan Jemadar, whom he follows.

"Sheikh Ahmed, son of Dawuljee Jemadar, formerly had a gang of fifty Thugs. I have not seen him since the time Mr. Munro arrested Thugs in the Zillah of Dharwar, but have occasionally heard of him.

"Chabreah Emaum Jemadar, and his brother Hoonoorgah, had formerly a gang of thirty Thugs. I have not seen them since the time of Mr. Munro's arrests;

arrests; but within the last two years I have heard that they were residing in the jurisdiction of some Rajah, near Bezwarah, on the road from Hydrabad to Masulipatam.

" Tippoo, the brother of Sheikh Ahmed, in whose company he is. I have not seen him since the time above mentioned.

" In former times, all these Jemadars, with many hundreds of Thugs, resided in the Arcot and other adjacent zillahs; but about twenty or twenty-two years ago, Sheikh Ahmed Jemadar, with a party of sixteen Thugs and four women, came to the Oorus of Peer Dustgeer, which takes place at the village of Neeloor, in the Pergunah of Goolburgah, where he met me and Khooddoo Jemadar, who had also come to attend the Oorus. Sheikh Ahmed informed us that he was an inhabitant of the Arcot Zillah, and that a great misfortune had befallen the Thugs of that part of the country; for, as the English Gentleman had commenced arresting them, there was no dwelling-place left for them there: he therefore wished to settle himself elsewhere. We further heard from Sheikh Ahmed, that his father, Dawuljee, Jemadar of Thugs, had been apprehended, and was then in confinement, either at Vellore or Bangalore. In the end, Sheikh Ahmed and his gang went into the Sorapoor district, and had an interview with the Rajah, through the intervention of Khooddoo Jemadar; and then fixed his residence in the village of Bullondghee. In the course of a year, nearly 100 Thugs were assembled at Bullondghee and the neighbouring villages, in consequence of the relatives of the others coming up from the Carnatic to settle there. I have heard that they paid large sums of money yearly to the Sorapoor Rajah. Some years after, the Thugs having amassed great wealth, the Rajah demanded a fine from them. They therefore left Bullondghee, and took up their abode at the village of Chinmullah, the Jageer of Raheer Patail, in the Afzoolpoor Pergunah. During this interval, the Thugs used to go out for "*Rozgar*," in the direction of Kurnool and Cuddapah, and on the road to Masulipatam.

"Several years afterwards, Sooltaun Khan Jemadar, the brother of Sahib Khan Jemadar, of Kukermulla, (now an approver at Sholapore,) was apprehended at Annygherry; and a Thug of his gang, named Mahomedaa, confessed his guilt, and pointed out the places of residence of the Thugs. He was sent to Mr. Munro, the Magistrate of Mungolee, in the Dharwar Zillah, who commenced arresting Thugs according to his evidence. Nearly forty or fifty Thugs were seized; from among whom, Sahib Khan Jemadar, of Kukermulla, Chunneeka Sahib Khan, and others, were sent to Sattara; and Mahomedaa, Lumboo Burreah, Giddoo Burreah, and others, to Dharwar, and there detained in confinement.

finement. Dreading lest they should be arrested, Sheikh Ahmed Jemadar, and the Arcottee Thugs, with their wives and families, left their homes in the Deccan, and went to Hydrabad; from whence part of them proceeded on the Masulipatam road, and the remainder on the Kurnool road, and fixed their residence in the vicinity of those places. Since that time the Arcottee Thugs have not again visited the Deccan during their Thug expeditions. They range through the country bordering on the sea-coast, by Masulipatam, Rajamundry, and Chicacole; or move, by way of Madras, up to Seringapatam, and then back again to their own abodes.

"The Arcottees are generally hereditary Thugs, by caste Mussulmans, are great eaters of betel-nut, usually wear Longies, like Sepoys, and often represent themselves to be in the Company's service, in order to secure themselves from molestation on the road. They bury the bodies of their victims securely, lest the secret of Thuggee should be divulged; and are much more deceitful than the Deccanee Thugs, so that rich travellers and Sahookars place confidence in them on account of their respectable appearance. Their manner of strangling with the handkerchief, mode of burial, and other rites, are similar to those of the Deccanee Thugs; though there is some difference in the slang language of the Arcottees. They generally use the

Hindostanee language in common conversation, though they also speak the Tamul.

"I recently obtained intelligence of Sheikh Ahmed Jemadar, and other Arcottee Thugs, in the following manner. There was an Arcottee Thug named Kasim, who formerly came and resided with Sheikh Ahmed Jemadar, in the Afzoolpoor district. He contracted a marriage in the village of Bullondghee; but when Mr. Munro began to seize Thugs, Kasim and his wife fled the country, in company with Sheikh Ahmed. About two years ago, Kasim's father-in-law, named Ismael, left Bullondghee, in search of his son-in-law. After some time, Ismael returned, bringing with him both Kasim and his wife; and they took up their residence at the village of Gour, in the Afzoolpoor Pergunah, where they were both residing at the time of my arrest, about three months ago; and if they are seized, they will be able to give correct intelligence regarding the place of abode of the Arcottee Thugs. I heard from Ismael and Kasim, that Sheikh Ahmed, Mahomed Hossein, and Emaum Sahib Arcottee, Jemadars, with sixty followers, were living in some villages four or five cose on this side of Bezwarah, on the Masulipatam road, appertaining to some Hindoo Rajah Zemindar, beyond the Hydrabad territory.

"There is also a female named Jugdumah, who is a Jemadarnee of Thugs, with a party of upwards of 200 persons, who reside in certain villages belonging

longing to some Rajah, situated three days' journey on this side of Bangalore. The Thugs of her gang proceed on expeditions towards Masulipatam and Chicacole. Jugdumah is about fifty years of age; and has two sons, named Sirdar Khan and Burree Khan, besides her own two brothers. She exercises the authority of Jemadarnee herself, but sends her sons and brothers out in charge of the gang: she has amassed great wealth by the practice of Thuggee."

Female Thugs are not common; but, in many instances, women take great interest in the unrighteous expeditions of these murderers; and one instance, at least, has occurred of active interference. Capt. Sleeman says: "I have heard of only one woman who has gone herself on Thug expeditions; and that is the wife of Bukhtawar Jemadar, of the Soosea class of Thugs. She and her husband are still at large, in the Jypore territory. She has often assisted her husband in strangling; and on one occasion strangled a man who had overpowered and stunned him. Mothers, I know, have often made their sons go on Thuggee, when they would not otherwise have gone; and wives, on some occasions, their husbands. I have heard of one woman in the Deccan who kept herself a small gang of Thugs: but Bukhtawar's wife is, as far as I can learn, the only woman that has gone on Thuggee herself."

CHAP. XVII.

GRATITUDE and good faith are qualities not to be looked for in persons following the profession of Thuggee. It has been seen too, that, like the greater part of mankind, they do not act up to their own principles, but that their practice is even somewhat worse than their creed. Of the murder of women, though strictly prohibited by the Thug Code, the records of the British Government in India contains several examples. In that which follows, cruelty is aggravated by ingratitude. The narrative refers to the murder of the family of Newul Singh, a Jemadar, in the service of the Nizam. One of the party engaged, thus related the circumstances to Captain Sleeman.

"The gang had brought on this family from Nagpore. They were, Newul Singh, a Jemadar in the Nizam's service, who had lost one arm; his brother, Hurbuns Singh; his two daughters, one thirteen, and the other eleven years of age; the two young men who were to have been married to them on reaching home, Kuleean Singh and Aman;

Aman; the brother of the two girls; a boy about seven years of age; and four servants. The house in which part of the gang lodged at Dhoma took fire; and the greater part of the gang was seized by the police, but released at the urgent request of Newul Singh and his daughters, who had become much attached to Khimolee, the principal leader of the gang, and some of the others. Omrow Singh Dufadar was a relation of Newul Singh; and he assisted in getting them released, as he can now tell you. Had the gang been then imprisoned and searched, we must have been discovered; as they had with them two bags of silk, taken from three carriers, on their way from Nagpore to Jubulpore, whom we had murdered in the great temple of Kamlee, where the Cantonments now stand. On reaching Jubulpore, part of the gang went on. Adhartal and the rest lodged in the town, with Newul Singh and his friends. The merchants at Nagpore finding that the men with the silk had not reached Jubulpore, and hearing of our gangs being pursued, sent to their correspondents at Jubulpore, who got the Cotwal to search those who were lodged with Newul Singh. Hearing of the approach of the police, Khimolee again availed himself of the attachment of Newul Singh and his daughters; and the girls were made to sit each upon one of the two bags of silk, while the police searched the place. Nothing was found. The next day they set out,

and

and passed us at Adhartal; and five days after this, they were all strangled at Biseynee."

On this narrative Captain Sleeman observes:— "The gang accompanied Newul Singh and his family from near Nagpore, through Seonee and Jubulpore, to Biseynee, a distance of more than 200 miles; and were with them about twenty days, on the most intimate terms, before they put them to death."

Another crime, equally marked by cruelty, by ingratitude, and by a departure from the ordinary rules of murder as received among Thugs, was perpetrated with regard to the family of a Moonshee who had rendered a party important service, in enabling them to escape justice from the hands of the British Authorities. Like most others, this story rests on the testimony of an accomplice. He says:—

"We fell in with the Moonshee and his family at Chupara, between Nagpore and Jubulpore; and they came on with us to Lucknadown, where we found that some companies of a Native Regiment, under European Officers, were expected the next morning. It was determined to put them all to death that evening, as the Moonshee seemed likely to keep with the Companies. Our encampment was near the village, and the Moonshee's tent

was

was pitched close to us. In the afternoon, some of the Officer's tents came on in advance; and were pitched on the other side, leaving us between them and the village. The Khulasies were all busily occupied in pitching them. Noor Khan, and his son, Sadee Khan, and a few others, went, as soon as it became dark, to the Moonshee's tent; and began to sing and play upon a Sitar, as they had been accustomed to do. During this time, some of them took up the Moonshee's sword, on pretence of wishing to look at it. His wife and children were inside, listening to the music. The *jhirnee*, or signal, was given; but at this moment the Moonshee saw his danger, called out murder, and attempted to rush through, but was seized and strangled. His wife, hearing him, ran out with the infant in her arms; but was seized by Ghubboo Khan, who strangled her, and took the infant. The other daughter was strangled in the tent. The Saeses (grooms) were, at the time, cleaning their horses; and one of them, seeing his danger, ran under the belly of his horse, and called out murder; but he was soon seized, and strangled, as well as all the rest."

A further instance of the breach of the rule which extends inviolability to the lives of females occurred in the murder of a Moghulanee, where the pecuniary temptation was comparatively small. Feringeea,

Feringeea, whose evidence has so frequently been quoted, stated, that this female followed the footsteps of his gang for several days;—that they were unwilling to kill her, but unable to shake her off. At Lolsont they met with several Mussulman leaders and their gangs, forming a party of about 125, who had just come up from Ameergur. The exploits of these gangs, previously to the meeting, had involved them in some danger. They had reached Ameergur with a single Mussulman traveller, who had joined them during the last stage. "Two shopkeepers," says Dhoorgha, one of the party, "came up from the Mow Cantonments, and lodged in our camp; and about nine o'clock at night they were all three strangled: their bodies were wrapped up like bundles of cloth, and taken by five Lughas to the Jheel, to the south-west corner of the Fort. We were encamped on the west side. It was a moonlight night in March; and some people on the bastion saw them, and came down to see what they were about. Two out of the five men ran into our camp, and three fled in the opposite direction. The four men from the Fort, without examining the bundles, followed the two men into our camp, and demanded the thieves. They were four Meena police-men, and they declared that they had seen five men making off with bundles of clothes; and as they ran into our camp, they insisted upon our giving them up. I addressed those

those about me in Rumasee, and proposed to strangle the whole four. Punna, approver, and Molloo, lately transported, seconded me; and our roomals were ready, when the Jemadars said that it could be of no use, as others must have seen the Lughas at the same time; and we should have them down upon us, before we could dispose of the bodies. I then told the Meenas, that I could not believe them, unless they shewed me the bundles. They offered to do so: and we proceeded on half way to the spot, which gave the gangs time to get ready to be off; when I pretended that I was afraid to go with them alone, and would go back for my sword and a friend or two. They went on to the bundles, and I returned to our camp. We all made off by different roads, having agreed to re-unite at Chouroo; and travelled all night, and all the next day, as we met a regiment of cavalry soon after leaving camp, on their way from Ajmere to either Neemuch or Mow. We were all re-united at Chouroo five or six days after; and there we rested, and divided the booty. Molloo pretended that he had thrown away, in his flight, all the valuables that he got from the two shopkeepers; but we suspected him. The booty acquired from eight men murdered by our different parties in their flight was here divided, with what we got from the Mussulman at Ameergur."

The party then proceeded to Lolsont; where, as has

has been already related, they met with Feringeea and his followers. They proceeded with them to Somp; the Moghulanee following, accompanied by an old female servant on a pony, one armed man-servant, and six bearers for her palanquin. This Moghulanee is stated to have belonged to a family of rank, but her conduct appears to have been marked with some levity. She is said to have eloped from her friends, and proceeded to the Neemuch Cantonments; from whence, at the period of the murder, she was on her way to the village of Ateer, near Agra. She seems to have become attached to Feringeea, who is described as being at that time a handsome young man, and having the appearance of a man of rank. He had told her that he was going to her village. The motive for this is not apparent; as before he met with the Mussulman party he became anxious to shake her off; and he subsequently told her, that she must go on without him, as he had met some old friends, and should be delayed. According to his account, she then insisted upon his accompanying her home, under the threat, that, if he refused, she would get him into trouble. His fears were thus excited; and being, as he states, a Brahmin, while she was of Mussulman descent, he was apprehensive that he might be suspected of improper conduct, and turned out of caste. He therefore resolved to get rid of her; and the necessary preparations for the murder were commenced.

commenced. The amount of property to be gained was not more than 600 rupees' worth, and the number of persons belonging to the congregated gangs was large. Several of them alleged, that they should not get more than two rupees each, and that it was the better policy to suffer the unfortunate girl to escape. But Feringeea was peremptory; and among Thugs, though arguments in favour of mercy may be urged without effect, firmness in the advocacy of murder is seldom unsuccessful. It succeeded here. "From Somp," says Dhoorga, "we sent on men to select a place for the murder, and set out with her before daylight; but the Belha, in the dark, lost the road; and we were trying to find it, when the young woman became alarmed, and began to reproach us for taking her into the jungle in the dark. We told Feringeea to come up and quiet her; but dreading that some of her party might make off, the signal was given, and they were all strangled."

It was with reference to this murder that several of the memorable maxims of Thug wisdom and morality, which have been already recorded, were uttered. It was to excuse it, that one, who had acted as a strangler on the occasion, said, "We must all have food; and I have never known any other means of gaining it." It was with regard to this murder, that Feringeea, whose manly beauty

beauty of person had attracted the partiality of the unhappy victim, consoled himself by the philosophic reflection, "It was her fate to die by our hands." It was the recollection of this murder which drew from the same person the exclamation, "We all feel pity sometimes, but the goor of the Tuponee changes our nature: it would change the nature of a horse. Let any man once taste of the goor, and he will be a Thug, though he knew all the trades and had all the wealth in the world. My father made me taste of that fatal goor when I was yet a mere boy; and if I were to live a thousand years, I should never be able to follow any other trade."

In this case, plunder was not the primary motive to murder; but the facility with which the commission of the crime was determined on, and the coolness with which the determination was carried into effect, afford but too powerful proof (if proof were wanting) of the utter and hopeless depravity of those who have been corrupted by the vile dogmas of an execrable superstition.

CHAP. XVIII.

THE Records of the Zillah Court of Chittoor contain various particulars connected with the proceedings of the Thugs, or Phansigars. The following is an extract from a Letter addressed by the Magistrate of that district to the Register of the Foujdarry Adawlut, in the latter end of the year 1809.

"The Records of Trials before the Courts of Circuit must have given to the Foujdarry Adawlut information respecting those extraordinary associations of persons called Phansigars (so called from the manner in which they put their victims to death), who take extensive journeys, under the disguise of travellers, for the purpose of committing murders and robberies. These associations, which consist chiefly of Moormen, were formerly extremely numerous, particularly in the Chittoor Pollums, and some parts of the ceded district; a gang sometimes consisting of from thirty to forty persons, who used to divide into small parties of about ten or twelve persons, and each party taking different routes. They had fixed places of rendez-

vous

vous in advance; where they all met and divided their booty, and again prosecuted their journey in the same way. The Phansigars received encouragement and protection from petty Polygars and Headmen of villages, who shared in their plunder: and fathers brought up their children to murder and rob, which constituted a regular profession, by which many families subsisted from generation to generation.

"The extension of the Company's Government, and the attention paid to the police of the country, has checked, in a considerable degree, this inhuman practice. There are now seldom so many persons in a gang as formerly. The plans of the Phansigars are now less systematic, and they are frequently obliged to change their places of abode; but they are still numerous, and a great number of murders are committed by them, every year, in the Company's territories.

"The release, within the last three years, of many persons belonging to these associations, from the prisons in the ceded district and the jail of Chittoor, has tended to encourage the Phansigars: they have become acquainted with the form of trial they will undergo if apprehended, and the nature of the evidence necessary to convict them: many of them are now aware, that they have only to deny the crime with the commission of which they are charged, and that they are certain of escaping.

"I

"I am particularly impressed with the necessity of some extraordinary means being adopted to suppress these associations, and to bring to justice the members of them: but on so important a subject it is with great diffidence I submit my sentiments to the Court.

"It is only necessary to consider the habits of the Phansigars, to be convinced of the extreme difficulty of discovering and convicting them, and how inadequate the ordinary measures of police, and the operation of the present laws, are for effecting those objects. The scene of their crimes is always out of their own district, and seldom within thirty miles of their usual places of abode: they are sometimes absent from their homes for several months together, and take journeys of many hundred miles: their victims are generally travellers, with whose circumstances they become acquainted at public choultries: they frequently change their names, and sometimes go by several names—the latter, to prevent detection: they murder their victims at a distance from towns or large villages, in public roads leading through jungles or uncultivated land, in which they bury their bodies: they sometimes take with them some of their children (boys under twelve years of age), the less to attract notice and suspicion: the head man of the gang sometimes rides on a horse; and they have generally with them some bullocks, or tattoo ponies, to carry

the

the plundered property; and by these means they more readily pass for merchants, the character they frequently assume. A gang is always sufficiently numerous to allow of several persons belonging to it being stationed at a short distance from the places where their victims are put to death, to give alarm in case of the approach of danger. They never commit a robbery unaccompanied with murder: they first strangle their victims, and then plunder them."

In 1812, the Magistrate of Chittoor thus addressed the Secretary to Government in the Judicial Department:—

"With respect to the crime of murder by Phansigars, it is not possible for any magistrate to say how much it prevails in his zillah, in consequence of the precautions taken by these people of burying the bodies of the murdered. Soon after my appointment, a large gang of Phansigars (many of whom lived in this zillah) were discovered; and apprehended on their return to their homes from a journey they had made to the Travancore country, where they had committed numerous murders, and brought home a rich booty, in money, and goods of all sorts. Since that period, particular endeavours have been made to discover any Phansigars residing in this zillah: a few have been apprehended, some convicted, and others have left the zillah. Many of of the Phansigars who have been brought to trial here were not inhabitants of the zillah. At present, I say with some degree of confidence, that there are now living in the zillah very few, if any, Phansigars, who have lately committed offences; but that murders are occasionally committed by Phansigars in this zillah, as in every other in the country, cannot be doubted. In 1810, the bodies of three Hindoo merchants were accidentally found buried a short distance from Vellore, which they left one morning very early, on their way to Salem, where they lived. From information received, there is reason to believe the Phansigars followed them from Madras (where they had been with merchandize), before they found an opportunity of murdering them. It may be generally said, there is no discovering Phansigars while travelling; though, a few months ago, a gang of eleven persons were fortunately apprehended travelling through the zemindary of Calastry, one or two of them having been recognised by a police Thanadar, as having been before in the jail of Chittoor for the same crime. Pardons, which have lately been given by Government to several of these people, have had a most beneficial effect. About forty Phansigars are now in this jail, of whose guilt (though they have been acquitted) not a shadow of doubt exists: many more have been apprehended in Cuddapah zillah, and many have fled from it: many have also

escaped

escaped from Salem into the Mysore country; where I have lately had some reason to suppose that a good many Phansigars, who have left the Company's territories, have taken up their temporary residence.

"It is not possible to conjecture, with any degree of accuracy, what number of persons have annually fallen victims, in the Company's territories, to the barbarous practices of Phansigars. That, for the last four or five years (to 1811), they have amounted to several hundred each year, I have no doubt; but it is certain that, formerly, a much greater number of persons were annually killed by Phansigars. This account will not perhaps appear exaggerated, if it be admitted (and the fact has been proved) that there are many considerable gangs of these people, who live by murder and robbery. If it should be objected, that we seldom hear of persons being murdered or missing, it must be recollected, that it is only in cases of large sums of money being lost (as when Lieut. Blackstone's people, seven in number, were murdered, and a thousand pagodas taken) that inquiry is excited respecting missing people. It is travellers only who are murdered; and many of them poor people, whose disappearance is probably never mentioned out of their own families, who may not attribute their death to the true cause. They murder even Coolies, Palanquin-boys, Fakeers, and Byragees: no one escapes whom they have an opportunity of murdering:

dering: the chance is, that every man has a rupee or two about him in money or clothes, and with them the most trifling sum is a sufficient inducement to commit murder. The property of the eleven persons lately murdered by the gang apprehended in the zemindary of Calastry did not exceed in value thirty pagodas; and though several of their bodies were found, none of the friends have been discovered."

Various depositions were, about the same period, transmitted to the Magistrate of the zillah of Chittoor. The following is a Declaration by Sheikh Madar of Goottapaliam, in the Talook of Vauvelpaudy, of the district of Cuddapah.

"My father, named Futteh Mahommed, was employed as a Cuttoobady peon, for a long time, by Paupe Naịck, Polygar of the said Goottapaliam. I went to Seringapatam; and was employed, in the service of the Sultan, in a battalion, for about five years: after which, on that country being taken possession of by the Company, I was discharged; and returned to my father at the village of Goottapaliam. Afterwards, I and my father cultivated land, and attended to Cuttoobady duties. About six years ago, my father died. Mr. Munro, who was Collector of that country, jufted (resumed) the Cuttoobady lands, and we became cultivators in that village. About five years ago, Gidda Bada Khan,

Khan, one Daudavala Bada Khan, one Fakeerah, one Ooneyah, four persons with their families, came from Cullore to the said village of Goottapaliam, for the purpose of living there, and asked the Polygar, Paupe Naick, to give them some ground for building houses upon; telling him they were merchants and traders: he, accordingly, gave them some ground in a little village called Gollapully, attached to Goottapaliam, where they built houses and resided.

"Being on very friendly terms with them, they asked me to borrow four pootties of grain any where, and to give it to them: and as I considered them, from their appearance, to be merchants and creditable persons, I borrowed the grain from an inhabitant named Gheregereddy, and gave it to them.

"About three months after, these four persons prepared for a journey; saying, they were going to trade in the Hydrabad country. I asked them for the price of the grain which I had borrowed on their account: to which they replied, they would give it as soon as they returned. I consented; and they went off; and returned to the village after three months absence, and paid me the money which was due to me. After remaining there for about three months, they again made preparation for a journey; telling me they were going towards Bellary, for the purpose of getting employment. They called me; and said, 'The women are living in our houses;

houses; and if you will lend whatever they require for their expenses, we will repay you as soon as we return.' I accordingly, during their absence, lent the women two pootties of grain. About four months afterwards they returned to the village: when I asked them for the price of the grain; and they said they were unable at present to give it, but would pay me by and bye. They delayed doing so for three months, and I continued to importune them for payment. At this time, a Jemadar, named Fakeer Mahommed (who is not present) came to them, from Nerrabayeloo; and seeing me pressing them to pay, promised that he would pay for them: and for this purpose he took me with him to a village called Nerrabayeloo; and after that to Jemadar Madar Sahib, son of Chargul Emaumboy, at a village called Coley Muttoor, in the district of Durmapoory; where I and Fakeer Mahommed remained in his (Madar Sahib's) house, for fifteen days.

"Tippoo Gaudoo, Zimmo Gaudoo, Paud Khan, Sahib Khan, Deena Gaudoo, Condacara Futteh, and ten other persons (whose names I do not recollect) of Coley Muttoor and other villages, and Fakeer Mahommed of Nerrabayeloo, united into a gang, in the house of Jemadar Madar Sahib: and Fakeer Mahommed told me, that 'he, and Jemadar Madar Sahib and the others, intended to go to the Trichinopoly country, for the purpose of procuring property by killing people by Phansee (strangling); and

and promised, that if I would go, and obey their directions, I should be paid monthly four rupees.'

"Having consented to what he proposed, we all assembled the next day; and at three o'clock A.M. left the said Coley Muttoor: and passing Durmapoory, on the road to Trichinopoly, we arrived at a choultry situated near a village called Deevettyputty, in the Talook of Salem. The day before we arrived, Mahommed Khan, his son Hossein Khan, both of whom are now before the Court, and Causeeram, Chengooram, Mancram, Parasooram, Lutcheram, and five or six persons whose names I do not recollect, and who are not present, came and halted at that choultry: afterwards, Fakeer Mahommed asked the said Hossein Khan where he had been, and what he had procured? To which he answered, 'We killed two *Committies* near a village called Vaurahamullah, in the country of Madura; and have brought 300 Sauvara Causooloo (or pure gold coin)':—this I heard.

"The two gangs of Phansigars remained together there that night; and after lamp-light, a Brahmin, with some things upon a white horse, came to the choultry, on his way from Seringapatam to Trichinopoly. The said Hossein Khan, Nerrabayeloo, and Fakeer Mahommed, advised him to halt; as we also were all going to Trichinopoly, and would accompany him in the morning: to which he consented, and halted there. During the night, Hossein

Hossein Khan, Fakeer Mahommed, and Chingooram, killed the Brahmin; and took the horse, twenty star-pagodas, and sundry other articles found upon him: and the two gangs having divided the property, gave me one rupee, telling me it was on account of my wages. Afterwards, two or three persons (whose names I do not recollect) of Mahommed Khan's gang took the corpse, and went away, saying they would bury it in the inner part of a tank situated near Deevettyputty. After their departure, I went to sleep; and, the next morning, these three persons told me that they had disposed of the body, as proposed, in the tank: after which, Mahommed Khan's gang went away, saying they were going to Nerrabayeloo.

"We set out from thence: and proceeding on the road to Namacull, with the intention of going to Trichinopoly, halted in a choultry near a little village situated about four or six miles distant, on the other side of Namacull; where another gang of Phansigars, consisting of Cala Emaum, Harala, and Hossein, who are now before the Court, and Allem Khan, Esmall Khan, Vencataramdoo, and three persons whose names I do not recollect, and who are not present, joined us. Fakeer Mahommed asked the said Cala Emaum, what country he had visited, and what he had procured? He answered, 'We have been towards Madura, and procured nothing.' Fakeer Mahommed said, 'We are going towards

towards Trichinopoly; come with us;' to which Cala Emaum, and the other persons attached to him, consented: and we remained there that day. The next morning, three Canara people came to the place, and Cala Emaum inquired their destination. They said they were coming from Madwarow Tuhseeldar of Bangalore, for the purpose of going to Caroor Caungayem. We proceeded with them about eight miles to the other side of Namacull; but as we had not an opportunity of strangling them within that distance, we returned again, and halted in a choultry situated near a tank near Namacull, and remained there three days. The three Canara people returned by the same road; and we saw, and followed them. They stopt in a choultry situated round a church of Mauree Annah, in the village of Taurooputty; and we went to them, and told them that we also were going tc Bangalore; and all lodged together, on very friendly terms.

"A minute afterwards, two Sepoys, one of them a Moor, and the other of the Balja caste, came and lodged in the same choultry, on their way from Hydrabad to Auttumputty. The Canara people, Sepoys, and ourselves, remained there that night: and at three o'clock in the morning, Cala Emaum and Harala Hossein, who are now before the Court, and Allem Khan, Sahib Khan, Condacara Futteh, and three others whose names I do not recollect, and

and myself, got up and awoke the Sepoys, telling them we were going to Auttumputty, and asked them to go. They accordingly set out with us; and proceeded as far as a dry water-course near a Buttee garden, in the neighbourhood of that village; where we stopt, and proposed smoking our hookas; to which they agreed. Shortly afterwards we strangled them, and took cloths, three gold rings, and twenty star-pagodas in ready cash found upon them; and having buried them in a dry water-course, we returned to the remainder of our people, who were in the choultry at Mauree Annah near Taurooputty. When we were about to set out from thence, the three Canara people left that place; and we followed, joined them, and went as far as the inner part of a lake near Agraharum, which is situated between Tarooputty and Deevetty-putty; where we strangled them, and took four or five seers of turmerick, five or six rupees, and clothes; and tying the bodies as bundles in blankets, we carried them to a Hanomuntaroy's church in a jungle, near Tapoor Canama (or Pass), where we buried them.

"From thence we went to a little village on this side of Andavund Cottah, and halted; when Cala Emaum, and Harala Hossein, who are now before the Court, and Allum Khan, Sahib Khan, Esmall Khan, Vencataramdoo, and three others whose names I do not recollect, took their shares, and went away; saying they were going to their village, Gootacul.

"From thence we went to Eradoo; and from thence along the road leading to Satteamungalum; when three Baljavars, with 100 rupees, who were proceeding from Seringapatam to Trichinopoly, came up: we joined, and went with them as far as a dry water-course near Chiuna Mala; where we strangled them, took the 100 rupees, clothes, and a bullock, found upon them, and buried the bodies in the water-course.

"We then returned towards Eradoo and arrived at a choultry in a tope on the side of the village of Chittadoo, where we remained three days. On the evening of the third day, two Baneyan merchants and silver-belted peons came and halted in the choultry, on their way from Bavanegoodul to Coimbatoor, and remained there that night. The next morning they set out; and we proposed accompanying them to Coimbatoor, for the purpose of purchasing cloths. After proceeding a short distance, we came to a dry water-course; where we strangled them, and took Veeraroy fanams amounting to about star-pagodas 2500, some cloths, &c., and the silver belts; burying the bodies in the dry water-course. Setting out from thence, we arrived at Baljarputty, where they divided the residue of the property; and Fakeer Mahommed paid me the wages which were due to me.

"Afterwards,

"Afterwards, all the persons, except myself, went away to their respective villages. I remained in the house of Esmall at Deevettyputty, for a period of two months. Mullock Khan, and Futteh Khan, who are now before the Court, and Essool Khan, and Sahib Khan, who are not present, came to Deevettyputty, where I was. I asked them where they had been? They said, 'We have been to Trichinopoly, and procured property by Phansigaree: we are now returning to our village, Nerrabayeloo: come with us to your village.'

"We then set out in company: and coming near a tamarind tope and well in the jungle near Tapoor Canama or Pass, saw a Brahmin sitting; whom we killed, and buried in an old well near that place: we found on him, tumballs, cloths, and eight rupees in ready cash, which we divided: and from thence proceeded as far as Durmapoory; from whence Mullock Khan, and others who were with me, went to their village. And when I was returning, by the road leading to my village, I saw Sahib Khan, Esmall Khan, Munja and his wife, in all four persons, of Bada Baljurputtoo, coming near Chinna Baljurputtoo; and I asked them whence they were coming. They answered: 'We have been to Royacottah: returning from thence, we met a Brahmin of Benares, carrying a Cauvedee to Ramaswarum; whom we killed, and found upon him 380 aushrafee (gold coins), which we took; and are now

now going to our village.' They went away to their village accordingly.

"The persons who used to go with the gang of Nerrabayeloo are about twenty in number, living in villages of Podala, Podakaners, Hoppene, and Gollaputty, in the district of Combom.

"Besides those Phansigars who are now before the Court, I can seize many others; and produce them in the Court, with proofs.

"The wife of Fakeer Mahommed of Nerrabayeloo, who is not present, told me, that her husband, and some others of that village, killed three Sowcar's people in the road leading from Conjeveram, Pondicherry; and brought Pauvele, or new double pagodas, of seven rupees value each.

"About three years ago, a person named Fakeer Naeckoodoo seized Modeen, who is now present, Akemen Khan, who is dead, Azza Khan, Emaum Cawn, Sheikh Emaum, and Mahommed Hossein, who are now in confinement in the jail of the Court of Cuddapah, and about ten other persons whose names I do not recollect, and myself, and carried us to the Court of Codecondat. In the mean time, as that Court was abolished, and included in the Zillah Court of Cuddapah, we were sent to that Court; and when we were examined, as we did not declare the truth respecting our having been concerned in the Phansi trade, some of us were released.

"About

"About twenty days ago, when I went to Gottapaliam for the purpose of discovering Phansigars, I heard that the gang of Daudavala, Bada Khan, and others of that village, had gone towards Bellary, by way of Cuddapah, for the purpose of Phansigaree.

"And I also heard that part of a gang of Phansigars of Nerrabayeloo had gone towards Bunder, or Masulipatam, for the same purpose."

The above deposition is dated February 1814. At the same period, the following declaration was made by a youth named Yerrogaudoo. He appears to have been thrown in the way of the Thugs, by one of those terrible instances of famine not uncommon in India: but, judging from his narrative, neither the novelty nor the atrocity of his employment made much impression upon him.

"When my mother and father died, during the famine which occurred about four years ago, I went, in search of a livelihood, to a village called Nerrabayeloo, in the Talook of Goorumcondah, attached to the zillah of Cuddapah; and lodged, during the night, at the house of a pot-maker named Moosalanah. The next morning, Mahommed Khan (of Nerrabayeloo), who is now before the Court, saw and asked me who I was, and from whence I came. I told him how I was situated, and that I came there in search of employ; and he promised me clothes

clothes and maintenance. I accordingly remained with him, and worked as he directed me.

"Some time after, Mahommed Khan, his son Hossein Khan, Sheikh Hussen, Sheikh Hossein, Sheikh Futteh, Sheikhjee, his son Goodooboy, Yacoob, Sied Emaum, his elder brother Sied Modeen, Ullah Buksh, and Madar, who are now before the Court, and Aub Khan, Sahib Khan, Emaum Sahib and some other persons, about seven in number (whose names I do not recollect), and who are now run away, of the village of Nerrabayeloo, assembled, with the intention of going to the Tauteputree country.

"Mahommed Khan desired me to go also; and, as I was employed in his house, I took a package with him. We all set out from Nerrabayeloo; and were going along the road leading to Tauteputree, when we met a palanquin-boy in the road, whom Mahommed Khan questioned as to where he was going: to which the boy replied, 'I came with a gentleman's palanquin; but being seized with fever, and unable to walk, I am going on slowly towards Gottee, in the hope of meeting the gentleman there.' Mahommed Khan said he would go also: so we all set out, and arrived at a river's side, situated near Tauteputree; where they killed the palanquin-boy, and took three rupees, cloths, &c. found upon him, and threw the body into the river. We all went from thence to the town of Tauteputree; and were

were proceeding from thence along the road leading to Cuddapah, when we saw a Moorman with a bullock, who was going along the road near a village called Padatoor. We went with him a short distance, and they killed him by Phansee (strangling); and, taking the bullock, one rupee, and clothes found upon him, buried the body in a dry water-course, which was near.

"We then left the Cuddapah road, and went along the road leading to Bundur (or Masulipatam); when we were joined by about ten persons who were concerned with another gang of Phansigars. Shortly afterwards we saw two Rajpoots, near a village called Paretaul, who were going to Bundur, from Hydrabad. From thence, the two gangs of Phansigars accompanied them as far as a village called Ebrampetten; where they killed them by Phansee, and took a large red mare, twenty or thirty pieces of cloth, four pagodas, 100 rupees in ready cash, two silver finger-rings, two swords, two firelocks, four chemboos, one tambalum, and two tapalies: the bodies were buried in a river which was near. Of these things, one sword and one tambalum are now before the Court: the other things were proportionably divided between the two gangs of Phansigars. We all went from thence to Rajamundry, and arrived at a choultry and a tank (about four miles) on this side of Bundur, where two Gollars and one Moorman had halted: we went to them, and from thence proceeded together as far as the sea-side, when they killed them by Phansee, and took 1000 rupees found upon the Gollars, 100 rupees found upon the Moorman, and ten or twenty pieces of jacket-cloths; and buried the bodies in a hole. The pieces of jacket-cloths were tied in this square wax-cloth, now before the Court. As the village at which the Gollars and Moorman were expected to arrive is but one day's march from the village which they had left, fearing that a search would be instituted by their relations, we left that road without going to Bundur.

"After this, all, except myself, went towards the Hydrabad country; but Mahommed Khan told me to go back to the village. I accordingly returned to the village of Nerrabayeloo, and remained there for one month; at which time a person named Emaum, who is not present, prepared to go off, with the intention of joining Mahommed Khan and his gang: and Mahommed Khan's wife asked me to go with Emaum, for the purpose of dressing her husband's victuals.

"I accordingly went with him, and joined Mahommed Khan near a village called Pedoogooralloo, situated in the road leading from Bundur to Madras. Where they went, or what they procured by Phansee, after I left them, I know not.—From thence we all went towards Madras; and fell in with three Mogulvalloos (or Moormen), who were going to Madras

Madras with cloths, &c. from Hydrabad. We went with them a short distance, and then killed them by Phansee. Some valuable white cloths, one keenkhaub jule, a bed, a large horse, and about 100 savnaraesaloo (or pure gold cashes) were found upon them: these we took; and buried the bodies in a dry water-course. Of those things, the keenkhaub jule is now present in the Court.

"After this, Sied Emaum, and his elder brother, Sied Modeen, took five or six men out of those who are now before the Court, whose names I do not recollect, and went towards Bundur. I remained with Mahommed Khan and others, at a village situated near the place where the Mogulvalloos were killed; and at this place the other gang separated from us, having first received their just share of the stolen property.

"A few days after this, Sied Emaum and others returned; when I heard Sied Emaum tell Mahommed Khan, that they had killed a Mogul-man near Hydrabad, and obtained Mahataubee topies, a white horse, and ten rupees found upon the boy. Of those things, that white horse, and two Mahataubee topies or caps, are now present in the Court.

"After this, Sied Emaum and ourselves assembled, and went from thence towards Madras: and, on the road to Madras, we saw a Baljavur man with a horse, one servant, and two Brahmins, who were going from Madras to Hydrabad: this was about one day's march from Pedoogooralloo: they killed them by Phansee, buried them in a dry water-course near that place, and took two jamakanahs, one black horse, five jumballs, one coosoomba or red turban, one patunchoo dovatee or cloth, one patunchoo red cloth, one patunchoo black cloth or sie cloths, 100 Hydrabad rupees, and one wooden box. I was present when all those things were taken; of which the two jamakanahs, and one patunchoo cloth, are now before the Court: I know their description.

"We afterwards went and remained at Madras one night; and were going to Pondicherry, whither three persons, belonging to a Sowcar, were conveying Pauvele (new double) pagodas in two purses, and passing near a choultry situated upon a sea-cauree's (salt-river's) side between Madras and Pondicherry; where the gang killed them by Phansee, and took the pagodas and cloths, &c., found upon them, and buried the bodies on the spot.

"About six months ago we returned to the said village of Nerrabayeloo. Besides those things which were divided before, they divided, in the said Mahommed Khan's house, all the other cloths, horses, and ready cash, &c., which were procured by killing persons by Phansee; but did not give me any share.

"When they were dividing the property, two Pauvele pagodas fell down; which I took up, and gave into the hands of Coommara, or Polmaker Moosalenna

Moosalenna of Nerrabayeloo, with the intention of giving them into the hands of my elder brother.

"I will point out, as far as I am able, the things which are deposited with such and such persons, by these persons now before the Court; but I do not recollect the names of the persons who keep the things.

"Subsequently, Goodooboy and Madar, who are now before the Court, Mahommed Khan's son-in-law, Laul Khan, and six persons whose names I do not recollect, and who are not present, assembled, and prepared for a strangling expedition. This was about a month ago; when Mahommed Khan told me to take and carry the package of the said Madar: and having taken the package, we all left Nerrabayeloo, and went, by way of Channel Ghaut, a little distance eastward; from whence Madar and Goodooboy returned, the omens not being favourable. I also returned with them. The other persons proceeded with the intention of going to the Pondicherry country, by way of Arcot. When we were returning towards Nerrabayeloo, Emaum Naick, the Thanadar, seized us in Naugapulla Channel Ghaut, and asked us to point out the Phansigars; to which I, and Gadamanepully Madar Sahib, who is now before the Court, consented; and pointed out the Phansigars who are now brought to the Court: the others, about sixteen in number, ran away.

"The

"The Phansigars who joined us when we went in the Bundur road, as above mentioned, and those who were concerned with these gangs, are living in four villages called Padala, Patacanoor, Hebelly, and Gollaputty, in the Talook of Cambom, attached to the zillah of Cuddapah. They now and then used to join the said Mahommed Khan, his son Hossein Khan, and others, who are now before the Court, in their strangling expeditions; and divided the property thus procured. Their names are, Caudavala Hossein Sahib, Oonegagaudoo, his younger brother Emaum Sahib, Aub Khan, and about twenty persons whose names are unknown to me. I am ready to point out all those persons.

"When some of the people of the Cambom gang joined us as aforesaid, I heard Oonegagaudoo tell Mahommed Khan and others, that 'they had killed one Subahdar, one Jemadar, and one Havildar, and a dog which was with them, within one day's march of Ellore, and took the bullock, cloths, and some ready cash found upon them; and that news of these murders having spread, a search has been instituted for the murderers.' They therefore advised us not to visit that part of the country."

The same witness subsequently made a second Declaration, to the following effect:—

"Four persons were passing near Paretaul in the

the road to Ebrampetten, on their way from Rajamundry to Golocondah, when the Phansigars strangled, and buried them in a dry water-course which was near; and took some doodies, and dooganies, and cloths, found upon the bodies.

"Two Committies and one Moorman were passing a village called Nagaracul, on their way from Madras to Hydrabad; when the Phansigars followed them a little distance, to a dry water-course situated between Nagaracul and a village called Huttaralagam; there killed them by Phansee, and buried them in the water-course. A black-and-white-coloured jamakanah, a silk paundam (a purse to keep betel-nuts in), two rupees in ready cash, two patunchoo (or silk-bordered) cloths worn by them, and one white cumbly, some tapalies, and chemboos (or pots), were found upon the bodies. Of those things, the black-and-white-coloured jamakanah is present in the Court.

"A person was passing along the road about one mile on this side of Nagaracul, coming to Hydrabad: the Phansigars killed him; and took one Gungasagarum dhotie (a sort of cloth), one pistol, twenty rupees in ready cash, and two black cumblies, found upon him; and buried the body in a dry water-course which was near. Of those articles, one fine black cumbly is present in the Court: the pistol is at Nerrabayeloo, in the house of Yacoob, who is now present.

"I forgot

" I forgot to mention these circumstances in my first Declaration.

" The white bullock which was found with a Moorman who was killed near Touteputree is now at Nerrabayeloo, in the house of Mahommed Khan, who is now before the Court.

" It is customary for the Phansigars to pretend friendship for travellers, and, going with them a short distance, to strangle them with their dhoties. When the cloth is thrown round the neck, the travellers are seized by their legs. Their dead bodies are cut open, and the limbs divided, to prevent their swelling, and emitting a smell through the crevices formed in the ground. This smell would attract jackals; and they would dig down upon the bodies, which would thereby be discovered. It is also the custom of the Phansigars to select a man especially to cut the corpse so, and to give him an additional share of the plundered property.

" The red horse with a white spot in the face, found upon two Rajpoot men who were killed near Ebrampetten, is a mare; and she is now present in Court.

" The said Mahommed Khan's cultivating servant, named Nullo Hossein, who is now living at Nerrabayeloo, was with the gang of Phansigars with whom I went. I forgot to mention his name in the first Declaration given by me.

" It is the custom of Phansigars to shew signs by

by the hands, and speak *bundoocuttoo mautaloo* ('words unknown by any others'): for instance, if the hand is put upon the whiskers, the meaning is, 'Be courageous; do not fear: you must not reveal: I shall not.' The meaning of the word *aukada* is 'one thousand.'

"I said before, that when the gang of Phansigars went a second time, Goodooboy and Madar Sahib left them, and returned to their village, in consequence of an *apascoonum* (bad omen); these omens were, a black crow sitting upon a dead tree, and, without making the usual noise with his nose, called '*keer*'; and Goodooboy's turban touched the branch of a tree, and fell off. If they had paid no attention to these two omens, they supposed, that though they might escape in one place, they would lose their lives in some others. I heard them when they were conversing in this manner.

"The horse which was found upon three Mogulmen, who were killed at a place four days' march from Madras, is of a red colour, a male; and is with one of the gang of Phansigars, named Oonegagaudoo, in Padala villages attached to the district of Cambom.

"A Yagoyepareetum (or holy string) was worn by one of those persons killed between Madras and Pondicherry.

"The black horse which was found upon the Balja-

Baljavur men who were killed near Pedoogooraloo was a mare, and had a colt; and as soon as they were brought to a village called Madataroovoo, they ate *moste aukoaloo* (poisoned leaves), and died.

"It is the custom of the Phansigars, before they march, in order to ascertain whether or not success will attend them, to keep the Vegraham, or the image with brass things, which are now before the Court; and to worship a god named Anyee; and to bring a sheep and wash it, and afterwards to kill it; and to place the head before the god, and to place a lamp upon the head; and to pray; mentioning, at the same time, the names of the four quarters (east, north, south, and west): and if the nose of that head tremble at the time when they mention the name of any quarter, they go in that direction; and if it does not tremble, they do not go, at that time, any where.

"I stated, that the Phansigars kill the people with dhoties which they wear on their hips: it is the custom of the Phansigars to keep dhoties, like the one now before the Court; which was worn by Madar Sahib, who is now before the Court.

"I do not recollect some places, nor do I exactly know other places, in which all the people murdered by the Phansigars, mentioned in my declarations, are buried; but I am able to point out the places in which the four persons who were murdered near Paretaul, in the road to Ebram-petten,

petten, were buried; and also the places on which the two Gollahs and the Moorman, who were going from Rajamundry to Bundur, were buried.

"Sied Modeen, who is now present, and five or six Phansigars of those who came from the Cambom country, killed three Gosayns, by Phansee, near Pedoogooralloo; and took home some ready cash and clothes, some Japala chemboos (or pots), one red horse, and three jubboloo (or kind of jackets), found upon them. I heard this near Nagaracul, where they were relating the circumstance to some of the Phansigars. Of those things, this chemboo (or pot) of Cuthee (Benares) country is present in the Court; and that horse is with the Phansigars living in the Cambom country."

CHAP. XIX.

It is certain, that in some instances in which accusations have been preferred against the Thugs, the course of justice has been reversed:—the guilty have been allowed to escape with impunity; while those who have ventured to accuse them have incurred the punishment which the real culprits have escaped. A fact of this nature is mentioned in the deposition of a man named Rujub, taken by Lieut. Brown, at Jubulpore, in November 1835. The deponent was not present at the murder which he relates: and this may furnish a better excuse for some incorrectness in his statement than India witnesses are at all times in a condition to offer. The deposition is as follows:—

"I heard from Niamut Khan and Madaree (both dead), Moosahib Khan (at large), Peerbuksh, and others, that they murdered the Mussalchee of Mr. Pringle, near Koonjie, in the Patna district. The Mussalchee had been to Calcutta with some gentleman, and was returning from thence. The body was

was thrown into the river Ganges. After the murder, the Thugs went to the go-down or grog-shop, and there got drunk; when a dispute arose;—upon which, Ghasee Khan Jemadar, Dookeea, Man Khan, and Joteea (the latter is Chuprassee with Mr. Pringle at present), gave information of the murder; and those concerned were arrested, and taken before the Court at Chuparah. After the depositions had been taken, the case was made over to Mr. Elliot, the Commissioner. The property of the murdered Mussalchee was produced in Court; and his wife came forward, to recognise it. Mr. Elliot told her, that if she did not speak the truth she would be punished; upon which she took fright, and would say nothing, although she knew the property to be that of her husband's. The wife of the Mussalchee is still at Chuparah. There was no evidence but the depositions of the approvers, and the case was not proved; and the approvers were sentenced to fifteen lashes, five years' imprisonment, and to be taken round the city, mounted upon asses, for five days:—the rest of the Thugs were released. Mr. Elliot, the Commissioner, told the Nazir of the Court who had arrested the Thugs, that he was ruining the country by seizing innocent people; and sentenced him to fourteen years' imprisonment. When in confinement, the Nazir swallowed some pieces of diamond, by which he caused his death."

In

In answer to some inquiries on the subject, addressed by Capt. Sleeman to Capt. Ramsay, Assistant-general Superintendant at Chuparah, the latter gentleman obtained the following communication from Mr. Pringle, Zillah Judge at Sarun :—

" The accompanying Extract from a Report which I addressed to the Superintendant of Police in the Lower Provinces, on the 9th of May 1827, will furnish you with most of the particulars of the case of Thuggee which the General Superintendant has inquired about; and, with the list of persons then apprehended, which is attached to it, will furnish to you all the information I could then collect regarding the crime of Thuggee, and the gang of Thugs in the district, together with the particulars of my operations against them; which, at that time, promised so well, but which were subsequently baffled by Mr. Elliot, the Circuit Judge: for the Thugs were acquitted by him, and the man I deputed, and who was so active in apprehending them, was not only imprisoned, but sentenced to exposure on an ass, and corporal punishment. My own conduct was visited with the severest censure; and both the Government and Nizamut Adawlut were led into a belief that there was no such gang of Thugs, and that the crime, if it existed at all, was very limited in its extent.

" My report will shew that the approver's statement, received from you, is not quite correct; which, indeed,

indeed, could hardly be expected, as he had his information from another person. But one part of it in particular, I am happy to observe, is not true, as you yourself are aware: for you have seen Nazir Abdool Ullee alive; and though I fear he has not long to live, from the effects of bad health, produced by the cruel treatment which he experienced, still I hope he will live long enough to obtain justice, by having the value of his services acknowledged by Government, and the Declaration, dated the 28th of February 1829, 'that he was incapable of serving Government in any public capacity in future,' cancelled. For myself, it is quite enough to know, that all I then brought to light has proved to be true, and much more: though it is melancholy to reflect on the loss of human life; which might have been prevented, had I obtained credit for my assertions, and been allowed to prosecute the researches which I had so successfully commenced more than eight years ago; and which must have speedily led to an exposure of the extensive existence of the crime of Thuggee, and to the apprehension of many of the Thugs themselves."

The Extract alluded to, from the Report addressed to the Superintendant of Police in the Lower Provinces, is subjoined:—

"The other case of highway robbery, attended with murder, was as follows:—Two of my servants, on on their way from Calcutta, where they have been with me, were ascertained to have come as far as Bankipore, near Patna; but no more was heard of them for more than a week: and I found out, on inquiry, that the road between Cheeran and Sheirpore Ghaut, a little above Dinapore, which is very lonely, being covered a good deal with water in the the rains, was reckoned unsafe, and infested with robbers.

"I knew the inhabitants of the Thannahs, through which it passes, to bear rather a bad character for plunder, particularly of boats, as is stated above; and was convinced that the men had been murdered, and that many others must have shared the same fate. As it was impossible that such crimes could have been committed, and never heard of, without the connivance and gross negligence of the police-officers of Gooltingunge and Cusmer, I suspended them all (with the exception of the Darogah of Cusmer, who had lately been appointed, and apprehended the Decoits in the foregoing case); and sent other officers to take charge of the Thannahs, with a party of Burkundazes and Chowkeedars, under the Darogah of the town of Chuparah, whom I put over the whole.

"The above party succeeded in apprehending six persons, going in a body, with property on them proved to have belonged to the people who were missing; also a quantity of property, evidently obtained

obtained by plunder, and cords, knives, and khoopees, such as grasscutters use, but which Thugs also use to bury bodies and property, being the most portable instruments for doing so.

"Mr. Fleming, who happened to arrive at this station to hold the Sessions there, very kindly informed me, that he had lately tried a case of Thuggee at Gorruckpore, in which there was no doubt that some of the persons concerned were inhabitants of this district: and he also was so good as to give me a perusal of his Rooeedad, or summing up of the case; from which, and from further information received from him, I found that there was a large gang of Thugs in this district, where it joins to Gorruckpore;—that they had been there, and carried on their depredations to an enormous extent and to a great distance, from generation to generation, with the utmost boldness, and hardly any molestation;—that five of the six apprehended, belonged to the gang;—and that one was a notorious Sirdar: his son was taken with him, and his father and one brother have been taken since. Another brother, named Shitaub Khan, is still at large, and is, I believe, at present with Sheikh Amee, son of Chund, who was concerned in the late murder of the Sipahees in Gorruckpore, for which two of the gang were lately hanged; and a third brother, named Mosahib, is at present in the Gorruckpore jail, having been con-

victed

victed of highway robbery, attended with murder. Another of the persons apprehended, is Buxoo, son of Jeeun Khan; and both father and son were imprisoned on the above murder. All this I have traced from the information given to me by Mr. Fleming: for, notwithstanding its being known to the Magistrate of Gorruckpore that the above persons were inhabitants of this zillah, no communication regarding them was made to me. What the consequence of such unaccountable want of cooperation might have been, I need not point out.

"The gang is composed chiefly of Mussulmen, and the leaders of it are almost all of that persuasion: there are Sirdars and Jemadars of it; and their head-quarters are in Purgunah Kowaree, in Thannah Hosseinpore. There are, however, many Hindoos and Dosauds in it; and a very leading character is named Anund Lall Bhat, who is not yet taken. I reckon their number to be about 200. I believe they have accomplices and correspondents in many parts of the country. One of them, when he was apprehended many years ago, said to one of the officers of the Court, that he could send a message to Calcutta, or any part of the country, and receive an answer in much less time than the dawk.

"They appear quite independent of the Seearmurwas of Burraitch; and were evidently unknown when the late Mr. John T. Shakespear wrote his Report

Report on Buddeek and Thugs. How much further their depredations extend, it is difficult at present to say; but so far I am certain, that they infest the districts of Gorruckpore, Ghazeepore, Benares, Juanpore, Mirzapore, Tirhoot, Patna, Behar, Shahabad, and perhaps Bhagulpore and Ramghur; and that many crimes attributed to the Seearmurwas of Burraitch have been perpetrated by them, appears certain.

"The records of this office, prior to 1809, are so very defective and confused, that I could not discover any account of this gang from them; but I found that in 1810, in consequence of information given by Khodabux Khan, sixteen of the gang were apprehended, as being notorious robbers, but, after an examination, were all released, in consequence of numerous witnesses, most of whom belonged to the gang, declaring them to be men of good character, and highly respectable; and I believe every man in the district would have said the same thing, for no man's life was safe a moment who dared to inform against them: but, independent of what is contained in the present inquiry, the bad character of many, that were then apprehended, has been subsequently proved. One of them, named Syfoo Khan, was a Goinda many years afterwards; having first, in conjunction with some others of the gang, murdered the above Khodabux Khan, the informer. In consequence of information given by Syfoo, the murder which took place last year in Tirhoot was discovered, and he died shortly afterwards. I need not, in this place, state any more, to shew that the terror in which the gang was held by people of all classes, prevented information being given against them; increased, no doubt, by the above sixteen persons being all released.

"In 1814, fifteen of the gang were taken in the Behar district, in consequence of a murder which was committed at Pandaruck near Bar; but in consequence of want of proof against them, they were all put on security for good behaviour. Eleven gave security; and were afterwards released by the Commissioner, under the provisions of Reg. 8, of 1818. An account of this murder will be found in your office.

"In the end of 1814, five of the gang were apprehended, in consequence of information, given on oath by the above informer Khodabux Khan, Ullum Noorbauf, and Hitcha Pasban; but were released in consequence of some of the gang coming forward, and giving them good characters: and Khodabux Khan was imprisoned three months; and a Mochulka of st. rupees 100 was taken from Khodabux, and a Mochulka of st. rupees 50 from each of the others, binding them to give no such information (apparently false) in future.

"It would have been well for Khodabux if he had conformed to this, and relinquished his hopeless trade

trade of informing against them; but a few years afterwards, he again volunteered his services in Zillah Gorruckpore, to hunt some of them down, and was murdered by them. The murder was proved against the gang; and some of them, I believe, are in jail for it now. Ullum Noorbauf wisely quitted the country shortly after undergoing his punishment, as related in the foregoing paragraph; and has not been heard of since.

"In 1821, one of the gang, named Muddaree, was taken up, and tried for throwing a noose over a man's head; which stuck on his nose, and cut it. He was committed; and the case was referred, by the Court of Circuit, to the Sudder Nizamut Adawlut; but he was acquitted, in consequence of a slight discrepancy in the evidence.

"In 1824, Bucktawar Khan, one of the gang, who was formerly taken and released in 1810, was again apprehended, in consequence of information given by a person named Ujjoodhea Roy: but the Magistrate, considering them both equally bad, ordered both to find security for six months, in the amount of 100 rupees. A great deal of suspicious property, which was found on Bucktawar, was confiscated; but he was able to give security, and was released; while the unfortunate informer was imprisoned six months, not being able to find security.

"In the end of 1826, one of the gang, named

Shumshair

Shumshair Khan, was apprehended for being with nearly fifty followers on the bank of the river Dewa at Manjhee for some days, and being suspected by the Darogah of having come there for nothing but plunder. The followers immediately dispersed. Nothing could be proved against Shumshair; and in 1826 he was released, by order of the Circuit Judge.

"Thus it appears, that, in two instances, the informers were punished, and the accused got off; and one informer met his death by persisting in acting against the gang. It is not therefore to be wondered at that no other person has since dared to come forward against them, until now. On any of the above occasions of part of the gang being taken, the whole might have been brought to light, as it is now, if the investigation had gone further, and confidence had been given to people to come forward, and if there had been any idea of the existence of the gang: but I hope the time is now over when no one dared to oppose or give information against them.

"After an attentive perusal of the trials above alluded to, and obtaining a good deal more information respecting the haunts and proceedings of the gang, I sent the Darogah of Chuparah, with a party, and an order to Baboo Chutterdharee of Sauhys, on whose estate most of the gang resided, to give every assistance the Darogah might require.

I gave

I gave the Darogah a list of persons to be apprehended and searched, and power to apprehend and search others who might be strongly suspected of belonging to the gang.

" The measure has been very successful, as the annexed list of persons apprehended will shew: and although it will probably be difficult to prove any thing further than notorious bad character against most of them, still the gang will not soon recover from the blow they have now received: and I hope to prove enough, to shew that very few that have been taken, can, with safety to the community, be released.

" To return to the case of highway robbery:—I committed the six who were first taken, and five others against whom three persons afterwards deposed. I fear I was a little too hasty in admitting those three persons as witnesses. That they were themselves a part of the gang, I had no doubt; but still, from the evidence they gave before me, and in the want of all proof of their being concerned, I took their evidence on oath, and committed the case for trial.

" It has been postponed to the next Sessions; and I hope before that time to be able to get more evidence against the prisoners. Most of the gang, I believe, that were at their homes when the Darogah of Chuparah was sent against them, have been taken. A number of them who were out on predatory

predatory excursions will return when the rains set in; and many of those who fled on the approach of the Darogah will probably return also at that time. I therefore remain quiet till then, when I hope to make another successful attack on them: and, in the mean time, I am not without hope of apprehending Amee and Shitaub Khan, before mentioned in this Report."

A list follows of twenty persons apprehended, and variously dealt with according to law. It is succeeded by another, containing the names and descriptions of forty-two Thugs infesting the Sarun and Gorruckpore districts.

CHAP. XX.

A CORRESPONDENCE which took place between some European officials in the year 1814 will illustrate the state of society and morals then prevailing in the Western Provinces.

"TO J. WAUCHOPE, ESQ.

"My Dear Sir,

"You will, I doubt not, be much surprised at being troubled by a person who had only the pleasure of being acquainted with you for a few days, at Allahabad. I trust, however, to your goodness for an excuse, and will at once proceed to the object of my writing.

"It is now almost a month since I was informed, that, a fortnight before, some Thugs murdered four persons in a nullah between Banda and Kaeta; and were apprehended, to the number of about twenty-five or thirty, almost on the instant of their accomplishing the murder, and sent in to you. Amongst those apprehended, are said to be Sumadhan Brahmin, Oodeeha, and Khooman Lodehs, and Nunda Bukal, all of great notoriety.

"From

"From the circumstances under which they were apprehended, I think it likely many may have confessed, not only the present charge, but former crimes. In this case, their confessions must throw great light on the system of Thuggee, and, as they are, many of them, originally inhabitants of this neighbourhood, perhaps implicate many persons whose names were hitherto unknown; as well as corroborate accusations made against some who have been seized, and others who have escaped.

"As I have several men now under investigation, charged with this crime, and with being accomplices of some of those you have in confinement, I hope it will not be thought an improper interference to request you will oblige me with copies of such confessions as may have been made before you. If of no use to the case I have under trial, they will be so as private memoranda. I should also feel much obliged by your favouring me with a list of the persons apprehended, including their caste and place of residence.

"My reasons for this second request are, 1st, That a number of Thugs were apprehended by Mr. Wright, and confessed before him; and their confessions implicate the men I above mentioned as so notorious. Were copies of those confessions inserted in the case in your Court, they would, perhaps, tend to corroborate any confession made before you; and would certainly shew that they have

have long since followed the trade of murder. As I have notes of these confessions by me, after being favoured with the names of those you have caught, I could mention the names of those by whom they were formerly implicated. If you were inclined to call for copies of those confessions from Cawnpore, by enabling you at once to mention those you wish to have, much trouble would be saved. 2dly, Amongst those now in confinement with you, are, perhaps, some for whom I have been, and am still searching.

"Should my intelligence be incorrect, you will be inclined to smile: but allow me to mention, that, in order to state my wishes and reasons, I assumed the whole as a truth. For the sake of humanity, I hope no such murder was committed: but if it have, I cannot but congratulate you on the apprehension of the gang. Hoping to be excused for the trouble,

"I remain, my Dear Sir,

"Yours very sincerely,

"G. STOCKWELL.

"Etawah, 14th Oct. 1814.

"N.B. Part of my information says, Khoshallro, Pursudooa, and Kurhora, were with the party of Sumadan, but escaped. As these three live in Banda, in my jurisdiction, if their seizure be desirable, I believe I can effect it."

"My Dear Sir,

"I had yesterday the pleasure of receiving your copy of Bhuga's deposition; and the day before, that of your Letter.

"Though I am astonished at his recognising so few, I do not despair of finding evidence against the persons and notoriety of the remainder, though not to their specific villanies. In the course of two or three days, I shall send you two persons employed as Burkundaze in the Thannah of Sindouse; one of them a Dhanuck, inhabitant of this place, and well acquainted with the Thugs formerly residing here; the other, an intelligent man who has been five years in the Thannah, under the very edge of which their houses were. My object in sending them is, to ascertain whether some of those apprehended are not old inhabitants of this village, mixed with the Cawnpore Thugs; which I understand to be the case, from their having taken refuge in the same places about Jhalone, &c., and thus formed an acquaintance. I have also another man in store, who is at present gone to endeavour to procure the seizure of Sumadhan. He has, to-day, told me, of his own accord, that four of the Thugs I wanted are in your jail, amongst the twenty-five; viz. Oodeeha Lodeh, a very celebrated character;

Omeda Lungra, ditto ditto;

Lullooa . . . . ditto;—against him are two cases, according to a confession;

"Sundooa

"Sundooa Lodeh. (I cannot find his name in the list.)

"I hope you will excuse me, when I start a doubt regarding the plan you have at present in view, of sending the persons to Cawnpore from this zillah, to be there tried for the respective cases. You will, I am sure, excuse my fearing the result, when I mention that Mr. Wright apprehended seventy-six, of whom seventeen made confessions, which strongly criminated the remaining fifty-nine who denied. Amongst these denials are several suspicious circumstances; and once or twice the property was produced from their houses, and recognised. Those who denied, and those who confessed, were alike released by one sweeping order of the Nizamut Adawlut, without security or any thing else.

"I cannot but think, that when the very suspicious circumstances are taken into consideration, under which the seizure was made, and the change of their names and place of residence and caste (evidently implying a fear of those under which they were known), and to these be added the confessions of Thugs apprehended five years ago, criminating them, little can be wanting to establish their guilt. It is on such strong circumstantial evidences that I cannot conceive any Court will release them.

"On the contrary, should they be sent to

Cawnpore,

Cawnpore, there being no proof but what they before had, I fear they would find the same lenity which was shewn to their companions.

"In the event of their being sent to Cawnpore, you would still wish to have copies of those papers accusing them attached to the case in your Court; for which purpose I copy the following, from Wright's notes.

"When the person returns, which will be, I fancy, about a week hence, I shall send him, in order to point out the four whose names he mentioned; and I believe he will recognise some of the rest, on their being shewn to him. I shall do myself the pleasure of addressing you a short note, when I send the Burkundazes.

"I am, &c.

"G. STOCKWELL.

"Camp Sindouse, Dec. 22, 1814.

"You would, perhaps, think it a shorter way to send one or two of the Zemindars of this place, to recognise the Thugs of their village; but, alas! the communication is still kept up; and they derive, perhaps, as much profit as ever from them. They are by no means to be trusted in this."

"My Dear Sir,

"I have to entreat your pardon for allowing your last Letter to remain so long unanswered; the principal reason for which was, my not having any subject worthy of communication. As Bhowany left me some days ago in a dooly, he has no doubt ere this arrived; and I hope you may derive some benefit from him. Toollacya has been unwell, and only just rejoined me: he shall be sent you in a short time. He will tell you all about Purshaud, who came to me as a spy, and introduced Toollacya. As he can give you the whole of my intelligence respecting Purshaud, I refrain from troubling you. Herewith inclosed is a copy of an Urzee presented by my spy; and as his source of information is a relation and Padree to the Rajah of Jugumunpore, it may very possibly be correct. It will, at all events, be as well to have a look-out after the party who went towards Chutterpore, and are expected to return in the course of fifteen or twenty days. There can be no doubt that such persons are allowed to reside in Jugumunpore; as in April last, when in camp near to that place, the Umlah of my Court visited the place, and the houses of the Thugs situated close under the Rajah's fort were pointed out to them, among the other curiosities. Nothing like concealment was attempted; they being told, 'There are so many of this caste, and so many of that; and there you see *one hundred houses of of Thugs.*' As the ancestors of Madhoo Singh, and himself also, when in charge of Sindouse, collected a tax at the rate of twenty-five rupees per house, there can be no reason to doubt that Mahaepat Sah, a brother of the Rajah, should do the same. Toollacya will give you a list of men concerned in four cases within your district, several of whom are in your jail; and will also mention the principal Thugs and their villages, living in Jhalone and some part of Soobah Gwalior. I am sorry to say Perry writes me of two or three Thuggees having lately occurred in the eastern extremity of the district; and you will have heard from Middleton, that they have favoured him with some visits.

"I have not heard the slightest hint at the perpetrators of the Dudwareh decoity. This silence appears to me very extraordinary; as, by one means or another, we have become acquainted with all the decoits but one which have been committed in this district, and with most of those in the neighbouring zillah; so that this must be some unknown gang. I was once told that strong suspicion attached to the Zemindars, but could get no good grounds for such an opinion. Two points had nearly escaped me;—one, That the Thuggees in your district are preconcerted; that is, gangs rush in at once from different quarters, and their crimes are committed almost all at once, or in a very short

short period:—of the truth or falsity of this, you can well judge. The second, That for the short time Bhowany has been in my employ, he has been more successful in apprehending than any spy I ever took in service. I mention this as a reason for believing his assertions.

"Believe me, My Dear WAUCHOPE,

"Ever yours faithfully,

"G. STOCKWELL.

"Camp, Jehekha, 10th June 1815."

The sum collected from Thugs at Sindouse was 5000 rupees per annum, making the number of houses 200; but most of these houses, in order to evade the tax, contained three or four Thugs, besides their women and children. The probable number of Thugs might, at a low rate, be considered 400! Merchants came from Benares to purchase their spoils at a cheap rate.

"To J. WAUCHOPE, Esq., Magistrate, Bundelcund.

"Sir,

"I beg to transmit, for your information, the accompanying Extract of a Letter from the Magistrate of Etawah, dated 7th of August last, together with a copy of a Letter, and its enclosure, from the Joint

Joint Magistrate of that district, dated the 11th of August, on the subject of murders by Thugs.

"I am, &c. &c.

"J. SHAKESPEAR,

"Acting S. P. Western Provinces.

"Office of S. P., Calcutta,
31st of March, 1816."

EXTRACT of a Letter from the Magistrate of Etawah, to the Acting Superintendant of Police in the Western Provinces, dated 7th August, 1815.

"Par. 20.—As far as I can depend on the information and experience which I have acquired during my residence in this district, the Thugs who have been in the habit of infesting this part of the Company's Provinces may, I conceive, be divided into three classes, entirely unconnected with each other. First, those who originally resided, under the protection of the Zemindars, on the large estates of Hurra Singh, Dyaram, and Bhugwunt Singh, in Allyghur; and of Himmut Singh, late Rajah of Etawah, in this district; including also a few detached parties who lived unmolested at or near to a village called Borasa, in Furruckabad; and the thannahs of Shahabad, Phurha, and Kuhleyee in Etawah, in three or four of the police divisions of Allyghur. The murders which were formerly so common on the road which lies between

between Etawah, Khas, and Agra, on the high road from Cawnpore between Nubbeegunge and Shahabad, and on that leading from Mynpooree to Coel, as well as in other less-frequented parts of Allyghur, Furruckabad, and Etawah, were chiefly perpetrated by men belonging to this class. If such criminals can be supposed to have any religion, they will be found principally, if not exclusively, to profess the Mahommedan faith. A number have been seized, and are now in the jails at Mynpooree and Coel; and a few are in confinement also at Futtehghur: many, however, are still at large, some of whom reside in the district of Allyghur; and I have reason to think that a party of nine or ten of the most notorious of these offenders, by whom the murder in Suckut was in all probability committed, have, for some time past, taken up their abode in the vicinity of Agra.

" 21.—The second class consists of Hindoos, who are, for the most part, of the Lodhee caste; and this is by far more numerous than the class I have just mentioned. They resided in great numbers in the eastern thannahs of this district, and the adjoining purgunahs of Cawnpore, until disturbed by the measures pursued against them by Mr. Wright and myself in 1810 and 1811, when many were seized, and others absconded. By cultivating a few beegahs of land, they were able, under the ostensible character of ryots, to follow the more

 lucrative

lucrative profession of Thuggee, without being suspected. Their depredations were consequently local; and the murders which were so numerous to the westward of Cawnpore, particularly in the vicinity of Kanoje, and those which occasionally happened in the lower part of this jurisdiction, may be ascribed to their activity. About twenty of these offenders are confined, on security, in the jail at Mynporee; but many of those committed by Mr. Wright have been released, and have returned to their old haunts in the Cawnpore district, neither reformed by the morals of a jail, nor less audacious from the experience they have had of the facility of escaping from the hands of justice. To this class my letter to you of the 7th of June last adverts.

"22.—The third is more formidable in point of number, and extends over a greater expanse of country than either of the foregoing classes. It includes that desperate association of men, of both religions and of all castes, which grew up under the fostering protection of the Zemindars of Purhearha, and of the villages contiguous thereto in the Gwalior territory. It is already known to you, that those who resided in the villages of Purhearha were dispersed when Mr. Halhed personally visited that purgunah. They have however, since, gradually returned; and now live in a number of the Gwalior villages, stretching over an irregular tract of country from the right bank of the Kooaree to the

the confines of Duttea. They travel in larger bodies, and are more bold and adventurous than the Thugs in the Company's Provinces. Their predatory excursions are chiefly confined to the country which lies eastward and southward of Gwalior, and to the districts of Bundelcund; and I have reason to believe that they rarely, if ever, visit the Dooab. Their number has been partially augmented from some fugitives from the second class; who may, perhaps, from their knowledge of the country, occasionally venture across the Jumna. Several of the most notorious of these offenders have been seized by Mr. Wauchope, and are now in the jail at Bandah."

"To T. Perry, Esq., Magistrate of Zillah Etawah.

"Sir,

"I had the honour of receiving your Letter of the 22d April last, covering a Copy of a Letter from the Superintendant of Police, relative to the Thugs of Purhearha.

"2. I apprehend that the Putwaries of this purgunah can give no information on the point required. From all I have been able to learn, it appears to me that the Thugs formerly residing in Sindouse, &c., have settled in the Gwalior territories, where they are sure of protection: at least, as the Aumils of that Government derive a revenue from their depredations, it is fair to conclude that they protect

protect them as formerly. I am told by the most respectable Zemindars, that 5500 rupees was the average payment made to these States for the Thugs, at the rate of twenty-five rupees per house, this being the number of 220 houses; but most of the houses contained three men.

"3. The villages at present most notorious, adjoining to Purhearha:—Jhalone, Suhoo, Rusoolpore, of Jhalone; Suraopore, Sooneh, Seloruch, of Jugumunpore, and I believe in Jugumunpore Khas; Mollickpore, Mohonee, Tetringare, Sonaweery, belonging to Scindia. There is also a Poorwa of Rampoor, said to contain about 200 houses of Thugs; at the head of whom is the famous Dhurm Khea, alias Dhurm Khan.

"The former Sirdar, Boodhooa, and about twenty of his gang, were caught in or about Ameer Khan's army; and that leader cut off their noses and both hands—no doubt an effectual way of preventing their recurring to this way for a livelihood.

"4. I am also informed that they seldom repair to the Company's territories to commit their depredations; and have, as yet, heard of few instances of their taking up their abode on the left bank of the Jumna.

"5. This intelligence appears to me to be true; for the gangs of Purhearha committed their Thuggees more like banditti, openly and in large bodies, attacking and plundering parties of travellers, not

taking

taking any care to conceal the crime by hiding the bodies; whereas the Thuggees of the Dooab are committed more by stealth than force, on two or three individuals, early in the dark of the morning, or late in the evening, at least leaving no marks of force being used. The piercing the throat, or ripping up the bellies, is frequently done to prevent any chance of life remaining; and the bodies are carefully concealed in wells or nullahs. The only thing in which the two descriptions at all coincide is, that of their plundering, and invariably murdering the plundered.

"6. I have every reason to believe that the Thuggees committed in Cawnpore, Furruckabad, &c., have been perpetrated by the old Lodha gangs, as well as by those who were released from Cawnpore: and the only Mussulman gang which has come to my knowledge, is that of Koodrooa, living in Bowary; which I mentioned to you some time since, in a private letter. As you are fully acquainted with the names and villages of the principals, there is no necessity to mention them.

"7. I have also the honour to subjoin another list of Thugs, and of the villages in which they reside; which may, perhaps, be useful. It was procured from persons perfectly unconnected with those from whom the above was obtained.

"I have &c. &c.

"G. STOCKWELL,

"Etawah, Aug. 11, 1815. "Joint Magistrate."

CHAP. XXI.

For many years after the British power had obtained the ascendant in India, the Thugs continued to practise their execrable trade, almost without interruption. Although, at various periods, their horrible deeds called forth the transient attention of the Magistracy, no systematic efforts were made for the suppression of practices which no civilized Government could be expected to tolerate, after it became informed of their existence. The evil seems, however, to have been regarded in much the same light as the fixed inconveniences of the climate, or the accidental inclemency of unfavourable seasons—as a thing greatly to be lamented, but beyond the hope of remedy, and which it was the part of wisdom to endure with patience. Means were sometimes taken to evade the Thugs; but little or nothing was done to suppress them. As late as the year 1810, we find the following general order addressed by the Commander-in-Chief, Major-general St. Leger, to the troops under his command:—

"Head-

"Head-Quarters, Cawnpore, 28th April, 1810.

"It having come to the knowledge of Government, that several Sepoys, proceeding to visit their families on leave of absence from their corps, have been robbed and murdered by a description of persons denominated 'Thugs,' who infested the districts of the Dooab and other parts of the Upper Provinces—and the insidious means by which they prosecute their plans of robbery and assassination having been ascertained—the Commander of the Forces thinks it proper to give them publicity in general orders, to the end, that Commanding Officers of native corps may put their men on their guard accordingly.

"It has been stated, that these murderers, when they obtain information of a traveller who is supposed to have money about his person, contrive to fall in with him on the road or in the serais; and, under pretence of proceeding to the same place, keep him company, and, by indirect questions, get an insight into his affairs; after which, they watch for an opportunity to destroy him. This they sometimes create, by persuading the traveller to quit the serais a little after midnight, pretending it is near day-break; or, by detaching him from his companions, lead him, under various pretences, to some solitary spot.

"It appears, that, in the destruction of their victim, they first use some deleterious substance, commonly

commonly the seeds of a plant called Duttora; which they contrive to administer in tobacco, pawn, the hookah, food or drink of the traveller. As soon as the poison begins to take effect, by inducing a stupor or languor, they strangle him, to prevent his crying out; when, after stripping and plundering him, the deed is completed by a stab in the belly, on the brink of a well; into which they plunge the body so instantaneously, that no blood can stain the ground or clothes of the assassin.

"As the Company's Sepoys who proceed on leave of absence generally carry about them the savings from their pay in specie, and travel unarmed, they are eagerly sought out by these robbers, as the particular objects of their depredation. With a view, therefore, to guard against such atrocious deeds, the Commanding Officers of native corps will caution their men, when proceeding on leave of absence—

"1. To be strictly on their guard against all persons (particularly those unarmed) whom they fall in with on the road, who evince a solicitude to keep them company on pretence that they are going the same way, and are inquisitive about their affairs.

"2. Not to quit the serais at a very early hour in the morning, before the rest of the travellers.

"3. Not to receive pawn, tobacco, sweetmeat, &c. &c. from such persons, or smoke their hookahs, particularly if offered to them in solitary spots on the

the road; and, lastly, to avail themselves of the protection of sowars (horsemen), when opportunity offers, or travel as much as possible with large bodies of people. This last object might be attained, in a great degree, if the men were persuaded, on occasions of periodical leave of absence, to keep together on the road; as long as the several destinations of such Native Commissioned or Non-Commissioned Officers, as may be proceeding the same way, will admit.

"It has also been intimated to the Major-General commanding the forces, that the Residents at Delhi and Lucknow, and the Collectors of Revenue, will be authorized, on the application of Commanding Officers of Paymasters, to grant bills, payable at sight and at the usual exchange, on any other treasury, for sums which may be paid into their own treasuries on account of Sepoys wishing to remit money from one part of the country to another;—a mode which, in conformity to the views of Government, is particularly to be encouraged and attended to by Officers commanding corps and detachments."

At a later period, these ruffians attracted the notice of the Marquis of Hastings; but only, as it appears, incidentally. Scindia had stipulated to provide a contingent, to aid in the suppression of the Pindaries; but having no great affection to the work, he had evaded the performance.

"To

"To compensate for such a delay," said the Marquis, "which I affected to consider as accidental, I pressed that the corps should be employed in extinguishing certain mischievous associations in Scindia's territories. The description applied not only to some bands of avowed robbers, but to a particular class, denominated 'Thugs.' This nefarious fraternity, amounting, by the first information, to above 1000 individuals, was scattered through different villages, often remote from each other; yet they pursued, with a species of concert, their avocation. This was, the making excursions to distant districts; where, under the appearance of journeying along the high roads, they endeavoured to associate themselves with travellers, by either obtaining leave to accompany them, as if for protection, or, when that permission was refused, keeping near them on the same pretext. Their business was, to seek an opportunity of murdering the travellers, when asleep, or off their guard. In this, three or four could combine, without having given suspicion of their connection. Though personally unacquainted, they had signs and tokens by which each recognised the other as of the brotherhood; and their object being understood without the necessity of verbal communication, they shunned all speech with each other, till the utterance of a mystical term or two announced the favourable moment, and claimed common effort. Scindia's tolerance of of an evil so perfectly ascertained, merely because the assassinations were seldom committed within his own dominions, may afford a tolerable notion of the vitiation of society in Central India, before this late convulsion. There is reason to believe, that, by this time, the pest in question has been rooted out; which, with the suppression of some bodies of horsemen under military adventurers (a service completely achieved by the contingent), will be no less a benefit to Scindia's own government, than to adjacent countries."

What sort of "reason" there was for believing that the "pest had been rooted out" at the period when the Marquis composed the Summary from which the above extract is taken, does not appear; but, at a subsequent period, there was abundant "reason to believe" that the Marquis was in error, and that, in fact, little or nothing had been achieved. Captain Sleeman having applied in 1835 to Major Stubbs, Superintendant of Scindia's contingent, for a list of the Thugs arrested by that force, and an account of the manner in which they were disposed of, received the following answer:—

"I have the honour to acknowledge the receipt of your Letter of the 13th ult. I have no records of any Thugs having been apprehended by the contingent horse; and I am, therefore, unable to furnish you with the list you require.

"I have

"I have no civil authority, and cannot apprehend any one without orders from the Resident; excepting those detected plundering by the horse stationed for the protection of travellers on the roads. But many people have, at different times, been apprehended by the contingent and by the native Aumils, and made over to the contingent, at the requisition of different political authorities. The prisoners are usually sent either to Gwalior, Sehore, Saugor, Kotah, or where the requisition comes from: no examination or trial takes place here; consequently, there is no record, to enable me to comply with your wishes."

These languid and desultory efforts were at length succeeded by a better system. About the year 1829, the British Government began to take decisive steps for the abatement of an evil, which, after so long a period of European rule, ought not then to have been known in the territories of the Company. Their exertions were properly extended to those Native States whom we have, by treaty, a right to controul. The trials of persons accused of the crime of Thuggee, within districts where our regulations are in force, takes place before the established tribunals. The investigation and punishment of similar crimes within the territories of the Governments of Hydrabad, Indore, and Oude, have, with the consent of those Governments,

ments, been committed to the British Residents and Agents, subject to the revision and controul of the Supreme Government.

In 1829, a large gang of these miscreants was arrested by Captain Borthwick, Political Agent at Mahidpore. After the gang was secured, one of them, named Amunoola, under alarm for the consequences, voluntarily presented himself to the Jemadar of the party sent on this service ; and confessing that he and his fellow prisoners were the description of persons they were suspected to be, offered to make a disclosure of their acts and proceedings. From that time he was kept separate from his companions, to prevent him from being dissuaded from this purpose by their efforts. The day after the arrival of the whole at Jowrah, Captain Borthwick took his depositions; and, for the purpose of corroboration, despatched him the day following, under a guard, to point out the bodies of certain persons stated by him to have been murdered at different places on the route of the gang between Mundesore and Dekola, where they were seized. This corroboration was fully afforded. A promise of pardon induced five other prisoners to present themselves as evidence against their associates.

The proceedings of Captain Borthwick were thus communicated to Government by Major Stewart, British Resident at Indore.

"I have

"I have the honour to transmit, for the information and orders of Government, the proceedings of Captain Borthwick, in the case of a large gang of Thugs, apprehended by him on their return from an expedition into Guzerat.

"These proceedings detail so fully the system pursued by these murderers, that any comment or observations on them seem quite superfluous, the guilt of the party being established beyond all doubt. With reference, however, to the quantity and trifling value of the articles found in the possession of the murderers, it may be proper to notice, that this is satisfactorily accounted for by the circumstance of the party having, only five days before their apprehension, sent off, under charge of one of their leaders, almost all the booty they had collected in their expedition; including, of course, every thing of value.

"The expeditions of these murderous gangs have, of late years, become the greatest calamities with which Malwa has been afflicted: and it will not fail to attract the notice of Government, that the very pacification of the country has led to the extension of this murderous system, to a degree unknown before.

"The invariable practice of putting to death the whole of their victims, the manner in which this is done, and the mode in which the bodies are disposed of, renders the apprehension and conviction of of these gangs particularly difficult; and therefore I consider the seizure of so large a body of them as a most fortunate event for this country, and likely, if capital punishment is inflicted on the greater part of them, to put a stop to such expeditions for a long period to come. The punishment, however, of these murderers, to be effective in this respect, ought, I conceive, to be inflicted at the different places from whence they come: and I cannot help trusting that Government will also adopt some measures, both in our own territory and in the dominions of our allies, to bring to condign punishment the village-officers, and other authorities of the country, who connive at the proceedings of these murderers, and participate in their plunder. These can hardly be considered as less guilty than the murderers themselves.

"I beg leave, therefore, to suggest, that the leaders, and all of the party whose employment in the gang has been that of stranglers, should suffer capital punishment, each at the village to which he belongs. Where the murderers come from places not within our jurisdiction, I can hardly anticipate any difficulty in obtaining the assent of our allies to make an example so requisite for the future safety of innocent travellers throughout Central India. The rest of the gang, with the exception of those to whom pardon has been promised, ought, I conceive, either to be banished from Hindostan, or confined for life."

Amanoolah, the earliest of the approvers, was a Mussulman, aged about fifty years. His deposition follows :—

"I am one of the gangs of Phansigars now in confinement, and, with my associates, was stopped, in the month of Bysak last, at the village Dekola, about seven or eight cose northward of Bheelwarah, as we were returning to our homes in Hindostan. At this place, a party of eight or ten horsemen came upon us, and said, that Captain Borthwick having heard that we were carrying opium out of Malwa, had sent them to stop us. On hearing this, our minds were relieved from suspicion or fear that the object of the horsemen was any other than what it professed to be, or had any reference to our habits and pursuits. We readily consented, therefore, to return to Bheelwarah with the horsemen, who, we thought, would of course allow us to depart, after searching us and finding we had no opium. After our arrival there, we learnt the true cause of our being arrested; not, however, before the authorities and inhabitants of the town had joined in aid of the horsemen, to secure us, and prevent our escape. We, of course, loudly protested our innocence, affirming our readiness to be taken before Captain Borthwick, where we should clear ourselves, to that gentleman's satisfaction, of the accusations which the horsemen cast upon us of being Thugs and Phansigars; at the same time, urging

urging the great inconvenience we would unjustly be subjected to, if obliged, on such unfounded suspicion, to retrace our steps to Jawrah. To these protestations of innocence, Oomrao Jemadar (prisoner) added, that he had an English passport; and that if the horsemen persisted in detaining us, they would bring themselves into difficulty. Seeing that the horsemen were deaf to all our entreaties and threats, I became alarmed; and, as the only chance that appeared of saving my own life, determined to confess the truth, and to make a full and true disclosure of our habits and acts. I accordingly went immediately to the horsemen, and offered, on assurance of my life being spared, to make a faithful avowal of all our doings. I received the assurance I required: on which I confessed to them, that we were actually the Phansigars they suspected us to be.

"From that moment they kept me separate from my companions: and now that the assurance of pardon has been repeated to me, my mind is at ease, and I shall not withhold the disclosure of one single act that has been committed by myself and companions since I became a confederate Phansigar, but freely and fully state all that occurs to my memory to mention.

"I have been connected with these Phansigars for about two years; during which period, robbery, preceded in every instance by the murder of the

 individuals

individuals robbed, has been our mode of life. I belong, properly, to the gang of Mandun Jemadar, now a prisoner, which consists chiefly of Mussulmans, and is called the Mussulman gang. According to the custom of all these gangs of Phansigars, of proceeding at certain seasons to distant countries in quest of plunder (generally after the rains), our Jemadar Mandun, having collected his men, set out from his country in Bundelcund, upon an excursion of that nature, at that season last year. Our course was southerly; and passing Dhuttea, on our sixth stage we came to the banks of a nullah where there was a good deal of jungle. There a Mussulman traveller, on his way to Baroda, who called himself a Moolah, was prevailed upon to join us. Shortly afterwards, every thing being arranged, he was murdered, and his property plundered. A Koran was found upon him, which, to avoid detection, we burnt. There was, besides, a labada, and a straight double-edged sword, both of which are amongst the things seized upon us: other things of trifling value, belonging to this Mussulman, fell into our hands.

"This was the first act we committed: after which, we pursued our course, and, without falling in with any thing further, arrived at Oogein. From Oogein we proceeded to Baroda, by the usual stages, without committing any murder or robbery on the way; with only one exception, about five

five cose from the latter town. This was upon the persons of a barber and a byragee, who fell into our hands at the stage before we reached Baroda, and were murdered a short time after night set in. A red woollen cloth jacket, now among the things taken upon us, and a tattoo, also present, fell into our hands. [The other witnesses do not confirm this, as to the tattoo belonging to the barber.] What was found upon the byragee, I do not now remember.

"The next day we arrived at Baroda; and there found a band of our brethren, consisting of twenty-five men, under their leader, a Brahmin, and an inhabitant of Etawah. This Brahmin and Mandun (prisoner) our Jemadar, consulting together, agreed that the two bands should unite, and act conjointly. We accordingly left Baroda together; and after traversing different parts of Guzerat, returned to Baroda, empty-handed. A day or so after our return to Baroda, Oomrao Singh Jemadar (prisoner), Makhun Jemadar (prisoner), and Ruttyram Jemadar, with their bands, arrived: and the day after that, the Brahmin, with his band, set out on his return to Hindostan. We, having hitherto been unsuccessful, determined to remain some time longer, and try our fortune in conjunction with the parties just arrived; and accordingly joined them. Our united bands, after this, left Baroda; and having obtained intelligence, from our scouts, of four travellers with property, we went in pursuit

of

of them; and coming up to them near an English cantonment, murdered them; but were much disappointed to find that they were only poor stone-cutters, without a rupee upon them; our scouts having been deceived by the bundles of tools which they carried. After this we returned to Baroda; where, after halting a day or two, it was determined that we should return to our homes. We accordingly left Baroda, and made a stage of about three or four cose, where a Hadjee (pilgrim) met with his fate at our hands. Our next act was the murder of two Besatties. After them, two men, whom I heard were Rutbans, and at a stage or two from that where the Rutbans met their fate, we fell in with one or two palanquin-bearers, with two women and a child, all of whom we murdered in the jungle, and took their property. After this, four Mussulmans, with Mynas, fell into our hands, and were murdered. It was, I think, at this stage where we halted a day, and settled a division of property: after which we resumed our route; and near to Rutlam effected our designs upon five merchants, who had become the object of them from the last stage or so.

"We passed Rutlam, few or none of us entering the town; and stopped near a village to the north of it, at a byragee's shrine, where we made a good meal, having killed three sheep for the purpose. Having finished our meal, we again took the road, without resting;

resting; and halted at a village to the west of Jawrah, having, to avoid that place, struck off the high road. On our second stage from this, we passed a large town (Mundesore) on the bank of a river, without stopping, after purchasing ata, ghee, &c. for our meal at the end of the day's journey; and halted at a bowlee, where there was a large birtree on the road side, and near a village, the gate or door of which was of red colour. Here a traveller, a Mussulman I believe, who, I was told, was a Telinga, fell into our hands, and was murdered. He had a tattoo, which we set loose; but besides this, I understood that little or nothing was found upon him. On our journey next morning, Jemadar Ruttyram, with twenty or thirty men, was sent in charge of some tattoos laden with plunder, to our country in Hindostan; while we proceeded, by Neemuch and Mewar, and that route, in order to pick up more. A few cose beyond Neemuch, four travellers, apparently Poorbies (soldiers from the Ganges), fell into our power, and were there murdered. Of the amount or description of property acquired on this occasion I am unable to speak. Beyond this two or three stages, at a village called Gongar, a spirit-dealer, who was proceeding, I heard, to Cawnpore, was murdered, and stripped of his property. A few Kuldar rupees were found upon him; and a hoondee, which was burnt. A small hooka belonging to him fell into my hands, and

and is now in my possession. About twelve cose further, at the village of Sanganour, where we halted, we formed an acquaintance with four travellers, apparently shopkeepers; and though we had prevailed upon them to join our company, no proper opportunity offered that night for executing our designs upon them. Our purpose, however, was effected, as they accompanied us on the journey early next morning; and their clothes and property fell into our hands; but of what these consisted, I am ignorant. Our apprehension following a day or two after this, no further act was committed by us."

On being cross examined, this deponent said:— "There may have been other acts of murder and robbery committed by the gang in custody, since we left our country on the present expedition, besides those above mentioned. I have unreservedly disclosed all of which I have any knowledge, and according to the recollection I have of them. The present is the second expedition that has been made by the Phansigars, and in which I have been, since I joined them. The first took place immediately after the rains preceding the last (after the rains of 1826), and proceeded to the Deccan. We passed through Kandeish; visited Aurungabad, Poonah, and Hydrabad; and, after traversing those quarters, returned with considerable plunder, acquired by the perpetration of acts similar to those committed on the present expedition. I can point out

out the spots where most of the above-mentioned murders were committed, particularly those more recently perpetrated, as being more fresh in my recollection. My connection with the Phansigars arose from the marriage of my two daughters with Bhuggy and Nuggoo, two of the gang, and brothers of Heira, alias Ruttyram, one of the Jemadars. Bhuggy was one of those who was detached with Ruttyram. Nuggoo did not accompany us; but remained at home, to attend to the cultivation of some land. I can identify the persons of the whole of the prisoners, and speak to the offices which many of them usually perform in the gang; also the names by which many of them are known: but, as it is frequently the case that one person uses different names, individuals may be known to me by one name, and to others by a different one. I do not know the proper name of the Brahmin leader of the gang we found at Baroda, on our arrival there; but, as well as I recollect, he was generally called Lala:—some of his band remained behind, with us. The band I belonged to, that is Mandun's band, is a branch of the gangs of Oomrao and Makhun, who are the principal leaders of the Thugs from the countries about Jhansy, Dhuttea, Sumptre, Puphon, Palir, and other quarters in Bundelcund. I cannot speak as to the exact number of Thugs which they could collect; but, from what I have seen during two years that I have been

been associated with them, 200 is about the number that has proceeded each season on predatory excursions. These have separated into smaller parties, and set out on their excursions at different intervals; uniting again when they meet, or keeping separate, as it may be considered advisable.

"I am a Mussulman; am about fifty years of age; and, before I joined the Thugs, followed the occupation of elephant-keeper, in the service of the Raja of Jhalone. In Jhalone I lived for many years, but am a native of Singy Rampoora. Mundesore is the name of the large town we passed; and, without stopping, proceeded four or five cose further, to a large bir-tree and well, where a traveller fell into our hands and was murdered. I did not, at the time, know the name of the town, having never before been in this quarter; but have since learnt it. This murder was the first, as far as I am aware, that was committed after that of the merchant and his attendants, to the southward of Rutlam. As on the present, I belonged on the former excursion to Oomrao's gang, which then left Bundelcund a few days before Makhun set out with his. Our course, on that occasion, was directed to the Deccan; and we arrived in that quarter before any thing considerable fell into our hands. On the way, several acts were perpetrated, as well on the persons of single travellers as small parties of two or three, but all yielding trifling advantage:

advantage: but in the Deccan, information was brought, by our spies, of treasure passing through the country, on Angriahs; which induced Oomrao to take a select band of about thirty men, and go after it; directing the remainder of his gang to remain in the neighbourhood of the place where we then were, until he rejoined us. I was not with Oomrao on this occasion; but heard from the party, when he rejoined us, that they had made a long and expeditious march of about eighteen cose, before they came up with the Angriahs; that, after they met them, they soon succeeded in murdering them, and possessing themselves of the treasure concealed on their persons, which turned out to be a very large sum. It consisted of gold in bars, poollies, and mohurs; and amounted, as well as I remember, to about 20,000 rupees. Makhun Jemadar was in the same quarter at that time, and some of his men were present with Oomrao at the seizing of the treasure; but I remember there was some quarrelling about the division of it, from Makhun and his men not being allowed to share in equal proportion with Oomrao and his. I cannot say that Makhun himself was present. Mandun Jemàdar is only the leader of the gang I belong to, in conjunction with Heira Jemadar, who is, properly speaking, the principal. Heira escaped at the time we were apprehended at Dekhola."

Khaimraj,

Khaimraj, another accomplice admitted to give evidence, was a Hindoo of Lohar caste, and his age about fifty years. He said:—"I was seized in the month of Bysack last, by a party of horsemen, at the village of Dekhola in Mewar, along with my companions, who form the gang of Phansigars and Thugs now in confinement, of which gang I am one. The horsemen, when they came to us, said they were sent with orders to stop us, on information that we had opium; and that we must therefore return with them to Bheelwarah, to be searched. Deceived by this subterfuge (as we soon found it to be), we readily accompanied them to that town, without fear or apprehension of any mischance befalling us. In this, however, we were soon undeceived; for, shortly after our arrival at Bheelwarah, the horsemen openly accused us of being Phansigars; saying, that Captain Borthwick had received positive information to that effect, and they had, in consequence, been sent by that gentleman to take us into custody. The people of the place had previously joined in aid of the horsemen, to prevent our escape; and we had nothing for it, but to submit to our fate. Some individuals of the gang, taking alarm on the first appearance of the horsemen, ran off, and escaped; but with the exception of them, and a party of twenty-five or thirty, who were some time before sent, with the plunder we had then acquired, to find their way

way home by a more direct route than the main body intended to take, the whole of the individuals who for the last few months have formed this gang are now here in confinement. From Bheelwarah we were brought to Jowrah; the people of the town and villages on the way joining the horsemen, as they had done at that place; by which means we have been brought here in safe custody.

"It is not usual with persons of our character, when apprehended, to make disclosures from intimidation or the application of severities; and I should never have made confession had such a course been resorted to with me: indeed, I was firmly resolved to keep silent; but finding that two or three of my companions had already told all, and had pointed out the spots and bodies of the different individuals whom we had murdered during the last few days previous to our being seized, I considered it would be very foolish in me to abide by such a resolution, particularly when I found I might probably save my life by a full and true confession, while remaining silent would not avail me, or any of my companions, any thing. I therefore now come forward to disclose fully and truly all that I know regarding the Phansigars and Thugs, and what has been done by them since the time that I have belonged to them, as far as my knowledge and recollection of deeds and incidents will serve me.

"The

"The fact is, that the gang of Phansigars now in custody is composed of men from the Bundelcund quarter. Makhun Jemadar (prisoner), and his party, are inhabitants of Sillanee Punharee, in the purgunah of Sumptre. Oomrao Singh Jemadar (prisoner), and his party, come from the village Mullaitra, purgunah Palir, and different villages in that purgunah. Mandun, another Jemadar (prisoner), and his party, all Mussulmans, come from the village Mote and thereabouts, in the Jhansee purgunah. My immediate superior, Brikbhan Dufadar, also comes from the village Mote. I am an inhabitant of Mullaitra; and for the last four years have been on intimate footing with Oomrao Singh and his party; but it was not until the last year that I actually joined them, and accompanied them on the present excursion. Previous to setting out upon it, Makhun Jemadar, and Dirkpal Subahdar (the leader of another gang), with their gangs or parties, together with Oomrao Singh's party, assembled at Oomrao's residence at Mullaitra and the neighbourhood; when Dirkpal and Mandun Jemadar, with their gang, that is, the Brahmin and Mussulman gangs, as their parties were usually designated, preceded Oomrao Singh and Makhun fifteen or twenty days, when the latter followed with theirs. To these parties I belonged; but more properly to that of Oomrao Singh. Of their acts and proceedings, therefore, all in which they have

have been concerned since I have been associated with them, I speak from personal knowledge. Our first stage from Mullaitra was three cose near to Jhandee; the next, ten or twelve; the third about the same to the Khar ghaut. Three stages more brought us to Seronge; where, on the night of our arrival, we murdered a traveller who had taken up his quarters at the same place that we did, namely, the Pundwankee Bowlee. The next morning we continued our journey, without doing any thing. The stage following, about the middle of it, we came to a river; where we found four Sepoys cooking their meal, whom, after making arrangements for the purpose, we murdered, and possessed ourselves of their property: this occupied some time, and was not effected without difficulty. When the Sepoys saw us, they seemed to have entertained suspicion of us; for having, in a hurried manner, got through their meal, they quickly commenced their journey, and stopped at a village a short distance from the river, where our spies followed them, and saw them fairly lodged. We halted at another village, at a short distance from the one they were at; and at night sent a select party to effect our object. The Sepoys commenced their journey the next morning, followed by our party, who, watching their opportunity, when at a distance from any village, fell upon them, and murdered them as they were going along the road: one of the Sepoys, who must at at the moment have perceived the design of the party, from his extraordinary efforts to save his life, got away a few paces, and raised his spear in his defence; but he was instantly overpowered, and murdered also. Two thousand rupees was the amount of plunder obtained on this occasion.

"The same stage, and as we were resting at no distance from where the Sepoys had just met their fate, (having come up with the party who had effected that deed,) a party of four Rasdharies (strolling actors) joined us. We spoke kindly to them, promising to hear their Ras at our halting-place, and to give them a rupee for their performance: they were persuaded to accompany and take up their quarters at the same place we did, a well-known temple and bowlee near to Bhopaul; where, at night, we murdered them, and plundered them of all they had, which was something about forty or fifty rupees. There is a meerdung (drum) among the things which were found in our possession, when we were seized by the horsemen, which belonged to these Rasdharies.

"After this, our next stage was to the Powa Nullah, a short distance from Bhopaul, where we made a division of the plunder which we had acquired: and after having settled each person's share, we sent four of our comrades to our country with what remained surplus to our immediate necessities, and settled that they should rejoin us somewhere in in the neighbourhood of Indore. The next morning, about a cose on our way, we met a gang of fellow-Phansigars, returning to Bundelcund from an excursion which they had set out upon two or three months before: they were chiefly Mussulmans, and between twenty and twenty-five in number. When we met them, they were following two water-carriers with a bullock, whom they had formed designs upon. For the sake of friendship, and to admit us to share in the booty that might be acquired from the water-carriers, they invited some of our men to join them. Accordingly, Oomrao Singh sent four men with them; who rejoined us the third or fourth day afterwards, bringing with them, as our share of the plunder, a tuslah or brass-pot, a saree, and the bullock, all which was given over to Oomrao. We were now four or five short stages to the west of Bhopaul. When preparing to leave the village we had halted at during the night, two Brahmins arrived, who had come from the Poonah quarter, and were going, they said, to Hindostan. Finding, by our spies, that they had property, we pretended that we were also going to Hindostan, and prevailed upon them to join our company and go along with us. They accordingly put up with us outside of the village; and in the evening, taking the opportunity which then offered for accomplishing our purpose, we murdered them, and took their property; the amount

 of

of which I cannot exactly state, but some gold, and one or two hoondies, were found upon them: the latter were burnt.

"The next morning we left the place; and proceeded two stages without acquiring any thing. Our third stage was to Rugoghur (in the Dewass purgunah): we there took up our quarters, in a tope near the village. In the course of the day, our spies formed an acquaintance with a Subahdar of Telingies (Sepoys of the Company's army), who, with two Sepoys, had arrived there, and taken up their lodgings in the bazaar of the village. Our spies so imposed upon them, that they prevailed upon them to quit the bazaar, and encamp along with us outside. In the early part of the evening, a party of our people, appointed for the purpose, fell upon them, and murdered them. I cannot speak to the amount of money and property found upon them; but I saw two red jackets and two Sepoys' caps which belonged to them, besides a a pony (bay colour) now amongst those seized with us, and three bullocks, which fell into our hands. The Subahdar and the two Sepoys, we understood, had come from some cantonment, and were proceeding to Hindostan on leave. The caps and the jackets were burnt; and the bullocks disposed of, some days afterwards, in the bazaar at Dhar. A chatta which belonged to the Subahdar is amongst the things seized upon us, when we were apprehended.

hended. Here also, and on the same night on which we murdered the Subahdar and Sepoys, a man of the Kachee tribe, who had come from the cantonment of Mow, and taken up his quarters with us, was murdered, and his property plundered. Four rupees in money, a thalee, and a lotah, were found upon him. The tope, where all this was done, being, we thought, too near the village, we had the four murdered bodies conveyed a short distance, about a quarter of a cose, and buried.

"The next day we proceeded by the cantonment of Mow, but without stopping there, and halted near a village at a good distance from it: the name of the place I do not know, but remember we made the town of Dhar in four stages from Rugoghur. There, at Dhar, we remained three days, waiting for our friends who were absent; namely, the four who were sent from the Powa nullah, to convey to our homes the plunder we had then acquired. They, after an absence of about twenty or twenty-five days, rejoined us a few stages beyond Dhar; we having loitered about, and made short stages, to admit of their overtaking us. Besides them, four others were left behind with the bullocks we took from the Subahdar and Sepoys; who also at the same time joinied us, having, as I have already said, sold the bullocks in the Dhar market, after we left that town. From the time we left Rugoghur until we reached Dhar, we had done

 nothing:

nothing: but after our arrival there, a Mussulman, who came from Mow, on his way to Baroda, was persuaded to encamp at the tope, along with us. In the evening, or shortly after nightfall, he met with his fate at our hands, and was buried near the spot where he was murdered. Having, after a halt of three days, left Dhar for Baroda, we proceeded by short stages, until, as I have just said, our absent friends joined us; after which, we quickened our pace. At Bora Hutty, a place on our route, so called, we met a banker, attended by four Sepoys, with a pony and a bullock, on his way to Baroda. The Jemadars and all our people, by the most pointed attention and civility, cultivated the banker's acquaintance, as well as that of his attendants, the Sepoys, with a view to the success of our designs upon them: still, we had to proceed three or four stages in their company, before these were carried into execution. At length, an opportunity offering, he and his attendants were murdered, and their property plundered. The name of the place where this took place I do not remember; but the village had two or three shops, and a stream of water flowed past it. We set the banker's bullocks loose in the jungle; retaining the pony, which was with us until we arrived at Juwud (after our apprehension); where it was poisoned, through the fear that, being discovered in our possession, it might lead to our detection: for we understood, from the banker

banker and his attendants, that they came from Ougien or Indore, I forget which; and it was thought probable that some of their friends or relations, hearing of our apprehension, would come and recognise it.

"From the place where the banker and the Sepoys were murdered, three moderate stages, as well as I remember, brought us to Oodeypore, where the Rajah resides. Here we found a gentleman who was on his way to Mow from Bombay; and not relishing to be seen by him, we studiously kept out of his way. The next morning he proceeded on his way to Mow, accompanied by a number of travellers who had sought his protection; and we took the road to Baroda. At a village the fourth or fifth stage beyond Oodeypore, we met with Dirkpal Brahmin, with his gang, returning from Baroda. They passed the night with us; and the next morning continued their journey homewards, and we ours towards Baroda. We proceeded from this very leisurely, at the rate of little more than a cose or two daily. At Makney, we halted a little distance from the town; and it happened that five Telingies (Company's Sepoys), from Bombay, arrived there the same day. Our spies seeing them, brought them, after using much deceitful entreaty and many false pretences, to the spot where we were. In the evening, we murdered them, and took their property. I am not aware of all

all the more trifling articles of clothes and brass pots that were taken, but remember that seven small bars of gold, and some rupees, were found upon them. I do not remember the exact number of the rupees, but altogether it was considered a good productive job: one or two hoondies were also found upon them; and a pony, which they had, was set loose in the jungle. From Makney we proceeded, in the same manner as we had done for some days previous, slowly, and making short stages; and arrived at Dubhoy. About a cose from this town we met a Mussulman and Brahmin travelling together, who had come from Dhoolia Mallygaum. Our usual artifices were practised upon them with success: they halted for the day at the same place that we did; and in the evening, were murdered, and their property plundered. They had a pony laden with opium, besides some brass utensils and other articles of small value, all which fell into our hands. The opium we disposed of at Baroda, where we proceeded the next day, for 100 rupees; out of which we had to give the Cutwal twenty-five rupees *mahsool* on the sale. We here found eighteen Phansigars of the Mussulman gang, with their leaders, Mandun Jemadar (and Heira's, the former prisoner) and Amanoollah (evidence) &c., who had been with Dirkpal and his party, but, not satisfied with what they had got, remained behind to acquire more, and joined us.

"We

"We remained at Baroda three days; during which, Makhun Jemadar (prisoner) purchased different articles, clothes, &c., to the amount of about forty rupees. We afterwards proceeded on the Baroach road. For the first four or five days following our departure from Baroda, nothing fell into our hands. We were within seven cose of Baroach when the day of the Hooly festival arrived, which we celebrated with due festivity, making a halt for that purpose. At this place, three travellers, two Mussulmans and a Byragee, passing the place where we were, were seduced into our power, and murdered; but I do not now remember what amount or description of property was found upon them. From thence we struck off the Baroach road, and proceeded upon that of Joanuggur and Dwarka; and, leaving the highway, made several stages in the direction of these places, without falling in with any thing; in the course of which, several fordable salt-water inlets crossed our paths, and one which cost us five rupees to be ferried over. As I have just said, four or five stages had been performed without any thing falling into our hands; when one morning, as we arrived at Piblownd, to which town we had been steering our course, some of our spies, who had been absent on the look out, returned with accounts that they had seen four travellers proceeding to Baroda with considerable property; and they calculated that

that they would reach Baroda the same night, from the distance they were when our spies left them. On learning this, twenty-five men, the stoutest and most active of the gang, were selected, and sent in pursuit of them; the rest following as they were able;—and after a long and fatiguing march, the detached party overtook the objects of their pursuit, a short distance from a cantonment belonging to the English; and, after accompanying them a little way, fell upon and murdered them, as they were walking along the road. To the great disappointment and chagrin of us all, no property was found upon them; for they turned out to be common stone-cutters; and their tools, tied in bundles, which they carried over their shoulders, deceived the spies into the supposition that they were carrying treasure.

"The next day, the principal part of the gang that was behind joined the party detached on this job, when we all took the road for Baroda. At one of our stages, and near where we had stopped for the day, some horse-dealers came with horses, and took up their quarters. At night, we held a consultation to murder them and seize their property; which we were only deterred from doing (though there were fifteen or sixteen, including attendants) by the difficulty of disposing of the bodies of so many men in an open and frequented country, such as it was where we were. In devising

devising plans to get over this difficulty, so much of the night had passed that we considered it advisable to forego our designs upon this party. The same night, thieves came amongst us, and carried off clothes and other things from Makhun Jemadar (prisoner). From this we proceeded to Baroda; and, after remaining there a day or two, set out on our return to Hindostan. At the distance of about three cose from Baroda, three travellers fell into our hands and were murdered: I do not remember what property was found upon them. Our next stage was to within a short distance of the town of Dubhoy, where four men, Bessaties (pedlars), with three ponies and their packs of wares, whom we had overtaken on the road, were prevailed upon to take up their quarters with us. In the evening, they were murdered and plundered: their wares consisted of various articles of trifling value; amongst which were a quantity of cornelian-stones cut into different forms, serrotes (betel-nut cutters, coarse scissors), &c. &c.; and in money, something about ten or twenty rupees were found upon them. At this place, also, our spies brought three men to our resting-place, whom they had enticed to come and take up their quarters with us; one a Byragee, and the other two having the appearance of Mussulmans. They likewise were murdered; and their bodies stripped of what was upon them, and buried. The next day we left Dubhoy, and met six palan-

quin-

quin-bearers, who had been in service at Baroda, and were proceeding to their country in Hindostan: with them were two women and two children, in all ten persons. We persuaded them to join us, and they accordingly proceeded along with us. At the first stage they took up their quarters in an old temple in the village, by which circumstance we were then prevented from effecting our purpose upon them: on the way the next morning, in the jungle, it was accomplished: the whole were murdered, and their bodies, after being stripped of every thing, were buried a short distance from the road. On this occasion, more previous arrangement was thought necessary than was usual, where the victims were fewer in number, and as it was resolved to despatch them on the journey while they were walking along in our company: accordingly, some of the most expert hands at the business were fixed upon to despatch them; and a party, whose business it was in the gang, was sent on before, to prepare graves at a convenient spot for the bodies. A pony, and pony mare, belonging to them, fell into our hands; also some ornaments of base metal were taken off the legs of the women, with neck and other similar ornaments of small value: besides, other articles were found upon them, which I cannot now specify. From thence we proceeded to our ground on the banks of a river, I think the Mhye; and encamped, in four separate parties,

parties, near to a village called Futtehpore. Here it happened, that four Mussulman travellers, from Bombay, on their way to Bhopaul, arrived, and halted near one of our parties (that which had its place under a kurney-tree): communication was immediately opened with the travellers, and an acquaintance soon formed, which terminated in their being murdered in the evening, and their property plundered. They had five minahs in a cage, and four ponies, which, with their clothes and other things, we took possession of.

"From thence our stage was Oodeypore; where we met a number of hackeries from Mow, laden with opium, and escorted by Telingies (Company's Sepoys). One of the Telingies remarked, on seeing us, that persons of the same description in appearance had been seized at the cantonment: this being made known amongst us, threw us into some apprehension; and we took up our halting-ground at a retired spot in the jungle, near a fountain of water. A party of horsemen from Baroda, with some Sepoys and a Zenana meeana (palanquin), arrived, and took up their quarters for the day in the bazaar, where the prisoner, Makhun Jemadar, happened to be sitting at the time. One of the horsemen, observing him rather attentively, remarked to one of his companions standing by him, that 'the Mala (necklace) upon that man,' pointing to Makhun, appeared to be exactly the same as belonged

belonged to his brother. This so disconcerted Makhun at the time, though the horseman did not follow up his remark by any question, that he immediately slipped off;—and, on hearing from him what had occurred, we were all thrown into such alarm, that early the same night we started, and proceeded many cose on the Jhabooa road before we thought it safe to halt. We afterwards continued our progress, and arrived at Jhabooa; from whence Oomrao and Ruttyram separated from Makhun, and preceded him a short distance on the Rutlam road. Their first stage, after leaving Jhabooa, was Pitlawud; and Makhun, with his gang, was in their rear a few cose. The next day they quitted Pitlawud; and Makhun, with our party, halted there. We took up our quarters at a bowlee outside of the town, near which we found a merchant with four attendants preparing their meal. The merchant, from his respectable appearance, his dress, and the ornaments he wore, became the object of our attention and design; but having hastily finished his meal, he and attendants set out, in prosecution of their journey, towards Rutlam, and we saw nothing more of them; but we afterwards found that they had fallen into the hands of Oomrao and Ruttyram. From Pitlawud we proceeded to the vicinity of Rutlam, encamping a little distance from the town. We there met some of the men of the advanced parties, who told us that they

they had despatched the merchant and his attendants a few cose from Rutlam, and that they had proved a rich prize: to which Makhun replied, in a dissatisfied tone, that good luck seemed to attend where the Mussulmans were. From Rutlam we took the Peeplodah road, with the view to avoid Jawrah. Oomrao also deviated a little from the Jawrah road; and met us at Dhodur, the stage on the high road beyond Jawrah; and we afterwards proceeded together. On our way, hereabouts, we were searched once or twice for opium; but none being found upon us, we were allowed to proceed without further molestation. It was at Dhodur that some slight misunderstanding that subsisted between Oomrao and Ruttyram was reconciled, and things went on as usual. Our stage from Dhodur was to a convenient spot, where we halted for the night. We next day passed Mundesore; and, proceeding about four or five cose further, halted near a village, under a large spreading bir-tree, and where there is a Nagora, kept by a Fakeer who resides there. A Mussulman traveller here fell into our hands, and was murdered during the night, in the early part of it; and buried a little distance from the road, on the banks of a nullah. The next morning we resumed our journey; and having proceeded a cose or so, we sat down at a well; where, after some consultation, it was determined to send Ruttyram, with twenty or twenty-five men, by the most

most direct route, to our country, with the plunder which we had acquired. Ruttyram accordingly here left us; and the next morning we took the Neemuch road. Our stage was about a cose or two on the other side (north side) of the cantonment, where we halted a day. On this day, four travellers were enticed by our spies to rest themselves at the spot where we were; when, an opportunity offering, they were murdered, and their property plundered. A stage or two beyond this, another traveller fell into our hands, and was murdered: and near the village of Sanganeer four shopkeepers were murdered. Of this last act I was informed by my companions; not having been present when it was committed. Nothing further occurred until we arrived at Dekollah; where, as I have already stated, we were arrested."

On cross-examination, this witness said:—

"I know of no other act of murder and robbery committed by the Thugs, besides those I have stated above.

"This is the first time that I have accompanied the Thugs on any of their predatory excursions. Brikbhan persuaded me to do so. I have frequently heard them, since I have been amongst them, talk of the acts committed by them on former excursions, but can only speak of my own knowledge of those I have above detailed. My occupation among them has been to watch at night against theft, and

also

also to keep a look out when murders were being perpetrated. Old men like myself were generally employed in this way: beyond this, I never took any part in the commission of the murders."

Another of these worthies was named Poorun. He was an old Hindoo, of Lohar caste. He deposed as follows:—

"My father was a cultivator in Buraicha and other villages in the neighbourhood; which occupation I also followed; but joined the Thugs when I was about thirty years of age, and have since continued to be more or less connected with them. I have not, however, accompanied them on every excursion they have, since that period, made; but, on the contrary, for intervals of two, three, and even six years, remained at home, and earned a subsistence by the cultivation of land. In short, I have been upon six predatory excursions altogether; four under a leader named Oodey Singh, since dead; and two (the present, and the one preceding it) with Makhun Jemadar (prisoner), to whose gang I belong. During one of the intervals above mentioned (the last) that I remained at home, I was apprehended at Jhalone on information of being a Thug, and was kept some time in confinement; but the proofs which I brought forward, of having for so many years been seen employed in cultivation, was the means of my regaining my liberty. This

This event, however, threw me into embarrassment; and to get rid of it, I went to Salany to borrow money from Makhun Jemadar, who, I knew, had generally some at command: but he would only agree to relieve my necessities on condition that I brought my family to Salany, and became one of his men; to which, from the destitute state my family was in, I was forced to agree: and I accordingly joined his gang, and, as I have already stated, accompanied him on the present and preceding excursions. Oodey Singh, my former leader, was beyond the prime of life: when I joined him, he was, however, an active and enterprising man; but his becoming, in due course, less fit for exertion such as his situation required, and his son Koman having been seized with other Thugs and thrown into confinement at Jubulpore, affected Oodey Singh so much, that he completely renounced the habit of a Thug, and shortly after died.

"After this, I joined Makhun. It was before the establishment of tranquillity over the country that I served under Oodey Singh; at which time our excursions were neither carried to so great a distance as they have since been, nor were so lucrative or certain; for in those days, travellers, particularly with much property, seldom ventured to go from one place to another without being well escorted, or in large parties; and we feared the Pindaries, and other mounted plunderers, as much

as

as other classes did, not connected with them. According to my engagement with Makhun, I joined his gang; and set out with him on an excursion to the Deccan, about three months after I had engaged myself to him. His gang, on this occasion, consisted of about forty men; and set out from Bundelcund in the month of Phagoon Sumbut 1883 (about March 1826), proceeding by regular stages; crossed the Nurbudda at the Cheepanair Ghaut, where we fell in with Chotee Jemadar (Brahmin), who joined us with his gang, which was about the same strength as our own. We proceeded towards Mallygaon; and at Jhokur, near that cantonment, celebrated the Hooly: after which we resumed our progress, and reached Mallygaon, where we struck off by the Nassuck road, intending to turn from Nassuck to Poonah and Aurungabad. After proceeding a cose or two on this road, we met a friend belonging to Oomrao and Ruttyram's gangs, a relation of Makhun's; who told us that these two leaders, with their gangs, were close at hand, on the Poonah road, in pursuit of some Augriahs with treasure. It was proposed to Makhun to send a party of his men to join them, in order to be entitled to a share in the spoil: and he thought of going himself; but recollecting that Oomrao and he were not on good terms, he sent twenty-five men with Chotee Jemadar. The next day we received a message from them, that they

 had

had effected the business; and they were going on with Oomrao and Ruttyram to Bhoranpoor, where they requested we would meet them. We accordingly proceeded to that quarter; and found Chotee Jemadar with the party at Bhoranpoor, Oomrao and Ruttyram having proceeded to their homes before we arrived. From them we learnt, that the Augriahs were attacked and murdered near Jhokur, where we had celebrated the Hooly; and that no less a sum than 22,000 rupees was found upon their persons, in gold, bullion, mohurs, and pootlies; and that, as the share of our two gangs, they had received 6000. This sum was immediately disposed of; so far, that Makhun received 2000 of it for himself and his gang, and a similar sum was given to Chotee Jemadar for himself and his gang: these two sums was despatched to our homes. That sent by Chotee reached in safety; but one of Makhun's men, who went in charge of our share, having got drunk at Jansy, blabbed out the secret that he was a Thug, and with others was returning with large amount of plunder; upon which the Sircar there had him and his comrades seized, and the money taken from them. The remainder of the prize, namely, 2000 rupees, was retained for the expenses of the two gangs. After this disposal of the share of the plunder acquired from the Augriahs (which was allotted by Oomrao and his brother Ruttyram to our two gangs), we left Bhoranpoor, and

and proceeded to Aurungabad; but meeting with little or no success, we returned, by Dhoolia and Bhopaul, to Bundelcund, and arrived at our different homes before the rains set in. About four months or so after the termination of the rainy season, in the beginning of the month of Mah, Makhun's gang having been again assembled, set out on an excursion towards Guzerat, and were accompanied by Oomrao and his brother Ruttyram, with their gangs.

"Such acts as those above mentioned being of too common occurrence, with people of our habits, to make much impression upon me or any of my associates who had long been familiar with them, or to excite a curiosity among us to inquire into the particular circumstances attending the acquisition of plunder by parties detached from the main body, it therefore cannot be a matter of any surprise if some of the murders and robberies committed may have escaped my recollection, or of which I have no particular knowledge; but I have without reserve stated all that my memory serves me to mention, with every circumstance attending them. I have never, since I have belonged to the Thugs, known one single instance of robbery committed by them without the previous destruction of life, almost invariably by strangulation. This is effected either by means of a roomal, or shred of cloth well twisted and wetted; or merely by the hands: though the latter is rarely practised, and only had recourse to from accidental failure in the former and usual mode. On a preconcerted signal being given, the victim or victims are instantly overpowered; and the perpetration, whether by the roomal or hands only, is the business of a moment. In perpetrating murder, it is an invariable point with the Thugs to avoid spilling the blood of their victims, but, if possible, to take their lives by suffocation. This point is attended to with a view to leave no traces of murder, by which suspicion of the deed might be excited in the minds of the people passing the spot, and detection ensue. In the hurry, however, in which it is necessary sometimes to dispose of the bodies, the holes are frequently not dug to such dimensions as to contain them in a whole state, particularly when there is a good number to be disposed of: the bodies are cut into pieces, and closely packed in them. When these holes are near the side of a road, which is generally the case, and especially when in an open and exposed spot, after they are filled up with earth, fires are burnt over them, in order to remove all appearance of the earth being newly turned. Murders, in the manner I have just described, are with equal facility and certainty accomplished, and are as frequently perpetrated, while the victims are walking along the road, as when they have been enticed to our places of encampment for the purpose, and, unconscious

scious of what is to befall them,.are sitting amongst us with every thing carefully and leisurely arranged for their destruction. These murders are frequently perpetrated contiguous to villages, where we encamp and have enticed strangers to take up their quarters with us: they take place generally before the twilight is completely over and night has set in; and always while the business is going on, the hand-drum is beat, and singing commenced, to drown any noise that might be made by the victims. The different persons actually engaged, commence their operations simultaneously, and by signal given; which of course is preconcerted, but at the same time quite arbitrary: generally, a common coarse expression is made use of, not likely to strike the attention of the victims, such as, 'Tumbakoo lao' (Bring tobacco). A roomal, or shred of cloth twisted on the occasion, is the only implement which the Thugs use for strangling. I have never seen the phansee, or noose made of cord, used; though I am well aware of the general supposition that it is by such an implement people are strangled by us: but if such an implement had ever been in use, of which I have great doubt, it has long since been laid aside; for the obvious reason, that, on any incidental occasion of being seized, it would inevitably lead to detection.—Oomrao, Makhun, and all the other Jemadars or leaders, keep up a direct understanding with the local authorities in Bundelcund,

cund, in whose limits they and their followers reside: and invariably, on their return from an excursion, conciliate their forbearance and favour by suitable Nuzzeranas. Assistance and support from English Authorities being likewise indispensable, these are, through artifice, also obtained. The Jemadars and leaders have no direct intercourse, themselves, in this instance, but through the medium of emissaries; who, by misrepresentation and falsehood, frequently contrive to extricate them from the difficulties which persons of our habits are constantly liable to be involved in. A relation of Oomrao's, named Motee, and a person named Lala Barber, an inhabitant of Secondra in Cawnpore, render important services in this way. Motee, who was formerly a practical Thug, has discontinued for some years going on predatory excursions. He first brought himself into notice with the gentlemen, by informing against a gang; which, in consequence, was seized and confined at Jubulpore, where I believe the greater part still remains. Motee has ever since advanced in the favour of the gentlemen, making them suppose that he acts as a check upon the Thugs and other plunderers; at least, he makes all this appear to us to be the case; and, in consequence, exercises great influence over us, making us pay well for his connivance, and the good offices he no doubt frequently performs in our behalf. Oomrao, Ruttyram, Heïra, Mandun, and

and their gangs, are those for whom he more especially exerts himself to protect and assist.

"Lala Barber is the patron of Makhun; and by means of representations to different persons of his acquaintance, in the service of the Adawlut at Cawnpore, he renders great assistance to Makhun, in getting him through matters of difficulty. Makhun, when he returned to Bundelcund from the excursion preceding the present one, after ascertaining the mishap that befel the share of plunder he sent from Bhoranpoor, had, as was usual with him in similar cases, recourse to his patron, Lala Barber. Lala lost no time in waiting upon his friend Mahdee Moonshee at Cawnpore; to whom he represented matters in such a light, that the Moonshee wrote himself, or had an injunction written by his superiors, to the Jhansee Rajah, saying, that it having been made known that he (the Rajah) had seized four travellers passing through his boundaries and plundered them of their property, the persons so treated being of respectable and inoffensive character, he was directed to set them at liberty, and restore to them the property he had taken from them. A day or two before the receipt of this letter of injunction, the Rajah released Makhun's men; having, in the first instance, made them give him an acquittance for money he had taken from them: but now, thinking, that as the matter had come to the knowledge of the English, he should get

get a bad name with them, and also lose the money, unless he could prove that the men he had taken it from were Thugs and that their true character had been misrepresented, he (the Rajah) sent after them, and had them again apprehended. I do not know what afterwards became of those men of Makhun's, or what was the final result of the business. Besides Lala Barber, who manages matters in his favour through his acquaintances at the Courts and Cutcherries at Cawnpore, Etawah, Humeerpoor, Auria, and Mynpoor, Makhun has a great friend and supporter in the Jhansee Vakeel who resides at Hummeepoorah, named Gunesh Lall. Oomrao may have other patrons besides his relation Motee, who watches over his interests principally at Jubulpore. Makay Sahib, at Kytah, is a great friend of Motee's; and it was from him that he obtained the English pass which Oomrao shewed to the horsemen, when we were apprehended at Dekhola. In passing through a country, so great a number of men together, as our gangs sometimes present, is certainly calculated to excite suspicion; but when this happens to be the case, we are always prepared with some story or explanation, to ward it off. Few of us carry arms: perhaps, among fifteen or twenty persons, two or three swords may be found, but not more.

"When Thugs meet, though strangers, there is something in their manner that soon discovers itself

itself to each other: and to assure the surmise thus excited, one exclaims, 'Ally Khan'; which, on being repeated by the other party, a recognition of each other's habits takes place, but this is never followed by a disclosure of past acts. We do use certain terms to distinguish particular circumstances and events connected with our proceedings, which are known to ourselves alone. These terms are known to all persons of similar habits to ourselves, as well to the Thugs of the Deccan, of the Nagpore country, of Malwa, of Kaunthul and Bagor, &c., as to those of Bundelcund and Gwalior. The numbers apply exclusively to travellers, and are used to communicate the number that fall into the hands of detached parties in pursuit of them. I believe there are few countries that do not produce Thugs: those I have just particularized did, I know, contain them; and do so, I believe, at the present moment. In the Oomrautee quarter there is a gang called Nasir Khan's Karoo or gang, a well-known Thug leader; but whether he is still the leader of it, I cannot exactly say. In Kaunthul and Bagor, Makeema and Dulla were formerly the Thug leaders; but who these are at present I do not know. The names of the leaders of the Malwa Thugs, or of those of the Nagpore country, I am ignorant of.

" In the division of plunder, the Jemadars, or principal leaders, receive seven and a half per cent, besides sharing equally with the rest of the gang; but

but before any division whatever is made to the leaders or their men, one of the principal of the former alienates a certain part, greater or smaller in proportion to the amount acquired, which is devoted to Bhowany, our tutelar deity. This, however, does not generally apply to clothes, or plunder of that description; indeed, it almost entirely refers to money in gold or silver: for when it consists of diamonds or pearls, the leader draws blood from his hands; and having sprinkled a little of it over them, the sanction of the deity to a division is thereby considered to be obtained, without any other alienation. But the omission of this ceremony, or neglecting, when success attends us, to propitiate a continuance of Bhowany's favour, by laying aside a part of our acquisitions to be appropriated to her service, would, we firmly conceive, bring heavy misfortunes upon us. The office of strangler in these gangs is never allowed to be self-assumed; but is conferred, with due ceremony, after the fitness of the candidate, in point of firmness, bodily strength, and activity, has been ascertained, and a sufficient degree of expertness in the use of the roomal, or long shred of cloth used for the purpose of strangling, has been acquired, by long sham practice of the process among one another.

"When thus qualified, the person on whom the office is to be conferred proceeds to the fields, conducted by his Gooroo, previously selected, who

carries

carries with him the roomal or shred of cloth; and anxiously looking out for some favourable omen, such as the chirping of certain birds, or their flight past the right hand, he knots the roomal the moment that either occurs, and delivers it to the candidate, imploring success upon him. After this, they return, and the ceremony is closed by a feast, or distribution of sweetmeats. It is the seniors only who confer this office; generally, old Thugs held in some estimation, but who from the infirmities of age have ceased to accompany the gangs on their expeditions, and who receive their chief support from the voluntary contributions of those on whom they have conferred the privilege of using the roomal."

The barber, who is so important a personage in the last narrative, met his deserts, having been executed at Jubulpore in 1835.

The Instructions of the Supreme Government, conveyed to the President at Indore in reference to the above proceedings, contained the following passages:—

"Captain Borthwick is considered to merit great praise, for the seizure of so large a gang of those atrocious criminals, and for the full and satisfactory evidence which he has obtained of their guilt. The depositions of Amanoolla, and the other four accomplices who came forward on the promise of pardon,

pardon, afford the strongest proof of the whole of the prisoners belonging to the gang, and of the numerous murders committed by them, in the course of their progress through the several countries which were the scene of their depredations. The discovery of the dead bodies in the places pointed out by Amanoolla, and the production and identification of some of the property found in the possession of the gang, as detailed in the proceedings held by Captain Borthwick, confirm the depositions of the five evidences, and established the guilt of the parties beyond the possibility of doubt. His Lordship in Council observes, that one of the evidences, Khaim Rauj, has deposed to no less than seventy-one murders.

" These murders having been perpetrated in territories belonging to various Native Chiefs, and the perpetrators being inhabitants of various districts belonging to different authorities, there is no Chief in particular to whom we could deliver them up for punishment, as their Sovereign, or as the Prince of the territory in which the crime had been committed.

" The hand of these inhuman monsters being against every one, and there being no country within the range of their annual excursions from Bundelcund to Guzerat, in which they have not committed murder, it appears to his Lordship in Council, that they may be considered like pirates,

to

to be placed without the pale of social law, and be subjected to condign punishment by whatever Authority they may be seized and convicted.

"Under this view of the case, and adverting to the relative situation of the British Government as the paramount power, the Governor General in Council has no hesitation in authorising and directing capital punishment to be inflicted on the leaders, and all the gang who shall be proved to have been employed as the stranglers. With regard to those who aided in decoying and enticing the victims to their fate, or to remove and conceal the bodies, they must be held to be accessaries both before and after the fact; they are equally criminal as the principals, and deserving the same punishment of death: but his Lordship in Council authorises you to commute the sentence of capital punishment into transportation for life, with hard labour, beyond seas, or confinement for a certain term of years, according to the circumstances of each particular case. Such of the prisoners as have acted merely as followers of the gang, employed in the performance of menial duties, such as syces or grass-cutters, and did not, as accomplices, share in the plunder; and boys, also, under fourteen years of age, of whom there are three or four amongst the prisoners; are to be kept in confinement for such periods as you may consider proper.

"His Lordship in Council conceives that much difficulty, with risk of escape, would attend the plan

plan suggested by you, of executing the individuals condemned to suffer death, each at his own village; and deems it more expedient that the whole, on whom capital punishment is to be inflicted, should be executed at the place where they are now confined. It will be proper to intimate to Holkar's Government the apprehension and conviction of the gang, and the orders which you have received for inflicting capital punishment on the murderers.

" Previously to deciding on the fate of each individual prisoner (seventy-four in number), the Governor-general in Council desire that you will instruct Captain Borthwick to call them up singly, in the order of enclosure No. 11 of Captain Borthwick's Letter, in which their defence is contained; and take the evidence of the five witnesses as to the identity of the individual, his degree of connection with the gang as leader, accomplice, or menial, and compare the evidence as given by each of those five approvers. Captain Borthwick will also hear whatever the prisoners may desire to offer further in their defence; and wherever a doubt may exist in his mind as to the fact of the party being one of the gang (notwithstanding the identification of one or more of the evidence), that individual is to have the benefit of the doubt, and his case to be reserved for further orders. In the deposition submitted with your despatch, the cases of the prisoners are not given in the same numerical order in each; and it becomes difficult, in some instances,

instances, to know whether the witness refers to one and the same individual.

"By the course of the proceedings now directed, the first prisoner to be identified, according to the list in enclosure No. 11, is Oomrao Singh. Each of the five witnesses should be called on in succession, and without the privity of one another, to identify and name him; and Captain Borthwick will keep a record of the proceedings, stating his own opinion regarding the establishment of the prisoner's guilt, and the punishment to which, with reference to the observation in a preceding part of this letter, the prisoner is subject. Captain Borthwick having completed these proceedings, will submit them to you; and you will pass final sentence on all those deserving of capital punishment, and direct it to be carried into execution. Those adjudged to transportation beyond seas, are to be sent, under a suitable escort, to Bombay; to be kept in custody there until the receipt of orders from hence, which will be sent without delay. The individuals who are to suffer temporary imprisonment will be retained where they now are; and you will receive the final instructions of Government on the receipt of your report, and Captain Borthwick's further proceedings as above directed.

"With respect to the five witnesses to whom Captain Borthwick promised pardon, it does not appear whether unconditional release, on the conviction

viction of their associates, was distinctly pledged to them or not. Considering the past course of life which these individuals, who have taken an active share in all the atrocities to which they depose, have led, his Lordship in Council feels extremely reluctant to let them again loose upon society, without security for their future good behaviour. If by pardon was only meant that their lives, which had been forfeited by their crimes, should be spared, they may be considered to be treated with great lenity if no severer punishment be inflicted than confinement until they can give good security: and you will be pleased to send them, under a guard, to the care of the Governor-General's Agent in Bundelcund; with whom you will arrange as to the time of their despatch, and the place where they may be delivered over to the escort which that officer may propose to send to the frontier of his jurisdiction, for the purpose of relieving the guard which may be sent from Mahidpore. The Agent to the Governor General will receive instructions regarding their disposal, until they can furnish such security as he may see proper to accept. You will apprise the five individuals of this decision, in order that they may know their destination, and adopt means for obtaining the security required."

Forty of the criminals were sentenced to death: the rest to transportation, or to imprisonment for various terms.

CHAP. XXII.

AMONG the persons whose information was instrumental in aiding the Government in suppressing Thuggee, was a leader named Inaent. The particulars of his capture are thus stated in a Letter, dated December 1829, addressed to Captain Sleeman, by Captain Oliver, 73d Regiment N. I.

"Having arrested, and placed in confinement, a man charged on suspicion of being the leader of a gang of Thugs, and having resolved to send him to Jubulpore to have the case investigated, I beg leave to report the circumstances under which he has been apprehended.

"Early on the morning of the 7th instant, when the regiment was on the march from Chaka to Sewagunje, two chuprassies of your establishment, named Doulut Singh and Dhun Singh, who are in company with the corps, suddenly came upon a party of about twenty-five men seated round a fire on the side of the road, who, from their appearance, they suspected to be Thugs; and, approaching near to them, this suspicion was confirmed,

 by

by their recognising among them a man whom they had formerly known to be a Thug. On the coming up of these chuprassies, this man made a signal to the party; upon which they dispersed, and ran into the jungle, which is close to the road. The chuprassies seized the man who made the signal; and although he attempted to draw his sword, and made a desperate effort to escape, they kept hold of him until the advanced guard came up, when he was secured. They also seized a tattoo (pony), which he attempted to mount on the party being surprised, and another tattoo belonging to another of the gang.

"The prisoner says his name is Sheikh Inaent; and describes himself to be an inhabitant of Bundelcund, and that he was proceeding to Jubulpore in search of employment; and denies that he was in company with any person at the time when the chuprassies seized him.

"The chuprassies, however, assert that he is a notorious murderer, and that they knew him as a Thug these several years ago; and they say that there are several men at Jubulpore who can confirm all they state regarding him.

"Under these circumstances, and as I have heard reports that several gangs of Thugs are supposed to be in the neighbourhood, I have thought it proper to detain him in custody; and shall send him to you to be examined. Thakur Bishun Singh

Singh has undertaken to provide a guard for his security; and he will proceed in progress to Jubulpore to-morrow.

"The prisoner having no money, and requiring subsistence, with his consent I directed his tattoo to be sold by auction. Sixteen rupees were obtained for it; which will be accounted for to you, when the prisoner is made over to you.

"The several effects found on the prisoner, and the second tattoo (of which he professes to know nothing), are sent with him. A list of them has been made out, and it is sent along with him."

The hero's own version of his apprehension has also been preserved. He says:—"After the Dusehra of 1829, several gangs united, from different points, at the village of Kohpa, between Jubulpore and Banda: about forty from the districts of Futtehgur and Cawnpore, under Rambuksh, Mihrban, and others; twelve under Bhola Buneea, from Jhalone, and twenty-five under myself, from Jhansee. We intended to operate that season upon the great road from Mirzapore to Jubulpore; and strike off to that between Saugor and Calpee, when necessary. We came on to Shahnugur; and there leaving the main body, I came on with Rambuksh, Bhola, and fifteen other Thugs, to the village of Pureyna, to search for *bunij*. Here we met two shopkeepers, two blacksmiths, and a Mussulman

 trooper,

trooper, on their way from the Deccan to the Dooab; and having won their confidence in the usual manner, we sent them on to our friends with four of our party, and a message to say that they would find them worth taking. At night we rejoined the main body, and found Dibba Jemadar entertaining the travellers. We set out the next morning, intending to put them to death on the road to Biseynee: but we found so many parties of Brinjaras, encamped, and moving along that road, that we could not manage it. The next morning we went on with them from Biseynee; and at a nullah in the jungle, three cose distant, we killed them, at about eight o'clock in the morning. The bodies were buried under some stones, where your people afterwards found them. We returned through Biseynee to Shahnugur; and thence came in upon the great road to Mirzapore, at the village of Sewagunje. In the evening, four travellers came up, on their way from Jubulpore to Banda, and were persuaded to pass the night with us on the bank of the tank. We were preparing to go on with them after the third watch, with the intention of killing them on the road, when we heard the *duheea* (the call or cry of the hare), a dreadful omen; and we let them go on, unmolested.

"Soon after, four sepoys of the 73d regiment came up, and sat down at the fire to warm themselves. The regiment was on its march from Jubulpore

Jubulpore to Banda, and the four sepoys were a little in advance of it. After some conversation, they went on; and we prepared to set out, having thrown into the fire some clothes and a churee (a painted stick, as a badge of office) belonging to the trooper whom we had murdered. While we were preparing, the two men whom you had sent on with the regiment, Dhun Singh and Doulut, came up, and sat down to warm themselves. We overheard Doulut say to Dhun Singh, 'This stick and these clothes must have belonged to murdered men; and these must be some of our old friends, and a large party of them': and both seemed to be alarmed at their situation, as they were then alone. I made a point of being the last off; and my brother, Sheikh Chund, who was lately hung, had already mounted his horse, and I had my foot in the stirrup, when they saw part of the advanced guard, and immediately made a rush at our bridles. We drew our swords; but it was too late. Chund Khan jumped off his horse, and made off. Both fell upon me, and I was secured. Had Doulut and Dhun Singh called out Thugs, the guard might have secured a great part of the gang; but they appeared to be panic struck, and unable to speak. By this time the regiment came up; and finding some of the remains of the trooper's clothes on the fire, the European officers found it difficult to prevent the sepoys from bayonetting me on the spot. I put

put on a bold face; and told them that they ought all to be ashamed of themselves, to allow a native gentleman to be thus insulted and maltreated on the high road; and that nothing but the dread of the same ruffianly treatment had made my friends run off and leave me. I had three brothers in that gang: they were all afterwards taken: two have been hung, and the third is here."

Bholea Buneea, a worthy coadjutor of Inaent, deposes thus:—

"Three and a half years ago, I joined Mehrban, Cheyn, Sheikh Inaent, Dibba, Sewdeen, Bhikka, and Nunha, Jemadars, with a gang of altogether eighty-five Thugs; and we reached the tank at Sewagunje, in the Myhir Jageer, where we passed the night. On the day we reached this place, the advance tents of a regiment, on its way from Jubulpore, were passing; and we consulted upon the propriety of quitting the road, and determined to do so. In the evening, two hours before dark, four Hindoo travellers came up, on their way from Jubulpore towards Bandah; and we invited them to encamp with us. One watch before daylight we were preparing to set out, and these four travellers with us, when we heard the voice of a hare; and this we took for a very bad omen, and allowed the travellers to pass on: their lives were saved in consequence. We remained there; and I and Sheikh

Sheikh Inaent were on our way to the bank of the tank near the village, when Rambuksh, the son of Runna, called out, and asked us to smoke. I returned to him alone, and sat down with him by the fire he had kindled to warm himself. Sheikh Inaent went on; and soon after four sentries came up, and sat down to warm themselves by the same fire, and soon after went on. One of them lost his regimental cap; and soon after they had gone, he came back, and asked me whether I had seen it. I said I had not; and he went back, on his road to Jubulpore, to search for it. After this, a gentleman (European) came upon horseback; and seeing a young monkey under a tree tied to a hackery, he ordered the driver to put it on the hackery; and the driver said that he got on and off when he liked; and the gentleman went on. The sun was now near rising, when Dhun Singh, approver, came up, and sat down to warm himself by the fire, with a spear in his hand: and immediately after him, Dowlut, approver, came up, and sat down to warm himself at the fire which the party of Mussulman Thugs had just left and gone on towards Belehree. He saw in the fire a black painted stick, which we had taken, three days before, from the five men whom we murdered at Biseynee on our way to Sewagunje, and the party of Mussulmans had torn up and thrown into the fire; and being such a stick as hurcaras commonly use, he concluded that

Thugs

Thugs had been there. He called to Dhun Singh to join him, but Dhun Singh told him to come to his fire; and he came, and they halted together; and we overheard them say, that we seemed a large gang of both Mussulmans and Hindoos; and though we did not personally know either of them, we concluded, from their discourse, that they were spies. By this time a great part of the gang had gone off, and the others were preparing to move, when Dibba the Buneea called out to Sheikh Inaent to move off. He replied, 'Go on, and I will follow.' On hearing this, the approvers rushed in upon Sheikh Inaent, and seized his horse by the bridle. He asked whether they were robbers; and while they were scuffling, the rest made off. Sheikh Chund, who was lately hung at Saugor, the brother of Sheikh Inaent, leaped from his horse as one of the approvers seized him by the bridle. and fled on foot. Sheikh Inaent was secured, and taken away. I, Chimma, and Omeda, ran off; and reached Guteearee in three days, travelling night and day. We rested there three days; and then went to our home, in Tirwa in Jhalone.

"Rambuksh, Dibba, and others, making a party of twenty-five Thugs, fled on the road to Mirzapore and Omurpatun; and in their flight, murdered the six Gosaens at Omurpatun. Three days afterwards, Bhikka and others, making a gang of twenty-five, took the road to Belehree in Jubulpore; and with seven

seven travellers whom they met there, they took the road to Biseynee, where they put them to death.

"When Rambuksh, Dibba, and others, went home after the affair of Omurpatun, I went to visit them in the village of Tirwa, in the pergunah of Phuppond, district Belha; and there I heard them relate the circumstances of that affair.

"The five men murdered at Biseynee were, a Mussulman trooper, from whom we got the stick, two blacksmiths, and two shopkeepers. Had the two approvers called out Thugs when we were running off, we must have been all taken; as the sepoys had come up, and there were many of the Myhire Rajah's horsemen present. They called out, and said 'the fowls had gone loose,' or something of that kind.

"The five travellers were from Hydrabad, on their way to Benares; and we fell in with them at the village of Pooreyneea, one cose and a quarter from Shahnugur, on the road to Belehree. I, Rambuksh, and Sheikh Inaent, with a party of two Thugs, had left Dibba and the rest of the gang at Shahnugur, when we met these men at Pooreyneea; and I sent back with them, Imanee, Dummee the son-in-law of Dibba, Bukshee, and another whose name I forget, with a message to Dibba to keep the travellers. They went to the Shahnugur, and Dibba went to his quarters; and we joined a little a little before night. We had come on to Poorey-neea in the hope of meeting some travellers of this kind. We passed the night at Shanugur, and in the morning set out with the travellers; and had sent on Bilhae, to choose a place to kill them at: but we found so many Brinjaras encamped along the road, that we could not manage it; and reached Biseynee, where some encamped on the bank of the tank, and others took up their quarters in the shops of the bazaar. In the morning we set out about sunrise; and three cose from Biseynee, at a nullah, Sheikh Inaent gave the *Jhirnee*, and they were seized and strangled by Mehrban, Dibba Cheyn, and Bhikka the son of Sunum Isuree; neither of whom is yet seized. Their bodies were buried under stones in the nullah; and we got from them 100 rupees in money, 400 rupees' worth of gota, besides clothes and brass pots. On a division, we got about five rupees each. The bodies were pointed out last year by Rambuksh, to Chunder Deen Subahdar's party. Chittooa got a mare in this affair: and she was taken from him by a sepoy of the Hadjegur Rajah, stationed at the village of Gonoura; as a pickpocket told him that Chittooa was a Thug, and he made off without his mare or pony. The nullah is about two cose and a half from Hoppa. No other village is near the place."

We have the testimony of several of the party, that

that they were not idle on their retreat. A man named Beekun Khan being asked, "What did you do after Inaent was taken," answered, "We Mussulmans of his gang took the road to Biseynee, through Belehree: the Dooab men went off on the road to Mirzapore; and Bhola and his party went to their homes. While we were resting at a village two cose on the other side of Belehree, in this district, two carriers of Ganges' water, two tailors, and a woman, came up, on their way to Banda; and having rested and taken some refreshments with us, they went on in our company to Shahnugur, where we passed the night: and the next day we went on together to Biseynee, where we fell in with two other travellers, on their way to Banda. These two men we found so poor, that we tried to get rid of them; as they might be some obstacle to our designs upon the five, and could yield us nothing. We tried to get off without waking them, but in vain: they got up; and we tried to persuade them that it was too soon for them to set out, but in vain. We then sent four of our party, with orders to take them along the high road; while we struck off on the bye-path by which we usually took our victims on that road. They soon after got alarmed, and insisted upon being taken to the main body, which they had seen strike off to the right. The four Thugs were obliged to consent, and they soon overtook us. It

It was now determined that they also should die; and six of our party were desired to attend them, and move on a little faster than the main body, to the nullah in the jungle where we usually killed people. We slackened our pace: and as soon as the six men reached the nullah, they put the two men to death, and concealed their bodies till we came up, when the other five persons were strangled; and the bodies of all seven were buried under the stones near the place where we had buried the five men whom we killed in our advance, and where we, the next year, killed the five Byragees and the sepoy. All these eighteen bodies I pointed out to Chunder Deen, subahdar of the 4th regiment, whom you sent with me from Saugor in 1832. From the two poor men we got only one rupee; but from the others we got 200; and in the division, Chund Khan and Dulele, who have been hung at Saugor, took the share of their brother Sheikh Inaent, who had been arrested by the 73d regiment."

The exploits of another portion—the Dooab men—are thus referred to by Captain Nicholson, in a Letter to Captain Sleeman:—

"I think it right to report to you, that six persons were last night murdered near this place, by a gang of Thugs.

"I heard of it on my arrival here this morning: and

and as it was not convenient for myself to go and inquire into the circumstances, I sent a man for the purpose. He has just returned; and states, that the bodies of six Gosaens were this morning found lying on the ground near a tank close to the road, about a cose to the north of the town. They had been stripped. Their long matted hair seemed to have been opened out and examined; and the only mark of violence apparent on the bodies was that of a string round the neck, with which they seemed to have been strangled. Some articles of clothes were found near; also a tattoo; and a bow and arrow, under one of the small drains that cross the new road.

"It is further stated, that last evening these poor wretches were seen to stop at the tank, in company with twelve persons, apparently Kauretties, or carriers of Ganges' water; and to them, some of the articles found near the tank are supposed to have belonged.

"The person who brought me this information called afterwards, by my desire, on the Cutwal of the town; and was informed that persons had been sent out in all directions in pursuit of the supposed murderers, but that no trace of them had been discovered. I also am informed, that immediate notice of the murder was sent to the Rewa Rajah, and his son Bulbudder Singh, under whom Omurpatun more immediately is."

A mem-

A member of the party here adverted to, says — "We did not rest till we had got thirty miles in advance of the regiment, on the Mirzapore road. We then halted, and spent the night at a small village; and were going on again the next morning, when we fell in with four Gosaens, a Brahmin, and a Rajpoot, on their way from Hydrabad to Mirzapore. They went on with us to Omurpatun in Rewa, whence we set out with them before daylight; and on reaching the place that had been chosen the evening before, they were all six strangled: it was about an hour before daylight. After we had examined the booty, and made the grave, we went to take up the bodies; but one of the six got up, and tried to run away: he had got off about 100 yards, when he was overtaken, and strangled again." Being asked if the victim did not call out; the witness said, "Yes; but he had been so much hurt in the neck the first time, that he could not be heard at any distance: and we had no sooner brought his body back, and put it down among the others, than we heard the servants of Captain Nicholson coming up. The Captain was coming from Mirzapore, and was to encamp that day at Omurpatun. As soon as we heard his servants coming up, we all made off, leaving the bodies unburied. A white pony, belonging to Esuree Jemadar, got loose, and ran toward the servants, who called out to know whose it was: and thinking they

they must come up before we could dispose of the bodies, we made off, and left the pony behind us. Whether they discovered the bodies or not, I do not know; but the people of the town must have seen them."

Rambuksh, another actor, thus testifies:—"Three years and a half ago, when Sheikh Inaent was taken at Sewagunje by Dowlut, approver, with the regiment of sepoys, I was with Mehrban and Dibba, Jemadars, and a gang of twenty-five Thugs of the Lhodie caste; and we fled on the road to Rewa, and reached a village under a hill ten cose from Sewagunje, where we rested. In the morning we left this place, and halted on the bank of a tank on the road to Myhur, and there dined; and about twelve o'clock, four Gosaens, and a Brahmin and a Rajpoot, came up, on their way from Hydrabad to Benares. The Jemadars went to them, and, in conversation, won their confidence; and we went on with them to Omurpatun, which we reached about four o'clock, and rested in the shops of the bazaar. We dined there; and some time after dark, we, after consultation, determined to kill these men, and to set out with them for that purpose after the third watch. We did so about a cose and a half from Omurpatun, under some mangoe-trees and mhowa-trees, which had been chosen by Budula. About an hour before daylight, we sat

sat down, on pretence of performing our ablutions; when Esuree gave the signal; and Heira, my nephew, Sumbhoo, Esuree, Mehrban, Dibba, and Pershaud, strangled these six men, while others held them down.

"These bodies were disposed of in some rising ground 200 yards from the place. Some gentleman's things were coming from Rewah; and a white pony, belonging to Esuree, got loose; and the people, with his property, asked whose it was. Upon that, we left the bodies exposed, and fled. We got from them two ponies, with some clothes upon them; and we went on with the booty to a village six cose distant, where we opened it; and found 150 rupees in money, and some gold beads, with 100 rupees' worth of silver, and eight selahs; two with gold lace, and six plain. We tied it up again; and went on with it to Tirwa in the Dooab, where we divided it; and each man got about twenty rupees. The whole amounted to about 900 rupees.

"The gang of Mussulmans took the road to Belehree after the seizure of Sheikh Inaent; and we did not meet again in the Dooab.

"On one of the Gosaens' heads the hair was long, but on the three it was cut off. The pony, Esuree let loose; and we never recovered it, nor did I learn who got it.

"When we were about to take up the bodies to bury

bury them, one got up, and attempted to run off; but he was pursued by Dibba, Kasee Lhodie, and Dooja, who seized him after he had gone a hundred paces; and Dibba strangled him. He could not make a noise, as his throat had been hurt in the attempt to strangle him before. As soon as we had placed his body with the other five, we saw the party of the gentlemen coming from Rewa approach, and made off. The people did not then see these bodies, but they were afterwards discovered.

The adventures of the rear of the destroyed band are related by an approver, named Zolfukar:—

"When Inaent was seized, I was with a gang of twenty-four Thugs at Shahnugur, coming up with the others. Mahommed Buksh was with another of seven, at Biseynee. Bhola Buneea, in his flight, came up, and told us of Inaent's arrest. We went, as fast as we could, through Saugor, towards Bhopaul; and at Sehora we fell in with Feringeea, coming from Bhopaul with a gang of forty Thugs. He returned with us; and we proceeded to Bhopaul without killing any person. From Bhopaul we retraced our steps towards Saugor; and at Omaree fell in with the Farsee and his servant, and two Buneeas, whom we killed. But before we killed them, we had fallen in with a gang of eighteen Lodhies from the Dooab; and having shared in the booty, they left us to operate upon the Seronge roads.

roads. We had also fallen in with Noor Khan Jemadar and his gang of seven men, and they also shared in the booty of the Farsee.

"After the Lodhies left us, we came on to Bhilsa; where we fell in with the three men and two women whom we killed near Manora—Ramdeen Sepoy of Bhopaul, and his mother, on their way home to Banda; a bearer, his wife and brother. Coming on to Baghrode, we fell in with two men; who told us that three of their companions had been plundered by robbers, and were behind. We came on to Bahadurpore with them, and killed them between that place and the village of Mirzapore. We had left people to detain the three who were coming up, as we thought they could have nothing left after the robbery. They asked after their two companions, and we told them that they were pushing on as fast as they could for Saugor.

"We now struck off upon the Hoshungabad road; and at Belehree met Mahommed Buksh's gang of seven Thugs; and went on to Raneepore, where we killed two men, and another at Kurheya Khera. Here, to our great surprise and consternation, my mare dropped a foal; and we all came under the *eetuk*, all contaminated alike. We separated, to return home. I, with a party of about thirty, came through Bishunkera, Bhopaul, Bhilsa, and Saugor, home."

From

From this period, misfortune seems to have attended the entire party—Feringeea attributing all to the neglect of omens. He says:—

"We were bathing at a river four cose this side of Bhilsa, when I heard, directly over my head, the *chireya*. I was much alarmed; and Kurhora, who is an excellent augur, told me that I ought to take the gang back, on the Gunge Basoda road, immediately, after so bad an omen; but I determined upon coming on towards Saugor, two cose to the village of Muree. On reaching this place, I tied my horse to a tree; and went into the village, to talk with the Puteel, leaving the gang near the horse. While talking with him, I heard a great uproar, and saw my horse running towards the village; and, on going to catch him, saw your Nujeebs seizing and binding my gang. There were forty, but they secured only twenty-eight. I made off as I was, half dressed, and got home; and twelve of my gang escaped. Had I attended to Kurhora's advice, you would have had none ot us; —another proof of the efficacy of omens, if attended to."

Mahommed Buksh, another dignified Thug, confirms this account. He says:—

"It was a very unfortunate expedition. At Biseynèe we fell in with some travellers, and should have secured them; but when Zolfukar came up,

 Bhola,

Bhola, who is always talking, could not help saying, in Ramasee—'After all, we shall not go home without something to please our wives and children.' The travellers heard, suspected our designs, left our encampment on the bank of the tank, and went into the village. This was our first *banij* (merchandize); and to lose it thus, was a bad omen: it was, in fact, like being seized. Then came the murder of the women at Manora; and to crown the whole, the foaling of Zolfukar's mare, which brought us all under the *eetuk*. Every thing seemed to go wrong with us that season; and I often proposed to return home, and open the expedition anew; but I was unhappily overruled."

Feringeea himself might have escaped, but for the strength of those feelings of natural affection of which the Thug fraternity appear no less susceptible than their more honest neighbours, though the influence of such feelings is seemingly so inconsistent with their detestable occupation. Being asked how he came to be taken, Feringeea answered—"Having lived among the clans of Rajpootana and Telingana for years together, I should have gone off to some of them: but you had secured my mother, wife, and child: I could not forsake them; was always inquiring after them; and affording my pursuers the means of tracing me. I knew not what indignities my wife and mother might

might suffer. Could I have felt secure that they would suffer none, I should not have been taken."

A remarkable feature in the history of this man is, the fact of his having been retained in the service of two distinguished British Military Officers. How this connection was brought about, and how it terminated, are thus told by Feringeea :—

" My cousin, Aman Singh Subahdar, after the death of his brother, Dureear, and my father, Purusram, became our guardian. His mother was one of the first families in the country; and her sister's son, Jhundee, àlias Gunga Singh, had the command of two regiments at Kotah. Having no sons of his own, he asked Aman to give him either me or Phoolsa, the son of Dureear, (for whom you have offered 200 rupees,) for adoption, as he had great wealth, and no child to leave it to. He suspected Aman to be a thief; but knew not that he was a leader of assassins, or he would have had nothing to say to us. Phoolsa would not consent to live with Gunga Singh Kuptan; nor should I, had I not had a dispute with Aman, while out on a Thug expedition. I went to him; and he became very fond of me, and got me made a Subahdar in the Grenadier Company of the Buldeo regiment. I could not live without some of my old Thug friends; and got Rambuksh, my cousin, for whom you have offered 500 rupees, enlisted, and made a Havildar,

Havildar, on my own security for his good conduct. He was always a very loose character; and when Gunga Singh went to Oudeepore with his two regiments, as the body-guard of the young Queen, who was the daughter of the Kotah Chief, Rambuksh seduced a young widow, the daughter of one of the most respectable bankers of the city, who became pregnant. As soon as the intrigue was discovered, she pounded and ate the diamond of her own ring, or something of the kind, and died; and Rambuksh was obliged to fly, to save his life, which was demanded, by her family, of the Chief. Having given security for his good conduct, I thought my own head in danger; and fled to Boondee, where I contrived to get into the service of Major Todd; recommended to him, by the Postmaster, as a young man of high birth and great promise. On going to meet General Ochterlony at Bheelwarah, soon after, he recommended me to him; and he made me Jemadar of hurcaras. I attended him to Delhi and to Ajmere; whence he sent me, in charge of the Post-office peons, to Rewaree. From this place I was sent, with four peons, to attend a young lady of the General's family from Delhi to Calcutta. Her escort consisted of a Havildar, a Naick, and twenty sepoys, under the command of Bhowanee Singh, Jemadar of the local regiment. We reached Muthura without any accident, and lodged in Colonel Gunge. At night, Bhowanee

Bhowanee Singh was caught in an awkward position with one of the young lady's women; and dreading the vengeance of the General, he, and all his guard, fled. He roused me, told me what had happened, and advised me to go off with him, and try our fortunes with Runjeet Singh. This I declined; but hearing that my cousin, Aman Subahdar, had gone that season with his gang into Rajpootana, I started; and passing through Hindone and Beeana, joined them at Kuraulee, after having been absent from him some years. It was, I believe, the year after I rejoined Aman that my gang was arrested at Kotah; and that we killed Ashraf Khan, the Subahdar Major of the 4th Cavalry, and his party. From that time till I was taken, or about ten years, I was always out with the gang, except in the season of the rains; and for several even of these seasons we were out in Rajpootana, where the rains offer little impediment. Indeed, in the western parts of Rajpootana, Thugs have an advantage in the rainy season; as at the other seasons, the most wealthy travellers move along in wheeled carriages, and cannot be so easily managed as on foot or on horseback, to which mode of travelling they are obliged to have recourse in the rains."

The histories of these men are as romantic as the most ardent lover of Oriental adventures could desire.

CHAP. XXIII.

It has already been mentioned, that Thuggee is carried on by water as well as land; and Bengal is especially infested by River Thugs. In a case related in an early part of this volume in illustration of the general mode in which River Thuggee is carried on, the offenders were brought to justice: and a few selections from the evidence will tend to throw fresh light upon the subject under consideration. The number of prisoners was eight; and they were indicted for the murder of two weavers and four other persons. Bholai Chung, after stating that he knew the prisoners, said:— "Early in April last, Nubeendeo (one of the prisoners) called me to his house, on intention to trade in rice: thence he took me to a boat: it was 100 maunds' panchway, and five other men were sitting in it, none of whom I then knew. I asked Nubeendeo what seven men could do in so small a boat. He answered, 'Bungsee Manjee has another boat, which he has gone to fetch; when there will be room enough.' That day we remained in the boat. Next evening, Bungsee Manjee, Soobuldam, Birjmohun,

Birjmohun, and Gungaram Mistree, came up, on a pulwar, near to our boat: then Kumul Das left our boat, and called a person named Ramgobind: night came on, and we remained. Next day, at dawn, there were six men in the pulwar, and ten in the panchway. At about one pas day, were about to set out; when Suroop Mistree called out, 'Stop; for when the boat was loosened, I sneezed':—so both boats stopped: and Suroop went ashore, and brought two Tanties (weavers), with several pairs of dhotees: and he said to Nubeendeo, 'O relative, you wanted to buy cloths; and I have brought you the men who sell them.' He replied, 'Bring the men on board the boat': on which they came in, with the cloths. Soobuldam and Suroop Mistree threw an *angoocha,* twisted, on the necks of those two Tanties, and threw them over on the floor; dipped them under water, and held them awhile, and then let them go.—We set out, after this, to the north; pulled fifteen days in the direction of Kakeenu, district of Rungpore, where we went. Thence we went towards Sura, under the hot *kholabooree.* In a bight, we found a boat laden with tobacco and hemp: both our boats put-to there. Soobuldam asked the Manjee (commander) of the tobacco-boat, whence he came; and he told him he was coming from Khillaighat, and going to Sheraigunje: on which, Nubeendeo said, 'Our houses are at Muth, and we will go to Manickgunje': thus

thus all three boats remained there that night: next day, all three set out together at noon. Nubeendeo, seeing a waste *chur* (sand-bank), said to the tobacco-men, 'O Manjee (commander), let us stop our boats here, and cook our food.' There was a pilot with the tobacco-boat; and we all put-to at this chur, and dined. After dinner, Nubeendeo said: 'I have made a vow to the god, Hurry Soot; let me here fulfil it. Call the Manjee, and his boat-men, that they may assist.' So he put a mat (carpet) before the first boat; and when the four sailors and the captain of the tobacco-boat came, Soobul said, 'Do you, I pray, sing the song of Hurry Soot.' They had sung one, and were beginning another, when Nubeendeo said, 'Now, Hurry, give us our plunder': on which, Birjmohun, and Suroop Mistree, and Soobuldam, and Kumul Das, and Lukhikunth Sen, these five men leapt on the throats of the four men of the tobacco-boat, and on that of the pilot; twisted angoochas, and threw them flat on the sand; others seized them at the same time; after which they punched them to death with fists and elbows, and sunk the bodies in the water. I, Ramgobind, and Soobuldam, were put on board the tobacco-boat: and then all three boats started, and went on together till evening, when we stopped. At night, the tobacco and hemp were changed into our panchway and pulwar; and Soobul struck the tobacco-boat with a hatchet, made

made a hole, and sunk it: next day we set out; and came in five days to Kishenpore, and fixed the boat. Thence Suroop went to Manickgunje, to ascertain the demand in the bazaar for tobacco: thence he came back, saying the bazaar was empty, because of a disturbance. Then Suroop put the hemp in the panchway, and took it home to his house. I, Soobul, Birjmohun, and Kumul, brought on the tobacco, and the rest went to their homes. We came to Manickgunje, and gave the tobacco to Bullai Sah, to sell for us. Next day I went away; and in fifteen days returned, and saw that the boat was still there. Suroop told me that sixteen rupees' worth of tobacco had been sold;—offered me one rupee, which I declined; and went home."

Kishenmohun, alias Ramgobind Chung, of Kanikola, Pergunah Chaundpertab, aged twenty-two, ploughman, said:—"I knew the prisoners. Frequenting the fair of Manickgunje, I became acquainted with Gungaram Mistree. Last Bysakh, he came to me in a field where I was ploughing, and asked me to go on a trading-boat. I declined at that time: he returned in six or seven days, bringing Kumul Das, who asked me if I had spoken with any person about going on a boat. I said, 'Yes; with Gungaram.' 'Will you go?' I said, 'I am poor:' on which he gave me one rupee and a half; which I left with my family, and went to the house of of Kumul Das, and remainded there four days: after which, at the River Jumona, at the market of Balia Chundra, there was the boat of Kumul Das, of the class *botom.* I went with him: saw Suroop, Gungaram, and Lukhikunth, in the boat: at one-and-a-half pas watch of the day, a pulwar came, in which wêre Soobuldam, Birjmohun, Nubeendeo, Bungsee, and Bholae Chung, and was fastened near ours. Then two Tanties, with cloths under their arms, came from the north, towards the south, along the river bank. Suroop called them on board the pulwar; after which I did not see those two men leave the boat. I heard from Bholae, that Suroop, and Soobul and others, had killed these two men, and sunk the bodies. That day we set sail on both boats; and reached in fifteen days the Hatbooree: remained there two or three days, and then set out. Under a hut, in a bight, we found a boat laden with tobacco and hemp. Nubeendeo asked the men whither they were going. Manjee said, 'The boat is come from Khillaigunje, and will go to Sheraigunje': on which, Nubeendeo and the rest replied, 'We also shall go in that direction: come, let us go together':—so that boat came along with ours for one day to Surarez. All three boats put-to at a chur; all cooked, and fed. Nubeendeo said, 'I have a vow to Hurry; let me fulfil it': so all sat on the chur (sand-bank); and those four men of the tobacco-boat, and one pilot with them, came and

and sat on a mat, and sung songs to Hurry Soot: on this, Nubeendeo, Suroop Mistree, Lukhikunth, Kumuldas, Birjmohun, Gungaram, and Bungsee, twisted angoochas on the throats of these five men, threw them down, killed them, and threw them into the water. Then we set out, the three boats together. At night, Soobul and the rest changed the property into their own boats; and Suroop and Nubeendeo cut a hole in the tobacco-boat with an axe, and sunk it: next dawn, our boat departed: in five or six days we got to Manickgunje, whence I fled.

Gungaram Mistree, one of the prisoners, made the following statement:—" With my own hand I have killed no person: on board the boat where the two Tanties and five Mullahs were killed, I was a boatman. In the beginning of Bysek last, Suroop, my relative, came to my house, and took me off to repair a boat. We went near to the village of Binanee, on the River Jumona. I saw at that ghaut a pulwar-boat; and in it were Nubeen Sircar, Birjmohun Biswas, and his wife's brother, and Bhola Chung. Kishenmohun Chung, Soobuldam, I, and Suroop, when two ghurries day were left, got on board that boat, and remained there that night: next day, at about one pas day (nine A. M.), the boat moved, but high wind; so, at one-and-a-half pas day, put-to at Bhataghaut Binanee, near Khooneepara, and on the banks of the River Jumona, and remained there that day: next day, at one pas nine A.M., two Tanties (weavers), one of whom had a bundle of cloths, came along the bank from the north towards Binanee, going south towards Dowlutpore. Nubeendeo went ashore from the boat, and called these two Tanties; who said they had been trying to sell in vain, and were taking their cloths home. Nubeendeo and the others offered to buy, and called them into the boat. These two Tanties went into the boat with their cloths: after which, Suroop said to me, 'Do you go on shore.' I did so, about three begas distant. I sat down; and on returning to the boat two ghurries after, one of the party called me on board the boat. I embarked; saw some new dhotees, but not the Tanties (weavers): asked how, and why. Suroop and Nubeendeo replied, It was no concern of mine; they would take the cloths on, and sell them; for they had bought them. The boat was loosened. I asked where they were going: they said, 'We always go to Kakeena and sell cloths; and thither will we now go. If you will not go with us, remain you at Seraigunje, and work.' In three days we got to Seraigunje, where we stopped; and remained at Kakeena, and about that part, for a month, and then went on towards Surarez. On the way coming, we found a panchway, with five sailors in it, laden with hemp and tobacco: asked whither going: they said to Seraigunje.

Nubeendeo

Nubeendeo said, 'We, too, are going thither; let us go together:' so the boats joined, and went down the stream. On this, all the men on our boat began to speak in slang terms, and used signs which I could not comprehend: but as they wanted to kill the tobacco-men, I remonstrated. They said, 'We always do thus; and so we support ourselves: be at your ease.' In Jeth (May), date forgot, at about one-and-a-half pas day on the border of the river, both boats put-to at a chur or sand-bank, cooked, and dined: then Soobul, Bhola, Kishenmohun, Suroop, and Birjmohun, cast on the throats of the five men of the tobacco-boat, angoochas, threw them down, and closed their breath and killed them, and threw the five bodies into the river. Nubeendeo, and Soobul, and Suroop, went on board the tobacco-boat; rest remained on our own boat: both boats set out together, pulled for two pas (six hours), came to a village, and put-to the boats, and passed the night there; and took out all the tobacco, hemp, a lotah, and some other things, to our own boat; and sunk that tobacco-boat some how or other. That night we moved on to Seraigunje, came near Binanee, and put up. They put me ashore, to go home by land: the others took the boat, and went to Manickgunje. They promised to give me something, after selling the property in Manickgunje. Fifteen days after, Suroop came, and said they had sold all to Jugnath Sah:

did

did not tell how much, but he gave me two rupees. He had before given me this new dhotee, which I deemed belonged to the two Tanties. As he did not tell me the price, I went in the middle of Asarh to Manickgunje, and asked Jugnath what he had paid; *i.e.* I asked of his Gomashta: he refused to tell me. While I was sitting down, I could see the two Tanties taken into the boat; but I never saw them come out again; hence I suppose they were murdered."

Suroop Mistree made the following confession:—"I have killed no person. I went on no boat: cannot say why Soobul and Gunga Mistree take my name. In June, Gunga Mistree came to my house, and said, 'We have brought some tobacco and hemp: do you take it to Manickgunge and sell, and I will pay you.' I came to the ghaut, and saw these articles in a pulwar, on which were Soobul-dam, Bhola Chung, Kishenmohun, Birjmohun, and Bungsee Chung. They said, 'We cannot ourselves sell it; do you come and sell our things for us.' So I went on board that boat: Gungaram and Birj-mohun went on shore. We took the boat to Manick-gunje, and sold the articles to Jugnath Sah. I forget the amount; but Jugmohun Biswas took the whole, and gave one-and-a-quarter rupee. They would have given me a red chatta; but I would not accept it; so Gungaram took it. That chatta was above

above my means.—I cannot write.—I denied all things in the Mofussil, because Soobul had terrified me. They said they had brought the things from the north, yet they did not trade in tobacco." Witness points out Birjmohun, and said, "It was his father Jugmohun who came to Manickgunje after us, and managed the sale and accounts of tobacco."

Another of the party thus deposed:—"On the 2d Bysakh last, I and others, on two boats, putteela and a pulwar, went from Jumonee and Brimhoter and Tistee, to Kakeena, in the district of Rungpore; I was on the pulwar, the Manjee of which was Bungsee Nundee: he had said rice should be bought, and all share in the profits of the sale. We lugao'd the two boats at Kukeena, but got no goods: in the beginning of Jeth we set out, and on the low ground of a chur (sand-bank), in the afternoon, we stopped the boat: next day, at ten A.M., there came a boat from the direction of Dinajpore, in which there was tobacco: our three boats followed it, and in Bhatee of Hatkholapoory all the boats lugao'd together: the tobacco-men, in reply to our question, said they had brought tobacco from Dinagepore for a merchant, and were going to Kakomaree: next day, the malicks of our three boats, viz. Radanath, alias Suroop Chung, Nubeendeo, and Mirthoo Chung, met and consulted; and when the trader's boat set

 out,

out, our pulwar of Binnoo Manjee set out also: our other two boats remained at a distance, following in rear. At one-and-a-half pas day, the pulwar and tobacco-boat lugao'd (put-to) at a chur. We went ashore and cooked, but the trader's men cooked and fed on their own boat. Then I and Gungaram went on the chur, to get fire-wood. In four ghuries, or perhaps 1 pas, we returned to our boat, but did not see the trader's men on their boat. Our men, Nubeendeo, Radhanath, and Mirtoo Chung, who were our boat's maliks (masters), said, 'Loosen the tobacco-boat, and bring it near ours.' We all did so. When two ghuries of the day were left, we took all the tobacco, hemp, lota, planks, tusla, and kutono, from the tobacco-boat; put them into our pulwar, and sunk the tobacco-boat. Then we set out with our boat; and shortly, our other two boats came up and joined us: they said, 'Sell the tobacco at Manickgunje, and we will, in a few days, bring rice or dal, or whatever we get': so we took our boat with tobacco to Manickgunje. Radhanath, Suroop, Kishenmohun, Bungsee Nundee, and Bholanath Chung, remained in the pulwar, to sell the tobacco: two men were sent homewards. That tobacco was sold for one-and-a-half per maund to Bulram, Tantee Muhajun: we got forty-eight rupees; and the hemp was sold for five rupees to a Beoparee: Suroop and the other men divided the amount, and gave me two rupees.

rupees. I remained at home, they at Manickgunje. About the end of Jeth, Radhanath, Mirtunjoe, Kadanath, and Chedam, hired my boat, and went to trade, I do not know where. I do not know whom else they took. When we were going to the north, our boat put up at the plain of Balahat Babna, at about one-and-a-half pas distance, on the right bank of Jumona river: there, at about fourteen ghuries day, came two Julahas (weavers), with several pairs of new cloths: they were travelling, by land, towards the south. On this, Suroop Mistree and Radhanath Sircar, on pretext of wishing to buy cloths, called them to the boat, and sent me ashore to buy vegetables: in two ghuries, when I returned with the vegetables, I did not see the boat, but in a moment after I saw it being towed up the stream: they told me, in reply to my inquiry, that the boat had slid away, and they were bringing it up. I got on the boat, and saw a bundle of new cloths. In reply to my question, they told me they had bought these cloths from the two weavers, who had taken the rupees and gone. There were seven pairs of plain dhotees, one Zenana saree with a red border, all tied in a settrinjee; also there was a blanket. In the tobacco-boat there were one Manjee, and four boatmen. I cannot say what became of them, whether they were beaten, or killed, or thrown overboard. Nor do I suppose the cloths were purchased, or that the weavers met

 with

with any other fate. I got a dhotee, which has been brought into Court. The boat seized in Manickgunje, by the police, is mine: I let it to Radhanath. When, leaving two boats behind, our pulwar followed the tobacco-boat, there were on the pulwar, I, Radhanath, Bholanath Chung, Mirtunjoe Chung, Nubeendeo, Suroop Mistree, Gungaram Mistree, Mirthoo Chung, Bungsee Nundee, and Kishenmohun Chung. This prisoner, Suroop Mistree, gave me the dhotee."

CHAP. XXIV.

The following narrative will illustrate the practices of the Thugs, as to sacrifices, as well as other customs. It is the deposition of a person named Runnooa Moonshee; taken before Captain Wade, Political Agent at Loodhiana, 25th August 1834.

"Deponent is an inhabitant of Behareeapore, in the district of Belha, and son of Seeta Ram Lodhie; aged forty-seven years; follows the profession of Thuggee.

"Last year, in the month of Bhadon (August) 1833, three or four days before Mr. Wilson came to secure the Thugs at Behareeapore, I quitted my home, and resided with others in the fields in the neighbourhood. Kehree Singh Aheer, Zemindar of Puhla and Russoola, had told me this. He had also told us, that we had all better assemble in one place in his village, and he would not allow any one to secure us; but we suspected that he would cause our seizure, and we all intended to remove to the Lahore country. One evening, I went to my house, and brought my family with me; and proceeded

proceeded to Bunsra, to the house of Buksheea Thug: but not finding him at home, I told his wife to tell him, when he returned, that I was about to proceed in a direction to the west: and should he be willing to come, he would find me at Koree Chetr (Thunesur). I then went on to Belha, and purchased some parched grain from the bazaar; and returned to the field, where I passed that night with my family. The next morning I went to Burdoo; where Buksheea and Newla, with their families, together with Jeyneea my father-in-law, who had escaped from the Saugor jail, joined me. From this place, we all proceeded towards Koroo Chetr (Thunesur); and in one month we arrived in its vicinity. From this place, Jeyneea and Newla returned back to their homes, for the purpose of learning some news of his own brother Kinnereha, still in confinement in the Furruckabad jail. I and Buksheea, with our families, went on to Gungpore, a village in Shahabad, belonging to Sirdar Khan Singh; where we found Ram Singh (formerly a resident of Kunouje in Cawnpore, and by profession a Thug), residing in that village. After relating all our past misfortunes to him, we asked him for some place of residence. In reply, he told us, that there had been a great alarm of thieves in that village; and we had better go to Ruttungurh, near Shahabad, where we should get a better place for our safe residence. We accordingly went on to

Ruttungurh;

Ruttungurh; and on our arrival, went to Suroop Singh, Thanadar, and Baleh, a gardener, and told them that we were cultivators, and, owing to the scarcity of grain and famine in our country, we had left our homes; and asked them for a place to reside in, and stated that we would cultivate lands, and pay them the rent for them. To this they consented; and gave us a house to reside in, where we all put up, and repaired the house. A few days after, I sent Buksheea back, to conduct Jeyneea and Newla from their homes, (as they were told to come to Koroo Chetr,) lest they might be disappointed. When Buksheea arrived on the bank of a kutcha tank, on the west side of Koroo Chetr (Thunesur), he found Newla, Dhunoya, and Jeyneea. Kusseea, Gonooa, and Omedwa, with their families, coming up from their homes to join us, he conducted them to Ruttungurh, and resided with us there.

"In Kooar (end of Sept.) 1833, when the rain had fallen favourably, we cultivated some fields, and planted sugar-cane in them; and in Kartick we had done with all the field-work.

"In Aughun Dojee (Nov.) 1833, *we sacrificed a goat to Davy;* and on the following morning, Buksheea, Newla, Seetula, Omedwa, Dhunooa (now arrested), Dhunooa (at large,) Gonooa, Kusseea, and nine Hinunchula, set out on an expedition on Thuggee, to the west. Five or six days after, I followed

followed, and joined them in the serai of Rajpoora, the place appointed. On my arrival, they gave me a share of the booty which they had obtained from some people whom they had murdered ere I reached them at Bunjaraka-serai. The booty they got from their victims were 22 kuldar rupees, and some clothes. I received my share from Buksheea.

"From this place we set out in a direction to Loodiana; and again returned to Sanoowal, where we lodged in the bazaar in a Buneea's shop. About two ghuries before sun-set, a traveller came up, of Rajpoot caste, on his way from Peshore to Allahabad. Owing to a heavy fall of rain, we all put up in one shop, and cooked and ate our dinner in it. About six ghuries before daylight, we set out with the traveller; and when he had got on about a cose east from the village, we strangled him.

"Dhunooa (at large) was the Bhurtote on this affair; 2d Dhunooa arrested. Seetula and Omedwa acted as Guthaee and Lughaees. His body was securely buried in a dry tank, about four fields south from the place where we murdered him. We got from him fifteen rupees kuldar, some Hindee chits (letters), one matchlock, one tattoo which the deponent received in his share, one puttoo, one white loee, one red woollen chudder, and some other clothes; one thalee, and one lotah; which were all divided between us.

"After this affair, we proceeded to Umballah; and

and thence we took a direction to Hurdwar. In seven or eight days we travelled only twenty cose, to the Hurdwar side; and afterwards we changed the route, and returned to a village (name not remembered), about five cose east from Koroo Chetr (Thunesur). From this village we went on to Kurnaul, and crossed the Jumna. While we were sitting on the other side of the river, Buksheea and Gunooa, who had been left behind, came up with two merchant travellers, on their way from Peshore to Nowdah in Oude: they had won their confidence, and they agreed to travel with us. We proceeded on to a village about two cose from the bank of the Jumna, and encamped outside of the village, near a well, with the travellers. About four ghuries before day-light, we set out with them; and about a cose distant from the village, on the bank of a river, we seized them as they went along, and strangled them. Newla, and Dhunooa (at large), were the Bhurtotes at this murder. Their bodies were thrown into the river. We got from them a hundred rupees in cash, one tattoo of dun colour, one thalee, one lotah, and one tulwar, which we divided between us. The tattoo was sold to Ghureeba, porter of Sahabad, for eleven rupees; but deponent does not recollect who took the thalee and lotah. Buksheea got the tulwar in his share.

"After this affair we committed no other murder; and

and returned to our new abode at Ruttungurh. Three days after our return, Dhunooa (arrested), and Omedwa, went to their homes in the Dooab; and Jeyneea soon followed them. In Magh (Jan.) 1834, about eight days had passed, when Omedwa, with his family, came back to Ruttungurh; and about the middle of the month, Dhunooa (arrested), and Issureea (ditto), came back from their homes; and soon after, Jeyneea.

" The tattoo we got at Sanoowall was sold to Sheikh Mahommed Ameen of Sahabad, for eleven rupees Kythalee. The Sheikh is in the service of Sirdar Runjeet Singh, of Shahabad, in the village of Komtee.

" The puttoo and loee were sold to Donyur Malee of Ruttungurh garden, for five rupees. Who got the lotah and the thalee I do not recollect. The matchlock is still with Dhunooa (arrested).

" In Magh (Jan.) 1834, when four days only remained of the month, *we again sacrificed a goat to Davy;* and on the 2d of Phagoon (Feb.) 1834, Khusheea, Dhunooa (at large), and Issureea (arrested), set out on another expedition to the west. Three days after, I, Iryneea my father-in-law, Himunchula son of deponent; Setulla, Omedwa, Mehngooa, Dhunooa (arrested), and Newla, proceeded to Umballah from Ruttungurh, and joined them there. From Umballah we all set out, leaving Issureea behind: and when we had got outside of the

west

west gate, Issureea joined us with a traveller, who was on his way from Lucknow to Lahore: we went on to a village one cose west (name not known); and thence to Mogul-ka-serai, where we encamped with the traveller. Six ghuries before day-light we set out from this place; and about one-and-a-half cose distant from it, we strangled him. Dhunooa (at large) was the Bhurtote on this occasion.

"Issureea, Dhunooa, Omedwa, Khusheea, and Seetula, acted as Guthaees and Lughaees; and Omedwa was a Belhaee also. We got from him one gold ear-ring worth sixteen rupees, one pair of silver bangles, fourteen rupees, one lotah, one thalee, one white blanket, and some other cloths, which were all divided between us: his body was securely buried, about four fields distant from the road.

"After this we proceeded to Sirhind; and thence to Khanna, where we encamped near a well. While we were cooking our dinner, in the evening, a Rajpoot traveller came up, on his way from Lahore to Biswara in Oude; and we saw him near the well. Dhunooa (at large) acted as Sothaee, and won his confidence; and accompanied him to the village, and caused him to put up in one of the temples (Shewalla), near the east gate, and returned to us. We all, after taking our dinner, removed to the same place where the traveller had been lodged.

Six

Six ghuries before day-light we set out with the traveller; and leaving the high road, we proceeded, by a bye-path, to the south; and when we had gone on about a cose from the village, we seized him as he went along, and strangled him. Dhunooa was the Bhurtote at this murder.

"Issureea, Khusheea, Seetula, Omedwa, and Dhunooa (arrested), acted as Guthaees and Lughaees; and his body was securely buried in a field, about four fields distant from the place. We got from him thirteen rupees (Raja Sahee), one lotah, one thalee, one towah, and some other cloths, which we divided between us; but I do not recollect who got these articles.

"After this affair we proceeded to Umritser, which place we reached in eight days: we passed two nights in that town, and then set out on our return; and in two days we reached a village whose name is not remembered, about twelve or fourteen cose from Umritser east; and encamped near the outer gate, at the Chubootra. While we were cooking our dinner, a Mussulman traveller came up, on his way from Mooltan to Biswara in Lucknow. Seetula acted as Sothaee, and won his confidence. He put up with us; and about one watch before day-light we set out with him; and about a cose from the place where we had encamped, we strangled him. Dhunooa (at large) was the Bhurtote: Omedwa acted as Belhae. Issureea

Issureea, and Dhunooa (arrested), Seetula, and Khusheea, also Omedwa, acted as Guthaees and Lughaees. His body was buried about six fields south from the road, securely, in a hollow. We got from him fifty rupees (Raja Sahee), one copper rikabee, and some other cloths, which we divided between us.

"After this we proceeded to a village about two cose distant from the place where we had committed the above murder: and while we were sitting and smoking, two travellers came up, on their way from Lahore to Seetapore; and sat down near us, to smoke their hookas. In consequence of a heavy storm, we rested there about a watch; and then proceeded to a village about three cose distant (name not known), where we lodged in a chowpar (a public place at a village), with travellers. One watch before day-light we set out from this village with the travellers, left the high road, and proceeded by a bye-path; and when we had got on about a cose, we strangled them.

"Dhunooa and Newla were the Bhurtotes; Issureea, Dhunooa (arrested), Omedwa, Khusheea, and Seetula, acted as Lughaees and Guthaees. Omedwa acted as Belhae also We buried their bodies about four fields from the place where we had murdered them, securely. We got from them twenty-one rupees in cash; of which ten Lucknow currency, nine kuldar and two copper rupees, one brass

brass lotah, one thalee, one white blanket, one old rajaee (quilt), one towah, one silk doputta, and two cords for drawing water from the well. After this, in the month of Jeth (May) 1834, we returned to our new abodes at Ruttungurh.

"The articles we obtained in the above affairs were thus distributed:—

"One tusla to Omedwa, for Tilhaee (Omedwa's wife), mortgaged to a Bunyah in the Lhodiana bazaar for ten annas, while we were in custody under Maharaja Runjeet Singh's sepoys; one lotah to ditto; Omedwa's wife got one ditto large; and a thalee to Dhunooa. These articles Chutter Zemindar of Kureea seized from Dhunooa, when he was arrested.

"One blanket to Dhunooa: he sold this to Ruttun Chowdree, near Ruttungurh.

"One silk doputta to Seetula: this was sold to Boodh Singh, Jaut of Ruttungurh.

"One woollen red chudder: this (a sheet) was given to the manager of Ruttungurh, in lieu of the land-rent, for eight rupees.

"In the beginning of Bysakh of the present year (April) 1834, Iryneea went to the Dooab, and promised to return back on the 2d Jeth: after waiting some days beyond the time, we conjectured that he had been seized; and, becoming alarmed, we quitted Ruttungurh. We remained for six days in the neighbourhood of Karoo Chetr (Thunesur); seven or or eight days at Kuthree, in Gholab Singh's territory. A guard, with approvers, came to Shahabad: and about one-and-a-half watch after sun-rise, one morning, we heard two men, residents of Ruttungurh, talking with the people of Kuthree, and stating that some Thugs had come to Shahabad for the purpose of securing the Poorbeea Koormies (this was what we were called in the village) who had lately resided at Ruttungurh. When we heard this, we left Kuthree; and proceeded, by Kythul, to Dhurum Kote: thence to Kureeal, where we again settled, and cultivated some lands. We conjectured that the approvers would come as far as Lhodiana, and not beyond; and we intended to move further on, in the direction of Lahore and Umritser."

The deponent stated some further particulars, implicating more clearly in the practice of Thuggee Ram Singh, mentioned in the above narrative.

" In the month of Magh (Jan.) 1834, when ten days of the month had passed, I, Issureea, and Dhunooa (arrested), went out to the jungle for wood. A Hindoo traveller came up, on his way from Lahore to the east. We three, together with Ram Singh, and Kulloa his son, followed the traveller, and strangled him near a village in the jungle, about five cose east from Kooroo Chetr (Thunesur). Ram Singh Aheer, was the Bhurtote at this murder: Kulloo, Issureea, and Dhunooa acted

acted as Lughaees and Guthaees. His body was buried in the Dhak jungle (commonly called Pullass), about four fields north from the road, securely. This place is about a cose east from the village, whose name not remembered. We got from him seventeen rupees, and one iron weight of two seers, one ditto of one seer, one lotah, and some old clothes, which were divided between us. The towah and lotah are now with Ram Singh. Except this, Ram Singh was in no other affair with us, but I well know him to be a Thug: he used to follow Kurhoree Ramkishen Mutholee of Behareeapore, on Thuggee: when Mr. Parry, the Magistrate of Etawah, gave orders to seize the Thugs, he ran off from his home; and for several years he resided in the neighbourhood of Gwalior, and afterwards at Ruttungurh. Since he left home, this was the first time that we had met him. Chunduna is not a Thug: we had brought him for the purpose of purchasing some bullocks for our homes."

CHAP. XXV.

In April 1836, a gang of Thugs were apprehended at Masulipatam, and depositions taken before the Magistrate. The gang had been carrying on their trade for several years, with the knowledge of the Zemindars, but undisturbed by them. This tolerance of professional thieves and murderers is a remarkable feature in the phænomena of Indian society. The facts are thus brought to the notice of the Government of India, by Capt. Reynolds; whose activity in the suppression of Thuggee has been most laudable and effective.

"I have the honour to submit, for the information of the Right Honourable the Governor-General of India in Council, the copy of a Letter to my address, from the Magistrate of Guntoor, in the Presidency of Madras; together with copies of the enclosures to which it gave cover, detailing his success in tracing and apprehending a gang of Thugs residing in the Masulipatam district, on the high road from Hydrabad to Masulipatam; intelligence of whose abode had been obtained from the confessions of approvers before me at Hingolee.

"From the depositions taken before the Magistrate at Guntoor, it appears that this gang of Thugs has been established in the Masulipatam district for several years, apparently with the cognisance of the Zemindars of the villages where they resided; who, though aware of their bad characters, and the arrest of some members of the confederacy at Guntoor under most suspicious circumstances, have considered it prudent to conceal the fact from the Magistrate of Masulipatam.

"In the month of September last, I applied, at Captain Sleeman's suggestion, to the then Magistrate of Masulipatam, to ascertain if any Thugs had been arrested at Ellore, as we had reason to suppose they had been: and in his reply, he informs me that not a single individual of the description alluded to in my letter had been taken in his district for years.

"I mention this circumstance with reference to Captain Sleeman's despatch to you of the 21st of September last, enclosing copy of one to the address of the Chief Secretary to the Madras Government, wherein he points out the good effect attendant upon the transmission to me of a gang of Thugs arrested by the Joint Magistrate of Hoobly, in the Southern Mahratta country. I conceive that more good will result from the gang now seized at Guntoor being

being made over to one of the officers employed in this department, than from any measures that the local authorities at the place of arrest can adopt for inducing them to confess. If they are detained at Guntoor, but a partial disclosure of their crimes can be expected from them; while, on the contrary, there is every reason to believe, that, when the prisoners are confronted with the approvers at Hydrabad, many of them will be induced to come forward willingly, to assist us with the information in their possession.

"I have accordingly thought it necessary to apply to the Madras Government to issue instructions to the Magistrate of Guntoor for the despatch of the prisoners to Hydrabad: and I beg leave to attach the copy of a Letter I have addressed to the Chief Secretary to that Government on this subject; a measure which I trust will meet with the sanction of his Lordship in Council."

The following is the Letter referred to, addressed to Captain Reynolds by Mr. Matheson, Head Assistant Magistrate at Guntoor:—

"As, in the orders of this Government which accompanied the copies of the Papers received from you regarding the existence of Thugs in the district of Masulipatam, the Magistrates of this Presidency are directed to communicate with you on subjects which relate to your department, I have now the

 honour

honour to inform you, that, by following up the traces afforded by the depositions taken by you, I have at last succeeded in tracing and apprehending a gang of Thugs, who were residing in the Masulipatam district, on the high road from Masulipatam to Hydrabad. The Jemadar, with fourteen followers, was residing at Tooreeapallem, a hamlet of Mooneegalla; five others at Kistnapooram, a hamlet of Aukpaumoolah in that neighbourhood; and four others, including the two sons of Sheikh Ahmed Jemadar, were living in the town of Ellore. I have since apprehended another of the gang, while crossing the River Kistnah into this district: so that the total number now seized, amounts to twenty-five, who, with one or two exceptions, are professed Thugs.

"The depositions given before me, and of which I now forward translations, seem clearly to prove that these people form part of the gangs under the Jemadars Emaum Sahib, alias Chabriah Emaum, and Sheikh Ahmed, mentioned in the deposition of Myan Khan, alias Lingooteea, given before you in October last. Emaum Sahib is now apprehended; and Sheikh Ahmed or Hommed, it appears, died very lately, but his two sons are now seized.

"The Jemadar Hoonooryah, the brother of Emaum Sahib, appears to have left this part of the country about the time of the famine, and to have gone southward; where he has probably been joined by by many of Sheikh Ahmed's followers, as their numbers in these parts are said to have decreased considerably within the last few years; and I believe I have succeeded in apprehending nearly all those now residing in this neighbourhood. The depositions do not contain much information beyond the proving the prisoners to be Phansigars; but I send them in the hopes that you may, perhaps, be enabled to identify the murders mentioned therein, with some of those confessed before you. I also send a descriptive roll of the prisoners, which may probably enable some of your approvers to recognise them.

"I have little doubt but that these people can give important information regarding the Thugs now residing in other parts of the territories under this Presidency; and, as the only means of obtaining this, I have written to Government to be allowed to admit some of their number as approvers. In the mean while, I should be obliged by your letting me know whether you are possessed of any information by which you could bring their guilt home to them, independent of their confessions. I should also feel thankful if you could give me any intelligence as to the measures pursued by you, in order to convict this class of criminals; and also for any directions as to managing them which your experience may enable you to suggest."

Sundry

Sundry depositions were enclosed. The first was made by a man named Avvaroo Gopalroydoo, son of Appiah, of the Brahmany caste, Vystnava religion, by profession Curnum, aged twenty-eight years, an inhabitant of Alloor, attached to the Joodjoor purgunah, in the zillah of Masulipatam, and stated to have been sworn on Tuesday the 4th, decreasing moon of Chaitrum, year Doormookhee, corresponding with the 5th April 1836. It is subjoined:—

Q. "What do you know regarding the Moormen seized and brought by Sheikh Baday, the Cutwal of Guntoor, from the villages of Moongal, &c., appertaining to the zillah of Masulipatam; and what are you given to understand concerning their circumstances?

A. "About eight years ago, the Moormen named Pedda Emaum Sahib, Pedda Fakeer Sahib, Sheikh Mahommed, Chinna Fakeerah, Chinna Emaum Sahib, Mooshkeel, Madaur Sahib, his three sons, named Goolam Sahib, Khausim and Emaum, and another Madaur Sahib, and Mohadeen Sahib, together with their families, came to reside in the village of Chetta Aunavarum, from Guddamadoogoo, appertaining to the purgunah of Maylaveram, in the zemindary of Soorananywar. I cannot positively tell whence they first came to Guddamadoogoo; but there is a report that they belonged to the

the western country, and that they had come from thence, that is from Cuddapah, &c. I am the Merassee Curnum of Chetta Aunavarum, where they had come to reside, and Alloor. For about eight or ten years past, I have been carrying on the duties of Curnum of those two villages. After they came to Chetta Aunavarum, they used to keep one or two ploughs each, and cultivate the Jeroyety lands. They have never tilled themselves, but have been accustomed to carry on the cultivation through the means of coolies and servants of their caste: the names of Pedda Emaum Sahib, Fakeer Sahib, and Sheikh Mahommed, have been entered in the Sircar's accounts. Ever since they arrived at my village, the men used to say that they had caused cloths to be woven at Mungalaghurry, Cheerala, Parala, and other places; and just before the commencement of hot weather, after the monsoon, that is, from the months of Maukhum and Phaulgoonum, they used to prepare themselves for a journey; saying, that they would export and sell the cloths in other countries, viz. Chittoor, and other southern districts, as well as in those of Rajamundry, &c.; and set out with one or two horses and bullocks. One or two of the men used to take their females with them. Afterwards, by report, it was understood that they had not gone for trade. It was also reported, that while they would pretend to go to one country, they would go to another; that

that is, when they said that they would go to the southern country, they went northward; and when they said they would go to a northern country, they probably went westward. These people used to return after four, three, or six months, and arrive in the village at some hour or other of the night. On their return, they were usually accompanied by more horses and bullocks, with loads, than at their departure; containing tuppalas, chimboos or brass vessels, arms, gold thread, cloths, &c.; which being generally in use among them, were seen by me. The cloths appeared to have come from distant countries, and were most valuable. When asked whence they brought them, they would mention the names of foreign cities, and say that they had purchased them there. I was given to understand that all the articles brought by them were divided between themselves, after they had returned. Whenever quarrels arose between them, in dividing the property, the persons of the neighbouring villages used to hear and inform me of it. Every day they used to spend three or four rupees, and drink much toddy and liquor. They eat flesh every day: they are also much addicted to chewing betel and betel-nuts. They had every kind of dress peculiar to different countries. Seeing their expenditure, I thought that they must have brought a good deal of money. From the above circumstances, it would not appear that

that they had acquired their wealth either by traffic or any other legal means whatever. It is reported that these people are Phansigars, and that, under pretence of going to different countries for the purpose of carrying on trade, they used to go and kill the travellers on the roads, and seize the property which was found with them. Their people have never connected themselves with the Moormen who have inhabited this country for a long time: they marry among themselves. It was usual for five or ten persons to come at once to their houses from the western districts, and to return again after having remained there five or ten days. Their arrival was concealed, and it was not known whence they came. When they were asked who these people were, they used to say they are our relations:—'One is my elder sister's son. One is my younger sister's son, &c. They have come from Chittoor and thereabouts. Our ancestors used to reside at Chittoor and thereabouts.' They usually spoke in Moor language. They can all generally converse in Tamul and Canarese. They can speak better Tamul than Teloogoo.

"They lived in Chetta Aunavarum, which is my Merassee village, for three or four years, in this manner. I understand that during their stay there, about five years since, some of them assembled together, and joined with those that resided at Guddamadoogoo; and that they all, ten or fourteen in number

number (whose names are not known), set off in the month of Maukhum (January), and entered the Guntoor zillah, having crossed the River Kistnahat Bezoara;—that at that time the females of the Sepoys of the battalions garrisoned in the northern districts as well as in some under the Bengal Presidency, carrying with them such sums as they had received from their husbands, had, on their way to the places of their residence in the southern districts, met the said gang, and arrived at Guntoor; and they (the Phansigars) put up in one Moor choultry, and the females in another;—that some of the Fakeers, inhabitants of the town of Guntoor, having seen the Moormen (Phansigars), had entertained suspicion against them, and informed the then Cutwal, Sheikh Luttief, of the same; who said that it was midnight; that he would inquire in the morning, and that they (the Fakeers) should take care of them;—that in the morning, upon inquiry, no traces either of the women or the Moormen remained; and that, notwithstanding all the search that was made, they had not been traced. At that time, the Phansigars, Emaum Sahib (who is called among themselves Jemadar), and Sheikh Hommed (who is more than fifty years old, and who is also called among them Jemadar, and said to be the son of Dauvuljee Jemadar), and one Emaum Sahib (he is among the persons now seized by the Cutwal), son of Sheikh

Hommed

Hommed Jemadar—these three persons had assembled the others (names unknown), and had gone for some expedition. The above-mentioned Emaum Sahib Jemadar is among the persons now seized by the Cutwal.—I heard that Jemadar Sheikh Hommed had, about five or six months ago, gone to Hydrabad, in the western country, and died there. —I understand that one or two months after the above-mentioned women and these persons had thus disappeared from Guntoor, the Jemadar Sheikh Hommed, his son Emaum, who has been seized, a servant of Sheikh Hommed (whose name is not known), and another Emaum, had come to Guntoor;—that while they put up in a choultry, the Fakeers, who had seen them before, again recognised them, and informed the Cutwal, Sheikh Luttief, of the same;—that during the examination, after they were seized, Sheikh Hommed, his son Emaum, and his servant, remained; but the other, called Emaum, had gone out with Chimboo, and thus ran away;—that the said three persons had been put in the Guntoor Cutwal's choultry;—and that the following articles were found in the bag of the one who ran away; viz. a cocoanut-shell used to put in tirchoornum (the yellow-mark stuff), one coomkooma bharena or box (holding woman's mark stuff), one silk sikhabandoo or ribband, used by Soodras in tying their hair, a piece of steel wire of a span length, and one lead flat. The said persons

sons having then stated that they were the inhabitants of my village, and that they had cultivation there, the then head of police, Nukkalapully Soobbarow, summoned me, to ascertain the same. On being asked regarding them, I declared that the circumstance of their having had cultivation in my village was true; that their cattle, &c., were in that village itself; and that their houses having been consumed by fire, they had resided at Joodjoor, one cose distant therefrom.—In about ten days they were released from the Cutwal's choultry. I first went and arrived in my village: while I was at Guntoor they were set at liberty; but they did not come to my village, either along with me or afterwards. I was given to understand that they had gone, and arrived at Guddamadoogoo.

"Some time afterwards, Sheikh Hommed came to Chetta Aunavarum, and inquired after his cultivation. I said to him, as well as to the others, as follows:—'Here and there they positively state that you are Phansigars. You must not remain in my village': and I positively told them that they must entirely go away; and they accordingly left the village, and went away to different places; but I did not know whither they had gone. At this time the famine happened. I understood, the year after the famine had ceased, that some of them had settled in Naraingoodem or Tooreeapollem, a hamlet of Mooneegalla; some in Croostnayapallem, a hamlet a hamlet of Aukpaumoola; and some in Ellore and Seetummapetta. I understand that about six years ago, while they were all residing in my village, the parties of the Jemadars Emaum Sahib and Sheikh Hommed had at one time left my village, and met two Chetties, merchants of Madras, and Cauvery man, at a place called Yeedoolakoontah, near Ellore; that the Phansigars had killed them, and robbed them of their property;—that at the time of their killing them, one of the gang, named Ally Sahib, had found a bag of usherafees or gold mohurs tied round the waist of one of the three, valued at about 600 rupees, and had seized it without being perceived by the other Phansigars; and that they had quarrelled afterwards among themselves, in consequence of his having taken it without giving a share to the others. Ally Sahib is not seized now; but the persons who had quarrelled with him regarding the said mohurs are now seized by the Cutwal. These Phansigars gave two most valuable rings, called Buttany Woongarums, set with diamonds, which were stolen from the said merchants, to Poottoombanka Venkiah, of the Cumma caste, an inhabitant of Dauchavarum, on some account or other. The said Venkiah gave the said two rings to two Banians, named Somah Venkatasem, and Pamedemurry Juggiah, inhabitants of Joodjoor, as he had no ready money to pay, in liquidation of the 600 rupees he had borrowed from them,

them, and took back his bonds. As the proceeding of giving the rings to the said Banians, and of receiving the bonds from them, passed in my presence, I am aware of it. I saw those rings: even now I can identify them. Those rings are now in the house of Somah Venkatasem;—four or five pairs of benaurs kundwas, or upper cloths of red colour, valued at rupees 100 or 150, having been found with these merchants who were killed. Venkatrama Gopaula Jagunnadharow, zemindar of Calavakolloo, on that district, was informed of it; and, knowing that these people in my village were Phansigars, sent, on his behalf, one Mauderauze Lutchemenuroo, inhabitant of Joodjoor; who came, and, having threatened them, caused the said benaurs kundwas to be conveyed away. I did not distinctly see the kundwas, but saw the bundle being taken away.

" About one year after the case of the Banians had taken place, that is, five years ago, a merchant came with horses to sell; and after selling some, I understand, that one horse having remained with him unsold, he had supposed that the Zemindar, the said Venkatrama Gopaula Jagunnadharow, at Joodjoor, would perhaps buy the horse, as it was the time of celebrating his marriage; and that as the merchant was going from Mylanerum, on his way to Joodjoor, through the pass called Canaya Gundy, he met the Phansigars, named Madaur

Sahib

Sahib and Hyder Khan of Guddamadoogoo, where they asked each other their destination;—that one of them, named Hyder Khan, had then said to the merchant that he would go to Hydrabad;—that the merchant had said he also would go, if the horse was not purchased at Joodjoor;—that one of the Phansigars (I know not which) had followed the merchant to Joodjoor;—that the other, thinking that it would occasion delay if he should go to Guddamadoogoo, where his party then resided, and bring the Phansigars belonging to that gang, had taken the Phansigars who then resided at Chetta Aunavarum (now seized), and met the said merchant and the Phansigars who accompanied him in the tope or grove of the village Keesara, from which time no trace of the merchant remained;—and that the Phansigars had then taken away the horse, and sold it at Hydrabad, or thereabouts. A small horse belonging to the said merchant had been kept by Madaur Sahib, who is now in custody; but I was told by him, after he was seized, that the horse had died one year back. I was given to understand that these Phansigars had found with the merchant, an umbrella, a knife, and some rupees, being the proceeds of the sale of some of his horses. The said knife and umbrella were given to Guddamadoogoo Veyenna, the Curnum of Guddamadoogoo, by the Phansigars; and the said Veyenna gave that knife and umbrella to his brother-

brother-in-law, Avva Venkataratrum. They are now in his possession. I saw them with him.— In consequence of their having committed these acts while in my Merassee village, Chetta Aunavarum, I drove them from thence, considering that they must not remain there. Thinking that it would be of no use if I informed the Zemindar, *as he is aware of these circumstances;* and fearing lest trouble would come upon me, in the event of their not being visited with punishment on my having informed the Authorities of these circumstances, I had never informed hitherto. As you have now taken active measures regarding them, I have represented what has passed."

On the 8th of April following, the witness identified twenty-one of the gang.

An accomplice, named Rahamoo, deposed thus:—

" I was about four years old at the time of my father's death. When I was six years old, my mother died: I do not know my mother's name. As long as my father was alive, I resided in a hut in the Khausymeyah bazaar at Hydrabad: after my father's death, I remained there about eight days; when I left the house, and earned my livelihood by begging. I have neither maternal nor paternal relations. Till I was about ten years old I earned my livelihood by begging alms at Hydrabad, whence I set

I set out with a view to live in the eastern country. When leaving Hydrabad, I met with three Soodra people with a female child, conveying (brass) tumballs, pots, boxes, &c., belonging to two Moguls, to Bunder, on four horses for hire. I used to take care of their horses when they halted, and do other work: the Soodra people gave me rice. I came as far as Cunchecachula village with them, when the above Moguls desired me to attend on them; but the Soodra people told me, that 'If you attend on them, there will be some trouble to you, and you should not serve under them.' I was afraid, and left their company at Cunchecachula: and from thence I went to Chetta Aunavarum, two-and-a-half cose distant from it; where I met Mohadeen Sahib, alias Emaum Sahib, who is called a Jemadar. He told me, that I should remain under him, to look after his affairs: that in the event of my attending on him for about ten years, they would perform my marriage ceremony, and that they would give me rice. I accordingly remained in their house, conducting their cultivating affairs; and taking my food there. After remaining about one year, or about five or six years ago, the above Mohadeen Sahib Jemadar, and others, viz. Mooshkeel (present), his elder brother Emaum Sahib (present), Khausim Sahib (about two months ago he went, as he said, to see his relations somewhere towards Madras, but I do not know where they reside

reside — his father's name is Madaur Sahib, now present, but he did not come on this expedition), his younger brother, Emaum Sahib (present), Fakeer Sahib (present), Sied Hossein, alias Pedda Fakeer Sahib (present), his son, Sied Khasim, alias Siedam (present), Madaur Sahib (present), Hossein Sahib (present), his younger brother, Goodee Sahib (present), Hossein Meeyah, alias Khadar Hossein (present), and myself, went, thirteen men in number, including Jemadar, to northern country. Mohadeen Sahib Jemadar said that we must go to Chicacole and purchase cloths. He collected all the men, and carried me too: seven of us, including Jemadar and myself, went in advance: the remaining six men came after, at a day's journey apart. Mohadeen Sahib Jemadar rode a horse: so we went on, some in advance and some behind, by way of Ellore and Sanevaurapetta, to a coontah or small tank situated on the other side or north of Ellore, where there are a number of date-trees: there was water in it. Two Moormen came and joined us, when we were eating our dinner. They were asked from whence they were coming: they answered, that they were coming from Hydrabad, and were going to Chicacole. They asked us whence we came: we answered, that we were coming from Condapully, and were going to purchase cloths. Our second party remained behind; and we, together with the above two Moormen, set out from thence,

thence, and proceeded as far as the Godavary river travelling for about four days in company with the above Moormen. When we reached the Godavary, it was almost sunset. Mohadeen Sahib Jemadar alighted from his horse near the bank of the Godavary; and as the second party, being six in number, joined us in the morning of the same day, he went down into the bed of the Godavary with ten men and the above two Mussulmen, going slowly. It began to grow dark. Goodee Sahib and myself were staying behind. When I told him that our party had advanced, and that we must go on, he delayed, and answered, that they would return here. Mohadeen Sahib Jemadar descended the bank of the Godavary with the remaining ten men, together with the above two Mussulmen; and went as far as the edge of the water, when they all sat down. One Mooshkeel, and one Khausim (who is at large), twisted their causy-cocaloo or sash-girdles, threw them round the travellers' necks; when the remaining people fell upon them and killed them: they said they threw their bodies into the Godavary. One traveller had a dagger, and the other a sword with a black handle. There was found a bundle, containing rupees, two loongies, two puncha-cloths bordered with red thread, three jackets, two talagooddaloo or pieces of head-cloths and one turban, one thread carpet, and one cumbly, which they brought

 with

with them. One of the above two travellers was middle-aged, neither tall nor short, and of brown colour: the other was yellow, short and fat: they appeared to be inhabitants of Hydrabad country. After they were killed, our party took the above things and parcel of money; and we all came to a tamarind-tope, situated near Cauvoor, on the bank of the Godavary, where we slept; and the next day we remained there. I went for grass for the horse; and before I returned, the rupees were divided: they told me that six rupees had come to each share. I being a slave of Mohadeen Sahib, he, the Jemadar, might have taken my share himself, but he did not say so to me: out of the cloths, one loongy was put on by the Jemadar: the remaining cloths were kept in a bundle. The dagger, including handle, was about one cubit long, and I saw it with Fakeer Sahib: the sword with black handle, called choory, was less than one cubit long; it was left with Mooshkeel. Goodee Sahib and myself were told to go away to Chetta Aunavarum in front: so we went on.

"After eight days, the other eleven men, including Jemadar, arrived at Chetta Aunavarum: this took place after the feast of Shub-e-barat (in November) was over; which we performed; and then quitted home three or four days afterwards; and returned prior to the Rumzan month, after this affair had been committed. These men are in the

the habit of going, now and then, on similar expeditions, to Hydrabad and those parts. A short time ago, or about a month after the last Mohurrum feast, nine men of the above-mentioned gang, headed by Sied Hossein, who was appointed Jemadar by Emaum Sahib, set out from home: they said they would go to Hydrabad, but I know not whither they went: they returned to the village after two months, passing by Faraukutgoodem, which is situated on the south of Toorakagoodem.

"After the two Mussulmen were killed, as above mentioned, near Rajahmundry, I returned, and remained for a few days in the house of Mohadeen Sahib; but disliking the hard work under them, when the 12th Battalion was proceeding from Vizayanagur to Jhalnah, I went with it; and was employed to drive the wood bandies there, at one time for Mahommed Sahib Jemadar of the 5th Company of Martin Battalion; and afterwards, I used to drive bandies of straw for Rungapah, Subahdar-Major in the above 5th Company. The Martin Battalion having come to Hydrabad from Jhalnah, I accompanied Emaum Sahib, snuff-shopkeeper, in the same battalion, and I remained for some days at Hydrabad: up to that time, a year and a half had expired, when I repaired to the eastern country. Mohadeen Sahib, who was sitting near the chowkee at Moonagal, saw and called me, and desired

desired me to serve under him. I agreed; remained; and came to Naraingoodeëm or Tooreapallem, a hamlet under Mooneegalla, along with him. When I asked why they had come from Chetta Aunavarum, he answered, that, prior to the famine, gang-robbers had come and set fire to their houses; consequently they left that part: and that some had come to Tooreapallem, some to Kistnapooram; and that Sheikh Hommed Jemadar had gone to Ellore. I accompanied them in one instance only—when the two Mussulmans were killed, but never again. I entered into their house for rice, which was given. I ate, and carried on their cultivation as they desired.

"I do not know more than this.—These men who are residing at Tooreapallem, as well as those at Kistnapooram and Ellore, are all called Phansigars: their fathers and grandfathers were successively Phansigars: they formerly resided in the Goolburgah country, as I heard now and then, when they were speaking among themselves. Of those now apprehended and brought by the Cutwal, with the exception of four, the remainder are all Phansigars: the four excepted are, one arrack-seller from the northern districts; his name is Veeradoo, and he is employed as husbandman by Mohadeen Sahib: one Bahadur Khan Moorman, came newly from Soonnumpaud last year, and set up a punjah, and ever since he is living under their protection: Chunder-

Chunderlapauty Sheikh Hossein came last year as a beggar, and is doing cultivating business, under Goodee Sahib, for his subsistence: Madaur Sahib came from Gungereddypallem; he is Bahadur Sahib's brother-in-law. The above four men are not Phansigars; but the remainder are. I can tell their names, if they appear before me. Besides these men, there was one who lived at Chetta Aunavarum, called Sheikh Hommed Jemadar: he left that place, and settled at Ellore: during the festival of last Mohurrum, he came to Tooreapallem, and fell sick and died: he was born of Reddy-caste parents, and, when a child, was adopted by Dauvuljee Jemadar, and called Sheikh Hommed: until his death, he performed the duties of Jemadar: he was above fifty years of age when he died: his father, Dauvuljee, is said to reside somewhere about Seringapatam, as I heard from the said Phansigars. The Sheikh Hommed had two sons; one, Emaum Sahib; and Madaur Sahib: they are now among those apprehended and brought by the Cutwal. Of those residing formerly at Chetta Aunavarum, all are now apprehended, except four: they are followers of Sheikh Hommed Jemadar, and therefore went with him. Of these, one Ally Sahib is said to have gone to Goolburgah, where he has relations: the remaining three, Emaum Sahib, Dingra Hossein Sahib, and Nussoo Khan, are not apprehended; it is not known where they are. Besides this,

this, Hossein Sahib, alias Hoonooryah Sahib Jemadar, the brother of Emaum Sahib Jemadar, who has been now apprehended, formerly resided at Guddamadoogoo village, in the Maylaveram Purgunah, near Condapully, with four or five families of Phansigars: they went away, during famine, to Madras or those parts, and I do not know where they are. One of them, called Hossein Khan, came to Tooreapallem before I returned there, after my accompanying the battalion: this man, and two or three families of those under Hoonooryah, resided formerly at Bhroogabunda, in the Guntoor Zillah. Hossein Khan had kept a woman called Mungulah Bhaugy, resident of the same village; and proceeded from thence, with the said Bhaugy, to Ellore or thereabouts. Hossein Khan then got married; but left his wife; and took Mungulah Bhaugy, whom he knew at Bhroogabunda, to Kistnapooram. After we were brought here by the Cutwal, the said Hossein Khan (how he was apprehended I do not know) has been brought to Guntoor. His father-in-law, who was formerly at Bhroogabunda, and who went to Ellore, by name Madaur Sahib, came lately to Tooreapallem, and is now apprehended: he is Phansigar under Mohadeen Sahib Jemadar. Hyder Khan, apprehended at Seetummapetta, was also resident formerly at Bhroogabunda. The father-in-law of Emaum Sahib (son of Kallie Bodhoo), who was apprehended at Tooreapallem, is said to keep

keep a shop for selling salt, chillies, &c., in the Chittoor bazaar; but his father-in-law's name is unknown.

"When I first arrived at Chetta Aunavarum, I used to hear Ally Sahib, Bada Sahib, Nussoo Khan, Emaum Sahib, Hossein Sahib, and one Dingra Hossein Sahib, and Sheikh Hommed Jemadar, quarrelling among themselves regarding the circumstance of Ally Sahib having, in some expedition, obtained a purse containing gold mohurs and embezzled it himself, of which they considered themselves entitled to have a share.

"The brass booddy chimboo, a tumball which was seized in the house of Mohadeen Sahib Jemadar by the Cutwal and placed in the choultry, was never seen by me formerly in Mohadeen Sahib's house; but has been in use ever since they returned from the last expedition, which took place eight months ago, as above mentioned.

"I entered into service under these Phansigars for subsistence, but I am not one of them: if the people of the said village are asked, it will be understood that I am employed as a servant in their house: as I entered in their house, I was apprehended, and brought here with them."

This deponent identified twenty-four prisoners.

Another

Another witness, named Bhaugy, deposed as follows:—

"About eight years ago, Hossein Khan, a Moorman, Hyder Sahib, Hossein Sahib, Madaur Sahib, his son Hossein, Murah and Vully Sahib, alias Vully Khan, came to Bhroogabunda, with their women and children: the villagers were afraid that they were gang-robbers: I was then ten years of age. They halted in a tope, and told Bungariah, Ramiah, and others, the Curnums of the said village, that they would settle in that village; and built four or five houses: they were altogether about ten in number. Hyder Sahib cultivated with two ploughs, but conducted it through his servants: they remained there for four years. On looking into their conduct, it was at first thought that they were robbers and burglars; but, by degrees, it was strongly rumoured that they were men who killed people by strangling. While they were living at Bhroogabunda, they used to say that they had relations and brothers at Chetta Aunavarum and at Guddamadoogoo, situated on the other side of the river; and they used to go thither and visit them: and so two or three men would start together from Bhroogabunda, and not return for ten or twenty days, or sometimes a month. They used to drink arrack and toddy, and eat as much meat as they required: under these circumstances, the village people said that they were Phansigars. After four years

years had elapsed, the famine happened: they then said that they could not carry on their livelihood there, and would go to Ellore, and get the said Hossein Khan married: and they all left one night from Bhroogabunda, and went away. As it was a time of famine, I was in need of rice; and went with them, with a view to earn my livelihood by working as cooly under them, leaving my mother and father. They arrived at Ellore, where one Sheik Hommed Jemadar had already come: these men left Bhroogabunda, and arrived at Gunjy Bazaar at Ellore. I neither touched their pots, nor lived with them: I beat and ground their rice, and they fed me for four months. They thus remained at Ellore; and from thence they went to Soonarpetta: it is usually called Sanynauraupetta. After they arrived there about four months, Hossein Khan was married to Madaur Sahib's daughter.

* * * * * * * * * *

They remained at Sanynauraupetta five or six months; and from thence arrived at Kistnapooram. Of the party who left Bhroogabunda, Hyder Sahib and Hossein Sahib remained at Sanynauraupetta: the remainder, Hossein Khan, Madaur Sahib, and Vully Khan, being three in number, took up their abode at Kistnapooram; where Beesaubooboo, the daughter of the uncle of Hossein Khan, her son Khader, Hossein, Mooshkeel his elder brother, Emaum Shah, and Mohadeen, an old man, had already

already come. Their relations were all living at Toorakagoodem, a distance of three and half cose from it. When they were asked in what country they formerly lived, they said in the Cuddapah and Karnaul districts.

It is said that Mohadeen Sahib, alias Emaum Sahib, is Jemadar to those at Kistnapooram and Toorakagoodem. The Phansigars at Toorakagoodem used to come daily to Kistnapooram; and those in the latter went to the former place; consequently I have seen the Phansigars at Toorakagoodem, and know them: if I see them, I will recognise them all.—These men, after the expiration of the moonsoon, prepare for a journey, and go to procure money, and return not for two and three months. Previous to setting out, the whole body, those at Kistnapooram, Ellore, and Toorea-pallem, about twenty, would come to the house of Mohadeen Sahib Jemadar, where they would remain five or six days, and perform certain ceremonies to their gods, who are called "Narsimloo Ammagaroo," as also "Misummah." When they are performing the ceremony, they put coomcoomah or red stuff, and sandal, on the wall; keeping three bottles of arrack, colicry chippaloo or cocoanuts and dates, and at the same time bringing gauraloo and booraloo, or cakes dressed: when worshipping before the wall, betel-leaves would be affixed. They kill a number of sheep, and thus perform

perform the ceremony; and they will go away at night. They never carry their young women along with them; but one or two old women, who are accustomed to go with them. When they start, if they meet with bad omens, such as the breaking of a pot, the sight of a cat, or if they hear the mewing of a cat or the cry of the owl, they never go that road, but return home for five or six days: afterwards, looking out for good omens, they start. They seldom kill women: they principally bring men's jewels, such as girdles and rings, which will be used by them: chiefly bring ready money, and not so much property: they also bring good and fine cloths of distant countries, which will be used by men and women: they wear cloth like those of Sepoys. Their men and women speak Malabar and Canara well: they always converse in Hindustanee themselves; but whenever they want to speak secrets among themselves, they use the Canara or Malabar languages. They used to say that their relations were living in the southward, at a distance of two months' journey, and that they had not met since these last ten years: they never permit the Mussulmen of this country, or any one, to have access to their houses; nor do they go to the houses of Mussulmen of this district, or any one else: they never contract relationship at all with the Mussulmen of this country: they say that they are going out to trade in cloths, but it does not

not appear so: they, the Phansigars, likewise talk among themselves that they should not allow the people—barber, washer, and goldsmith castes—to join their company; and if they do, that some calamity will befal them.

I was connected with them about three years ago: these people, with the exception of Hossein Shah, went on an expedition with Mohadeen Sahib Jemadar; and returned in four months with the Jemadar, and arrived at midnight. They said that they had been to the western country, on the other side of Golcondah: they likewise said, that a sum of rupees, to the amount of three times twenty, was allotted to each share. When Mohadeen Sahib returned, he brought a certain number of women's cloths, called chandracala cheeraloo, valued at five rupees each, and gave them to his wife; and the same description of cholies were brought, which he gave to his wife and daughters: the other people also brought similar cloths, and delivered to the people in their houses respectively. They used to go out in gangs now and then, and return in three or four months, bringing much money gained by killing people; and divide it among themselves, and spend at a great rate. When returning from their journey, some of them wear (Sepoys') jackets of red broad-cloth. They also bring tumballs, pot, and weapons, which they use in their houses.

"Two

" Two or three months previous to the Mohurrum feast last year, they went to the other side of Golcondah, and returned about ten days after the Mohurrum feast: at that time, Mohadeen Sahib Jemadar was accompanied by about twenty Phansigars. Hossein Khan * * * also proceeded with them; and it was talked, that they had shared at the rate of twice twenty rupees to each man. Hossein Khan brought a chandracala cheeraloo, or woman's cloth, valued five rupees, for his wife; and he also gave two cholies of the same sort, one to his mother-in-law, and one to his wife. Mohadeen Sahib Jemadar brought a woman's cloth of the same size, valued ten rupees, and gave it to his wife; this had a broad border of silk thread at the sides as well as the ends: the remaining people also presented one woman's cloth to each of their wives respectively: the rupees which came to Hossein Shah's share were given to his mother and father-in-law, and not to me: they used to give me one measure of paddy, but nothing else; no jewels were given to me.

" The men and women purchase betel-leaves, which they keep in bags; and are continually chewing them. The Phansigars did not go out again between the time they returned, after the Mohurrum feast, and the time I quitted them and came to my village.

" All at once, Hossein Khan, who kept me, appeared

appeared to be mad, and began to beat every one: and one day he made a knot in the corner of a sella cloth, and, throwing it round my neck, twisted it four or five times, and endeavoured to strangle me. I was already senseless; when some of those residing at Tooreapallem who happened to be present, as well as Mooskheel and others of Kistnapooram, together with Hossein Khan's mother and father-in-law, came and released me: they gave me a Hydrabad rupee, and, saying that if I remained he would kill me, told me to go away. Mohadeen Sahib Jemadar allowed me, at the same time, a chuklor, called Paupegadoo, to accompany me. When sending me out, the Jemadar sent a message, that if any one questioned me, I should not reveal the circumstance of the strangling; that I should say that I ran away because they beat me, and that I must not tell any of their secrets. If I remained there, I thought he would kill me; and I therefore crossed the river, and came to Bhroogabunda, my native village.

"After my return, about twenty days ago, Hossein Khan came to Bhroogabunda for me, and desired me to come along with him: I answered, that I would not. He then wanted to take me by force. I told the same to the Curnums, who sent him away: when returning again on my account, he was apprehended by the Ghautty peons at Custalah: as he had Hydrabad rupees with him, this raised

raised suspicions, and they apprehended him. From thence he was escorted to Bhroogabunda, by a peon: they carried me, too, to Nursarowpetta, where the Aumeen took a deposition from me; and sent me to Guntoor, together with Hossein Khan: we came accordingly. The sword without the scabbard, now before you, and produced before me, which is said to have been seized by the Guntoor Cutwal, has been used by Hossein Khan since he returned from the last expedition, about the time of the Mohurrum feast last year: this sword was not in his possession before that time; he brought it with him at that time. The dagger and shield, which were now found with Hossein Khan, were also brought at that time: he also brought another dagger, but I do not know where it is.

"The basary, or nose-ornament, now produced before you, was worn by Sojah, the wife of Hossein Khan.

"The silk-woman's cloth was brought by Mohadeen Sahib Jemadar when he went to Hydrabad or thereabouts, and was given to his young daughter: she is married to Sydah. I have seen her wear it.

"One of these Phansigars, named old Mohadeen Sahib, went away three months before; saying, that his son is at Nundula, to the southward, and that he would go to see him.

"Mohadeen Sahib Jemadar's elder brother,

 called

called Hoonoor Sahib, is in the southern country, at a distance of two months' journey, as I heard from them."

This witness identified the whole of the party.

CHAP. XXVI.

As the greater part of the details that have been submitted, consists of depositions taken before various tribunals, it will be apparent, that for several years the Ruling Powers have not been indifferent to the suppression of the atrocious practices of the Thugs. Their proceedings, combined with the abolition of Suttees by the Government of Lord William Bentinck, and both following the extirpation of the Pindaries by the Marquis of Hastings, may be received as indicating an advancing regard to the principles of public morality in the Government, which, it is to be hoped, will gradually extend to the governed. According to a statement made by Captain Sleeman, the result of their proceedings is as follows:—Between the years 1826 and 1835 (both inclusive), 1562 prisoners were committed by various Magistrates. Of these, 328 were punished by death, 999 by transportation, 77 by imprisonment for life; from 21, security was required; 71 were sentenced to limited periods of imprisonment;—making a total

 of

of 1450 convicted. Of the remainder, 21 were acquitted; 11 contrived to escape; 31 died before sentence; and 49 were admitted evidence for the prosecutions.

But, though the practice of Thuggee has thus received a serious check, it must not be supposed that the whole of its followers have been apprehended, or any portion approaching to the whole. It is carried on with so much caution—and, if the expression may be allowed on such an occasion, with so much *decency*—its ramifications are so widely-extended, and reach so far into the very heart of Indian society, that the difficulties of dealing with it are almost inconceivable. Men whose decorum, regular habits, and fair character place them above suspicion, are connected with Thugs, and frequently active members of the fraternity. It would here strike us as extraordinary, if tradesmen in Cheapside or Bond Street united with their respective occupations that of murder: yet this state of things exists in India. In carrying into effect, in the Deccan, the means resorted to by the British Government for suppressing Thuggee, the Officer employed to superintend them was surprised to recognise a noted Thug in the person of one of the most respectable linen-drapers of the Cantonments of Hingolee. This person was so correct in his dealings, and so amiable in his deportment, that he had won the esteem of all the Gentlemen at the

the station, who used to assist him in procuring passports for his goods, in their way to Bombay; yet he was carrying on his trade of murder up to the very day of his arrest, being convicted with gangs on all the roads around, and close to the cantonments: and when he pretended to be proceeding to Bombay on mercantile enterprises, he was actually leading out his gangs of assassins, to strangle unsuspecting travellers. This fact may serve to shew how erroneous are the impressions of native character frequently received by European residents in India.

A portion of the *autobiography* of this bandit linen-draper may not be uninteresting. He says:—

"A year and a half before I was arrested at Hingolee, in June 1832, I set up a shop in the bazaar of the Golundazes, in the Hingolee Cantonments. I used before to bring cloths from Berar to the cantonments for sale; and became intimately acquainted with Maha Singh, Subahdar of the Golundazes. I told him that I should like to set up a shop in his bazaar; and he advised me to do so, and got the Cutwal to assign me a place. I set up a linen-draper's shop; and I went several times, with other shopkeepers, to Bombay, to purchase a stock of broad-cloths and other articles. The people of the cantonments knew that I used to deal to the extent of several hundred rupees.

"When

"When I resided at Omrowtee about seven years ago, I used to come to Hingolee and lodge in the house of Ram Singh, Thug, who has since been seized and sent to Jubulpore. Sometimes I came with the gangs on Thuggee; and sometimes as a merchant, with cloths for sale. When I came with cloths, I used to stay for fifteen or twenty days at a time in the Moghul Sowar Lines, and other places. After the release of Hurnagur and his gang from Hingolee, after the Girgow murders, I, with Makhun, the two Nasirs, Chotee approver, and others, killed three Manwaries: and after this, Imaum and Chotee got seized at Saugor; and this was reported to me by Kureem Khan and others, who came to Omrowtee from the Nurbudda valley; and I thought I might be pointed out and arrested. This was my reason for leaving Omrowtee for Hingolee. When I was arrested, I had determined to leave off Thuggee, and intended to go and reside at Bombay. I used to go out occasionally on Thuggee after I settled at Hingolee; and when the gangs of Thugs encamped on the tank or lodged in the Dhurumsalah, I used to converse with them; but I never let them know where I resided. Ismael, Thug, who is now an approver, used to reside in the bazaar of the 5th Regiment, and he served Captain Scott as a Gareewan. Mohna, alias Ruhman, used also to reside here sometimes. Bahleen also used to live and work in the bazaar; but they used

used all three to go on the roads, as many travellers used to pass, and no one sought after Thugs. Any skilful party might have had three or four *affairs* every night, without any one being the wiser for it. People knew not what Thuggee was, nor what kind of people Thugs were. Travellers were frequently reported to have been murdered by robbers; but people thought the robbers must be in the jungles, and never dreamed that they were murdered by the men they saw every day about them. I never invited a Thug to my house, nor did I ever expose any of the articles obtained in Thuggee for sale. I was much respected by the people of the town and cantonments, and never suspected till arrested."

The history of this man affords proof, that though, from the lax state of morals in India, many persons countenance Thugs with a full knowledge of their occupation, yet many, who associate with and protect them, act in ignorance of the character of those to whom they thus afford encouragement and support. It is at the same time indisputable, that the trade has not only been tolerated by Native Authorities, but deemed a fitting source of Financial replenishment. This appears from a multiplicity of evidence; and especially from the following deposition of Suntoke Rae, son of Laljoo Kuchwaha, Thakur, Zemindar of Sindouse, Thanah

Sindouse,

Sindouse, Zillah Etawah; taken the 24th of August, 1834.

"I am about sixty years of age; and am the son of that Laljoo who was confined for life in the Bareilly jail, for having been an accomplice in the murder of Lieutenant Mansell, near Murnae, A. D. 1812, when Mr. Halhed came down from Agra to arrest the Thugs. I have been asked to give a list of Thugs who paid tribute to the Gwalior State; and I have accordingly brought the latest list with me. It is dated Aghun Sumbut 1854 (November A.D. 1797). Sheik Mahommed Jumma, who was styled Colonel, was Aumil under the Gwalior State of the purgunahs in which the Thugs resided, viz. Pureehar, twelve villages, and Sursaudhur, fifty-two villages, at that time; and he sent for my father Laljoo, and between them this list was made out. Each of the three hundred and eighteen houses were taxed at St. Rs. twenty-four and eight annas, and the agreement was to last three years. My father collected the tribute, which amounted yearly to St. Rs. seven thousand seven hundred and ninety-one; and after the collections, he was allowed to deduct one hundred rupees for himself, and fifty rupees for the two Putwaries: the remaining seven thousand six hundred and forty-one rupees he forwarded to the Aumil's treasury. Whenever the Thugs returned from an expedition,

expedition, my father used to receive a present of one rupee from every house. The Sindouse Thugs were in the habit of making very long expeditions. They never returned in less than six months; and if they were unsuccessful, they sometimes remained absent two years, and on this account my father did not make a very large sum by the presents. The list I have now brought is the latest made. It is dated, Aghun Sumbut 1854 (November 1797). Colonel Mahommed Jumma was dismissed from the Aumilship, Sumbut 1857 (A. D. 1800); and owing to the confusion which existed in the Gwalior State, the Rajah of Rampoora seized upon the Purgunah Pureehar, and stripped the Zemindars and the Thugs of their property. The Thugs fled to the Purgunah Sursaee, in which half of the Thugs formerly resided, and which was still under the Gwalior Government; and the Zemindars went to complain to the Collectors of Mynporee and Agra. Matters stood in this way till Sumbut 1864 (A. D. 1807), when a Tuhseeldar, Lala Sunkerlal, was sent from Agra to Sindouse, and the Purgunah Pureehar was attached to the British dominions;—the Purgunah of Sursaee, in which half the Thugs always resided, and to which the other half (who had resided from time immemorial in Purgunah Pureehar) had fled on account of the oppression of the Rampoora Rajah, in Sumbut 1857 (A. D. 1800), still remaining under the Gwalior Govern-

Government. The greater number of the Pureehar Thugs then returned to their villages; and every thing went on comfortably for the next five years; when Mr. Halhed, who was Deputy Superintendant of Police, came to arrest the Thugs in December 1812. Into whosoever hands the purgunahs of Pureehar and Susaee have fallen—viz. Nuwab Vizier, the Rana of Gohud, the Rohilla Chieftains, the Bhudoreea Rajah, the Rajah of Bhurtpore, and the Gwalior State—from time immemorial has a tax of 24-8 on every house inhabited by the Thugs been levied and paid to the respective Aumils."

The names of the various Thug families follow, to the number of three hundred and eighteen.—On this, Mr. J. C. Wilson observes:—

"In each of these three hundred and eighteen houses, we may allow an average of three men capable of going on Thuggee. Thus the Sindouse Thugs may be fairly estimated at nine hundred and fifty-four, particularly as the tax was levied on the houses, and not on the persons."

Captain Sleeman adds:

"The lists received, were those rendered by Laljoo and other Zemindars to the Aumils, as the Thug *rent-rolls;* but they did not contain all the Thug families from whom the tax was levied. The Zemindars often collected from several independent members

members of one great family who had separated, while they inserted in the rent-rolls only the reputed head of the whole. The heads of families who paid the tax were, therefore, more than three hundred and eighteen; as will be seen by the following lists, which contain one hundred and twenty-two families more than are named in the lists of Suntoke Rae, forwarded by Mr. Wilson; and are very complete and correct, I believe."

A very long list is added by Captain Sleeman, with full particulars of all the principal persons, whose names are contained in it: the compilation of which is as creditable to his research, as the practice which it illustrates is disgraceful to the Native Princes by whom it was pursued.